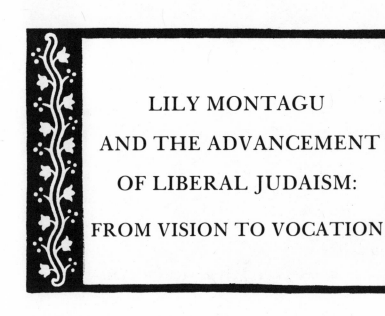

LILY MONTAGU

AND THE ADVANCEMENT

OF LIBERAL JUDAISM:

FROM VISION TO VOCATION

ELLEN M. UMANSKY

Studies in Women and Religion
Volume 12

The Edwin Mellen Press
New York and Toronto

Library of Congress Cataloging in Publication Data

Umansky, Ellen M.
    Lily Montagu and the advancement of liberal Judaism.

    (Studies in women and religion ; vol. 12)
    Bibliography; p.
    Includes index.
    1. Montagu, Lilian Helen, 1873-1963. 2. Reform
Judaism--Great Britain. 3. Jews--Great Britain--
Biography. I. Title. II. Series: Studies in women
and religion ; v. 12.
BM755.M57U46 1983   296.8'34 (B)   83-22005
ISBN 0-88946-537-1

Studies in Women and Religion ISBN 0-88946-549-5

                    The Edwin Mellen Press
                       P.O. Box 450
               Lewiston, New York   14092

            Printed in the United States of America

For Alan

TABLE OF CONTENTS

PREFACE

Early in the spring of 1976, I asked my graduate school advisor, Joseph Blau, for help in selecting a dissertation topic. My interests were in modern Jewish history and the role of women in Judaism. I was hoping to find a topic that would touch on both of these concerns. My advisor suggested that I begin by looking at the kinds of activities that modern Jewish women have pursued. We thus made up a list of every well known modern Jewish woman that came to mind. With the list completed, I turned to leave, but as I did so, he called me back, saying, "Wait, I have one more name to add to your list--Lily Montagu."

At the time, I had never heard of Lily Montagu. In fact, as I later learned, with the exception of one brief biography by her nephew, Eric Conrad, published in 1953 (and long since out of print), no study of her life had ever been undertaken. Neither had anyone written a history of the Liberal Jewish movement in England, a movement (as I later learned) that she founded and eventually led. For these reasons, Lily Montagu remained to me--and to the numerous American Jewish historians with whom I later spoke--somewhat of a mystery. Even my advisor was unsure about Lily Montagu's accomplishments. Indeed, his only recollection was personal in nature. Once, he told me, as a small boy in London (where his father was serving as rabbi), he attended a synagogue service at which Lily Montagu was preaching. He didn't know who Lily Montagu was or why she was preaching, but the memory of looking up at the pulpit and seeing--and hearing--a woman had remained with him for over fifty years.

After doing some preliminary research on the other Jewish women on my list, I turned my attention more fully to Lily Montagu. It was then that I discovered that her contribution to the Liberal Jewish movement in England had either
been glossed over or ignored. Not finding any books on her
(the Columbia University library did not have Conrad's biography in its collection), I turned to the *Encyclopedia Judaica*. There, in volume twelve, page 265, as one of several
sub-listings under "Montagu, banking family," I read:

> Lilian Helen Montagu. Social worker and magistrate,
> founded the West Central Girls' Club in 1893. A pi-
> oneer of Liberal Judaism in Britain. In 1902, with
> Claude Goldsmid Montefiore, she established the
> Jewish Religious Union which sponsored the Liberal
> Jewish Synagogue and in 1926 the World Union for
> Progressive Judaism. She conducted Liberal Jewish
> services, wrote on religious subjects, and also
> published a biography of her father.

I was intrigued by the listing. *Pioneer* of Liberal Judaism?
Leader of religious services? *Author* of works on religious
subjects? Even more intriguing was the picture that appeared
below the listing itself: a photograph of Lily Montagu
preaching at the Reform Temple in Berlin in 1928. It was at
that moment, I think, that I decided to write my doctoral
dissertation on Lily Montagu.

In the months that followed, I experienced many periods
of doubt. A number of the historians to whom I spoke agreed
that Lily Montagu had played some role in the development of
Liberal Judaism in England, but they doubted whether her role
was central. As one historian, not atypically asked me: "If
she's so important, why don't we know about her? Why hasn't
anyone written about Lily Montagu before?" More encouraging
were those who knew her. I spoke to a number of American Reform rabbis in New York and Cincinnati who had known Lily

Montagu during her years as President (or, later, Honorary
Life President) of the World Union. They spoke of her vitality and strength--despite her advanced age--and assured me
that Lily Montagu was, at the very least, an "interesting
character." But, not knowing of her role in the founding of
the Liberal Jewish movement in England (and unsure of her
role in the founding of the World Union), they too questioned
whether I should devote my entire dissertation to her.

By the spring of 1977, I had discovered that Lily Montagu's biography of her father (entitled *Samuel Montagu, First
Lord Swaythling*) was only one of eleven books that she had
written. The others (almost all of which I was able to find
either in the New York Public Library or in the Klau Library
at Hebrew Union College--Jewish Institute of Religion in Cincinnati) included: two novels, *Naomi's Exodus* (1901) and *Broken Stalks* (1902); *Thoughts on Judaism*, a theological treat-
ise published in 1902; a collection of short stories called
What Can A Mother Do? (1926); an autobiography, *The Faith of
a Jewish Woman*, published in 1943; commentaries on the Hebrew
Bible written for children (*Letters to Anne and Peter*, 1944),
and *My Club and I* (1953), a history of her involvement in
communal service. She also had edited a number of books including *God Revealed* (1953), a devotional work containing a
number of prayers that Lily Montagu herself had written; *A
Little Book of Comfort for Jewish People in Times of Sorrow*,
edited with Rudolph Brasch in the late 1940s; and *Prayers,
Psalms, and Hymns for Jewish Children,* edited with Theodora
Davis in 1901. I further learned that Lily Montagu had published a number of articles, on topics as diverse as Liberal
Judaism, socialism, the influence of Joseph Mazzini, and a
character sketch of the late nineteenth century Russian Jew.

After reading these works, I had a greater understanding
of Lily Montagu's interests and ideas. But I still wasn't
certain what role she played in the development of Liberal

Judaism in England. Later, I would discover that Lily Montagu's lack of self confidence, sense of modesty and perhaps
exaggerated respect for others, led her to downplay her own
contributions. While she occasionally alluded to her own
work, it was in the writings of Claude Montefiore, Israel
Mattuck and others that I first discovered that Lily Montagu
was, in fact, the founder of the Liberal Jewish movement in
England and the individual most responsible for its growth.

This discovery was confirmed in the summer of 1977. I
had decided to go to London in order to see whether any additional information on Lily Montagu could be ascertained.   In
particular, I was hoping to find unpublished sermons, letters
and/or documents further detailing her involvement in the
Liberal Jewish movement. I began my search with a visit to
Eric Conrad, Lily Montagu's biographer and the literary exec-
utor of her will. In 1967, Conrad had published a number of
extracts from Lily Montagu's letters and addresses in a book
entitled *In Memory of Lily H. Montagu*. The extracts were
brief (often no more than a sentence) with no reference either to their source or date of composition. My hope was that
Eric Conrad would be able to supply me not only with this information but also with the letters and addresses themselves.
To my chagrin, I found that he was able to do neither. He had
long since discarded his note cards (containing all biblio-
graphical references) and had given most of the letters and
addresses away. Unfortunately, however, he wasn't sure where
the material was or what, exactly, it contained.

Subsequently, I turned to John Rayner, rabbi of the Liberal Jewish Synagogue, on the "hunch" that some of Lily Montagu's letters and addresses might well be in the synagogue's
possession. While Rabbi Rayner admitted that, to the best of
his knowledge, none of Lily Montagu's unpublished materials
were there, he encouraged me to look through their archives--

a series of cardboard boxes in a closet in a classroom.* For
a week, I painstakingly went through each box, discovering a
fascinating array of synagogue records and private correspondence but, with the exception of letters written to Lily
Montagu by Israel Mattuck from 1912--when he became rabbi of
the Liberal Jewish Synagogue--until shortly before his death
in 1953, I found nothing either by or relating to her. Yet
as luck (or fate) would have it, as I opened the last box
(situated, I remember, in the bottom left hand corner of the
closet), I discovered over one hundred sermons by Lily Montagu, dating from the late 1890s through the fall of 1962 (only
months before her death). Through these sermons, I gained a
clear picture of Lily Montagu's religious vision--its source,
its development (or lack of development), and its centrality
in her life.

The discovery of the sermons encouraged me to look further. At my instigation, Hannah Feldman, a former member of
Lily Montagu's West Central Club and founder of a social organization called the Montagu Circle, discovered over two
hundred open letters (most of which are brief sermons) written to members of the West Central Club from 1939 to 1961.
She found these letters in a closet in the Club building.
Further, I asked Eric Conrad if I might go through any papers
by Lily Montagu still in his possession. Though he agreed,
neither he nor I anticipated the significance of this material. Most important were a series of documents revealing that
Lily Montagu had, in fact, founded the Jewish Religious Union, the organization out of which the Liberal Jewish movement developed. Included was a draft of a questionnaire written in 1899 to several leading members of the Anglo-Jewish

---

*I understand that the material contained in these
boxes has since been catalogued.

community attempting to ascertain how much support her intended association might receive; the draft of a letter
(dated November, 1901) calling for a future meeting, which
Lily Montagu herself identified as the "Letter Which Started
[the] J.R.U.," and the paper that she read at the J.R.U.'s
first "conference" in 1902, inviting those present to "Start
[a] Movement" with her.

My doctoral dissertation drew heavily on these (and
other) unpublished materials. I have since arranged these materials and had them microfilmed, depositing the original mi-
crofilm at the American Jewish Archives in Cincinnati and a
copy at the Liberal Jewish Synagogue in London. This book
grew out of my dissertation. Though broader in its scope and
conclusions, it remains the first critical study of Lily Montagu as a religious thinker and leader. Hopefully, it will
encourage future scholars to investigate Lily Montagu's
equally important contributions as a magistrate and social
worker, while encouraging others to write a history of the
Liberal Jewish movement itself.

My study of Lily Montagu is divided into two parts, preceded by an introduction and followed by a conclusion. The
Introduction sets out the historiographical assumptions underlying my work and clarifies its relationship to other
studies of nineteenth century Anglo-Jewish history and of
emancipation and its impact on Jewish religious life. Part
One then traces the historical, literary, and intellectual
background facilitating Lily Montagu's rise to prominence.
Without ignoring developments that occurred throughout Western Europe as a result of emancipation, it focuses on specific developments in England, all of which helped to create--
directly or indirectly--an atmosphere of tolerance and acceptance of Lily Montagu as a religious organizer and leader.

The most important development, detailed in chapter one,
is the rise of British feminism in the late nineteenth

century. As we shall see, this movement helped increase educational opportunities for women and encouraged their participation in English communal life. Jewish women benefited from these gains and began to demand greater participation within the Anglo-Jewish community as well. The social acceptance of upper class Jews and their own nationalistic fervor (leading in most cases to an anti-Zionist stance), coupled with the devaluation of religion and the concept of religious leadership among the Anglo-Jewish elite, created a new willingness to make the religious position of Jewish women more commensurate with that of women in Great Britain as a whole. Thus, as Christian associations encouraging women's participation were formed and as a number of Christian denominations began to accept women in religious leadership positions, so the Anglo-Jewish elite consciously or unconsciously began to redefine its traditional understanding of women.

Chapter two focuses on the rise of Jewish liberalism as a historical development that gave Lily Montagu's desire to revitalize Anglo-Jewish life greater support and direction. Discussed here (though briefly since both have been detailed elsewhere*) will be the origins of Reform Judaism in Germany and America and, at somewhat greater length, early attempts at Reform in England and their specific impact on Lily Montagu and the Jewish Religious Union that she established. Chapters three and four focus more clearly on Lily Montagu herself. Though it may well be that for most British Jews, even among the elite, the redefinition of Jewishness and Judaism was unselfconscious, Lily Montagu *consciously* sought to redefine not only what it meant to be a Jewish woman but also

---

*See, for example, David Philipson, *The Reform Movement in Judaism*, rev. ed. (New York: Ktav Publishing House, 1967); Gunther Plaut, *The Rise of Reform Judaism* and *The Growth of Reform Judaism* (New York: World Union for Progressive Judaism, 1963).

what it meant to be a Jew. Consequently, chapter three describes her literary background and chapter four her intellectual background, examining those works and people that most
influenced the development of her thought.

Part Two details more fully Lily Montagu's own life and
understanding of real religion. Beginning in chapter five
with a description of her family background and the encouragement that she received to express her ideas about religion
and to share those ideas with others, it focuses in chapter
six on her early efforts as a social worker and author.
Chapter seven describes Lily Montagu's spiritual awakening as
well as her concepts of mission and vocation and chapter
eight deals with the creation of the Jewish Religious Union
and the World Union for Progressive Judaism in which she assumed both organizational and leadership roles. Finally,
chapter nine traces the evolution and content of Lily Montagu's religious thought, including her responses to Zionism
and the Holocaust, and an evaluation of her religious ideas.

The conclusion assesses Lily Montagu's historical significance as a religious thinker, organizer and leader. It also
suggests a number of paradigms which a study of her life reveals. These paradigms help clarify the spiritual quest and
dilemma of many Jewish women in the eighteenth, nineteenth
and twentienth centuries. Taken together, they provide us
with new insight into what it means to be a Jew in the modern
world *and* to be a Jewish woman.

There are a number of people without whose assistance
this book might never have been written. I am indebted to my
dissertation advisor, Joseph L. Blau, for first bringing Lily
Montagu to my attention; to Ira Youdovin, former Director of
the North American Board of the World Union for Progressive
Judaism, for believing in the importance of my research; and
to John Rayner, Eric Conrad, Bertram Jacobs, and Hannah Feldman for making the research possible. I would also like to

thank Arnie Eisen and Gillian Lindt for reading earlier drafts of the manuscript and helping me to focus my study; Jaime Henriquez and Debra Reed for their help in the manuscript's final preparation; my editor, Elizabeth Clark, for her insights, enthusiasm and patience; and my colleague, David Blumenthal, for his honest and critical readings of the text and for his many invaluable suggestions.

In addition, I am grateful to my friends and family for their personal encouragement and support. I am particularly grateful to my mother, Dorothy Umansky, and to my husband, Alan Kannof, who, for the past six years, repeatedly have listened, not just to my "story," but to Lily Montagu's "story" as well. This work would not have been completed without their interest, support and affection.

Finally, I want to thank the following organizations for their financial assistance, which made the researching and writing of this book possible: the National Foundation for Jewish Culture, the Memorial Foundation for Jewish Culture, The National Federation of Temple Sisterhoods, the World Union for Progressive Judaism, the Center for Israel and Jewish Studies at Columbia University, and the American Jewish Archives in Cincinnati.

Ellen M. Umansky
Emory University

LILY MONTAGU
AND THE ADVANCEMENT
OF LIBERAL JUDAISM:
FROM VISION TO VOCATION

Introduction

On June 21, 1909, a distinctively Liberal Jewish movement was created in England. Its aim was to consolidate and
promote Liberal Judaism primarily through the formation of an
independent, fully organized congregation. Although many of
the group's theological beliefs were identical with those espoused by German and American Reformers, the origins of the
group were unique. It emerged out of an already existing organization called the Jewish Religious Union, an association
of Orthodox, Reform,[1] and Liberal Jews which sought to rein-
vigorate the religious life of the Anglo-Jewish community.
In order to do so, it instituted supplementary worship services on Saturday afternoons, conducted along Liberal Jewish
lines. Its intent was to ensure the future existence of a religiously committed Anglo-Jewry by offering a new understanding and appreciation of Judaism as a spiritual inheritance to
those for whom traditional forms of Jewish belief held little
if any appeal.

The Jewish Religious Union was established in February
of 1902. Its founder was a twenty-eight year old woman named
Lily H. Montagu. Encouraged by earlier--albeit unsuccessful--
British efforts at Reform, and greatly influenced by the theological works of Claude Montefiore, she formed an association of "sympathizers" who shared her belief that the growing
tide of religious indifference could best be stemmed through
a sustained and united community effort. Membership in the
association did not imply a personal commitment to Liberal

Judaism but simply a recognition of its ability to awaken within many Jews a sense of spirituality and personal responsibility to God.

Unlike such works as Albert Hyamson's *A History of the Jews in England* which view Anglo-Jewish history as a "history in miniature of the Diaspora,"[2] my study of Lily Montagu focuses on those developments that made Anglo-Jewry unique. Without ignoring important similarities between Anglo-Jewry and other emancipated Jewish communities on the continent, it necessarily asks: what was it about the late nineteenth and early twentieth century Anglo-Jewish community that, *unlike emancipated Jewish communities elsewhere*, enabled an exceptional woman like Lily Montagu to assume a religious leadership position? While emancipated Jewish communities throughout Western Europe offered women new educational and social opportunities and while the Reform movement, established in Germany by the mid-nineteenth century, offered new religious opportunities as well, religious leadership within these communities *de facto* remained within the hands of men. Neither the attainment of legal equality nor the conscious redefinition of Jewish self-identity propelled even exceptional women into actual positions of religious leadership. What, then, made the Anglo-Jewish community different and more specifically, which factors best explain Lily Montagu's rise to prominence?

In attempting to answer these questions, my work begins with an historiographical assumption implicitly shared by Cecil Roth, Lucien Wolf, and V. D. Lipman in their narrative and social histories of modern Anglo-Jewry and explicitly articulated by Todd Endelman in his study of the Jews of Georgian England. Endelman maintains that despite important similarities between the Anglo-Jewish community and Jewish communities elsewhere, one cannot simply subsume the history of modern Anglo-Jewry "under the general category of Western

European history,"[3] for unlike emancipation on the continent,
the integration of Jews into British political, economic and
social life was primarily unselfconscious and achieved before
legal equality had been attained. Thus, he argues, while
tracing struggles for legal equality or conscious reevalua-
tions of Judaism and Jewish self-identity may provide appropriate perspectives from which to examine eighteenth and
nineteenth century Jewish communities on the continent, neither is appropriate in studying the emancipation of British
Jewry.

According to Endelman, the uniqueness of modern Anglo-
Jewish history is rooted in the particular "political culture
and social structure" of eighteenth and early nineteenth century England (which, he notes, bore "little resemblance to
those of France and the German states"). He therefore focuses
his study of British Jewry from 1714 to 1830 on specific developments within England and their impact upon the social
and religious behavior of British Jews. Having done so, he
concludes that the gradual and largely unselfconscious integration of Jews into British society was rooted in the unusu-
ally "high degree of [religious] toleration prevailing in England," leading to the "growing secularization and acculturation of eighteenth and nineteenth century Anglo-Jewish life.[4]

If we extend Endelman's thesis through the late nineteenth and early twentieth centuries, we can begin to understand why Lily Montagu, unlike exceptional Jewish women elsewhere, was able to become a religious leader. Focusing on the
effects of growing secularization and acculturation on the
Jewish community in which she lived as well as on new patterns of behavior that subsequently were created, my study
attempts to show that it was not simply the personality and
drive of Lily Montagu that propelled her to the forefront of
the Liberal Jewish movement. Rather the community, and more
particularly its leaders (members of what Chaim Bermant has

called the Cousinhood, a "union of exclusive brethren with
blood and money flowing in a small circle"[5]), more secularized and acculturated than their counterparts on the continent, created a climate in which an exceptional woman like
Lily Montagu could function as a lay minister and leader of
her own congregation. This climate, created self-consciously
or, extending Endelman's thesis, unselfconsciously, helped
broaden the community's understanding of women's religious
role. In so doing, it enabled Lily Montagu to participate in
a number of activities from which traditionally she would
have been excluded.

My first historiographical assumption, then, is that the
Anglo-Jewish milieu was unique among other modern European
Jewish milieus in the degree to which its leaders reevaluated
and redefined women's religious role. Their reasons for doing
so were largely unselfconscious, rooted in the leadership's
understanding of themselves as "British." Through the forces
of secularization and acculturation (which, as Endelman argues, had a deeper impact upon eighteenth and nineteenth century Anglo-Jewry than upon emancipated Jewish communities on
the continent), the Anglo-Jewish elite began to adopt new
patterns of behavior. One of these patterns, emerging by the
end of the nineteenth century, was a willingness to expand
women's "proper" sphere of activity, making their communal
roles more commensurate with those of women in British society and their religious roles more commensurate with those assumed by women within the Victorian Church.[6]

GENDER, CONVERSION AND LIBERAL JUDAISM

In focusing on the religious activities of women, my
study of Lily Montagu contains a second historiographical
assumption. While a number of historians (including Endelman)
have discussed the geographical ramifications of emancipation

and have clearly elucidated the importance of economic and social class, they have largely ignored the extent to which gender helped shape the impact of emancipation on European (and even American) Jewry. Yet as my study of Lily Montagu reveals, the nature of Jewish emancipation takes on new dimensions when viewed from the perspective of women. My second historiographical assumption, then, is that just as one needs to differentiate between the impact of emancipation on British Jews and French Jews, and between wealthy Jews and those of the lower classes, so one needs to differentiate between the impact of emancipation on Jewish men and on Jewish women. Some historians have alluded to these differences. However, with the exception of Charlotte Baum, Paula Hyman and Sonya Michel's *The Jewish Woman in America*, historical studies have minimized (or misunderstood) the significance of Jewish women's own experiences and perceptions.

In the eighteenth and nineteenth centuries, emancipation forced both men and women to reevaluate their sense of Jewish self-identity. Some searched for ways of becoming fully modern while remaining fully Jewish. Others converted to Christianity as a way of ensuring their acceptance within the non-Jewish world. Several historians have noted that, among Jews who converted, women were the first to do so. The case of women, it would seem then, was different. Unlike their brothers, whose education remained confined to religious texts, middle and upper class girls frequently studied piano, foreign languages and a variety of secular subjects. Their education served as a visible sign of acculturation, proof that their families had indeed adapted to modernity. According to Jacob Katz, women's "access to enlightened education and culture" helped create an early sensitivity among Jews toward their inferior social status, leading many Jewish women to try to escape this status by means of baptism and intermarriage. [7] Claiming, then, that the major motivation

behind conversion to Christianity was social elevation, Katz
maintains that women converted first because their familiarity with Christian literature and their participation in mixed
social circles created an early awareness of all that Jews
were missing--socially, culturally and presumably politically
and economically as well.

Although the status of the Jew as pariah undoubtedly did
lead some women to undergo baptism (see, for example, Hannah
Arendt's study of Rahel Varnhagen), I am not convinced that
it was the perception of this status that lay behind most
female conversions to Christianity. Indeed, I would argue
that the assumption that women and men converted for the same
reasons is largely unfounded, based on a universalization of
experiences that were primarily if not solely the experiences
of Jewish men. Primary sources seem to indicate that, among
women who converted, many if not most converted for *religious*
reasons. I would, further, suggest that these religious conversions were not rooted in personal idiosyncracies but in
women's own understanding of themselves *as Jews*.

Women's limited Jewish education and their exclusion
from much of public worship may not have diminished the external Jewish identification of emancipated middle and upper
class women but it may have led them to *feel* less Jewish than
did their brothers. As they, like their male counterparts,
began to reexamine their sense of Jewish self-identity, they
may have begun to recognize that Judaism had little to offer,
not just in terms of social status but (and for some, more
importantly) as an outlet for religious self-expression.
Perhaps for women, even those who continued to identify themselves as Jews, the "problem" was not one of becoming fully
modern while remaining fully Jewish, but becoming fully Jewish while remaining fully modern. As one eighteenth century
observer noted, wealthy Jewish women were "100% better than
the men," that is, they were more acculturated, more at home

in the non-Jewish world.[8] And yet, ignorant of most Jewish
texts and barely able to read Hebrew, they felt *less* at home
in a Jewish environment that had begun to equate Judaism with
religion. Thus, they may well have asked themselves, if all
Judaism provided was a sense of religious self-identity, why
remain within a tradition in which one had little access to
knowledge and limited access to prayer?

The conflict between tradition on the one hand and self-
actualization on the other led many Jewish women, like Dorothea Mendelssohn, Moses Mendelssohn's eldest daughter, to
convert to Christianity. Dorothea, as Michael Meyer writes in
The Origins of the Modern Jew, was religious by nature: "She
possessed an inner life, creativity of the spirit, and a
feeling for the universe."[9] However, he maintains,

> There was really very little that was Jewish about
> Dorothea. In the manner of Jewish girls at the time
> she apparently received no extensive Jewish train-
> ing although . . . her father had personally taken
> an interest in her general education. In the Veit
> household [referring to her first marriage to Simon
> Veit] the major holidays were celebrated but there
> is no indication that Dorothea's observance of the
> Jewish tradition was anything more than perfuncto-
> ry, if indeed she did not already despise it. Her
> father's definition of Judaism as "revealed legis-
> lation" served to make Judaism a non-religion in
> her eyes. For this young woman, who thought, acted,
> and felt out of her own self, an externally imposed
> code, like a loveless marriage, had to seem like a
> weighty, senseless yoke, a kind of "slavery."[10]

Dorothea, in other words, not only was religious but also
claimed to possess an understanding of "religion." Yet having
little understanding of the ways in which Judaism defined the

religious, she was forced to develop a concept derived almost exclusively from non-Jewish sources.

Meyer suggests that Dorothea Mendelssohn rejected Judaism because it was too rational. Perhaps she rejected Judaism because she knew so little about it. Had she been more familiar with Jewish texts she might have been able to discover *for herself* a Jewish understanding of the religious that was compatible with her romantic nature. Even more likely, however, Dorothea rejected Judaism because she recognized—with justification—that even if she *had* redefined Judaism in a personally meaningful way, her participation within Jewish religious circles still would have been limited. The Jewish (Orthodox) community would not have made a public place for her. Even Jewish mysticism, which might have attracted her, remained closed to women altogether. Dorothea rightly concluded that Judaism simply did not offer women a means through which they could fully express their own religious nature. Such a means, she believed, could be discovered only through conversion to Christianity.

Meyer's description of Dorothea as religious but minimally Jewish sounds strikingly similar to other descriptions of eighteenth and nineteenth century middle and upper class Jewish women. Henriette Herz, one of the famous "salon Jewesses" of Berlin, received an extensive general education, studying Latin, Greek, Sanskrit, mathematics and physics. Her Jewish education, however, was more limited. She read the Bible in Hebrew along with some rabbinic commentaries (thus exceeding the religious knowledge of most of her female contemporaries) but knew far more about contemporary literature and philosophy than she did about either Jewish literature or thought. As Henriette herself wrote, "Children, particularly the girls, were not at all really instructed in the faith of their parents, but were constrained to observe its *forms*."[11] Judaism therefore became for her, as it had for Dorothea, a "dull practice of mechanical observance" of which she had little if any understanding.[12] It is not surprising, then, that Henriette found in Christianity "the consolation of a higher order."[13] Like Dorothea, she came to equate religion with inner piety and faith, which she could cultivate freely as a Christian, but not as an Orthodox Jewish woman.

Many eighteenth and early nineteenth century Jewish women, including Henriette Herz, Dorothea Mendelssohn and her sister Henriette, the daughters of Moses Isaacs of Berlin,[14] and perhaps even Rahel Varnhagen, found it impossible to remain fully modern while becoming fully Jewish for they identified that which was fully Jewish with Orthodoxy (or traditionalism) which, according to the modern sources to which they had been exposed, was antithetical to real religion. With a minimal understanding of Judaism and little emotional attachment (in part, I think, due to their limited education and a religious role which they perceived to be subordinate if not inferior) these women were confronted with a choice: either to continue to identify themselves as Jews and forgo the development of their inner spiritual nature or to become religious (and in the process, more socially acceptable) through conversion to Christianity.

We find in the writings of Lily Montagu a similar understanding of religion as inner piety, based on a familiarity with contemporary literature and philosophy and an almost complete ignorance of traditional Jewish texts. Though raised as an Orthodox Jew, she found Orthodoxy to be an "external fact" of her life which held neither inner beauty nor meaning. Consequently, she found it impossible to be *both* Orthodox and religious, claiming that Orthodoxy, and in particular that which it offered to women, only served as a hindrance to the development of true religious faith.

Yet in reading the theological works of Claude Montefiore and in learning of Reform Judaism in Germany and America,

Lily Montagu, as we shall see, discovered that one could be fully Jewish and fully spiritual without being an Orthodox Jew. She recognized that by redefining Judaism it was possible not only to remain modern but also to find, within Judaism itself, that which she had come to identify as the religious. Had she lived one hundred years earlier, Lily Montagu might well have converted to Christianity. But by the end of the nineteenth century, with the success of the Reform movement in Germany and America and the development of female religious leadership in the British setting, a new option appeared, namely to identify oneself as modern and Jewish by harmonizing Judaism with the spirit of the modern age.

PART ONE

BACKGROUND

I. Setting the Stage: Legal and Social Background

The Jewish community of late nineteenth century England was a community that had long been subject to the forces of emancipation, secularization, religious indifference and skepticism. For many, Judaism had long ceased to be an inspiring moral force. Among the wealthy, synagogue affiliation had become little more than a sign of respectability while religious laxity--among rich and poor--had increasingly become less the exception than the rule. To those, like Lily Montagu, who viewed this growing spiritual degeneration with alarm, Anglo-Jewry had lost sight of the dignity, beauty and truth of its religion. In vain, she wrote,

> we seek to gloss over the facts, in vain we point
> triumphantly to our charity-lists, to our learning,
> to our position in the front of every profession.
> We have yet to confess ourselves unable to impart
> to our children a strengthening faith.[1]

Emancipation and the Anglicization of British Jewry

In part, the religiously apathetic nature of the Anglo-Jewish community stemmed from the desire of its members to achieve political, social and economic emancipation. By the latter half of the nineteenth century, this struggle for equality was largely over. Political and civil equality had been attained, participation in England's economic life had increased, and there was little evidence of social discrimination, especially towards the native (predominately middle class) Jewish population. Of the 40,000 to 45,000 Jews living

in London in 1880, about half had been born in England.
Ninety percent were voluntarily affiliated with one of the
many synagogues in west, northwest and southwest London. Of
these, approximately seventy percent belonged to the United
Synagogue, "a union of orthodox (but highly anglicized)
middle-class congregations."[2]

As an increasing number of privileges were achieved,
Jews became eager to demonstrate their adaptability to English society. Their major source of identification began to
shift from religion to nationality and by the end of the century, members of the upper classes had begun to view themselves primarily as Englishmen and only secondarily as Jews.[3]
Secularized and acculturated, they identified themselves as
Englishmen of the Jewish persuasion, with Judaism seen less
as a spiritual force than as a social agent, important to the
community because it "continued to serve externally at least
as a delineation from the non-Jewish world."[4]

The leaders of the Anglo-Jewish community were wealthy
men who had taken advantage of Britain's commercial and political expansion. They discovered that "capitalism, private
enterprise, open competition, *laissez-faire*, and the reduc-
tion of control by the state to a minimum," ideas which were
in vogue during the early Victorian era,[5] provided great opportunity for personal financial success. Particularly at-
tractive was the emerging banking business, centered interna-
tionally in London. The Cohens, the Rothschilds, the Gold-
smidts, the Samuels, the Mocattas, the Montefiores and the
Montagus--those families from which the Anglo-Jewish leadership emerged--rose to become bankers and brokers in bullion.
Their commercial success not only eased their acceptance into
British society but also contributed to a growing sense of
nationalism among them.

The achievement of civil and political equality during
the nineteenth century also strengthened the nationalistic

identification of British Jews, especially among those of the
upper classes. Following the Resettlement in 1657, royal dis-
pensations had enabled Jews to establish synagogues in London. Parliament, however, did not formally legalize the profession of Jewish religious beliefs until 1846 and did not
provide for the registration to synagogues until 1855. Religious oaths, under Parliamentary enactment, limited Jewish
economic and political activity. Until 1831, for example,
Jews were required to take an oath upon the New Testament in
order to become citizens of London. They were consequently
excluded from engaging in retail trades within the city because the by-laws of the corporation of London had limited
such businesses to "freemen."

Admission to the legal profession also depended upon
one's taking an oath of abjuration. Up until 1833, Jews were
unable to omit the oath's final words, "On the true faith of
a Christian," and therefore could not be called to the bar.
By 1844, they had attained most rights of British citizenship
but until the Statute Law Revision Act was passed in 1867,
voters could be requested to take an oath of abjuration, professing their Christian faith, before their votes would be
recorded. Jews could be elected to Parliament, but until 1858
they could not be seated, again, because the oath of admission included the declaration of one's faith as a Christian.
The House of Lords successfully opposed Jewish membership until 1885. In July of that year, Sir Nathaniel de Rothschild,
the first Jew elevated to the peerage, "was sworn in and took
his seat accordingly."[6]

Although emancipation was not dependent upon the renunciation of one's Jewish national identification, the majority
of native-born Jews stood in opposition to both Zionism and
the concept of Jewish nationalism. Believing that their cultural and political integration rested upon an adjustment in
identity, they maintained that they were united not by race

but by the "bond of common religion."[7] Thus, they echoed the
conviction of the Chief Rabbi, Dr. Hermann Adler, that,

> we are simply Englishmen . . . certainly holding
> particular theological tenets and practising spe
> cial religious ordinances; but we stand in the same
> relation to our countrymen as any other religious
> sect, having the same stake in the national welfare
> and the same claim on the privileges and duties of
> citizenship.[8]

For this reason, a significant number took part in the human-
itarian movements of the day. Affirming the brotherhood of
all people, they worked to alleviate such social problems as
gambling, drunkenness, and prostitution. Many expressed interest in socialist organizations and newly formed trade unions and claimed that one could lead a moral life without attachment to any particular religious group. Thus, like many
of their Christian neighbors, many nineteenth century British
Jews believed that the criterion of a meaningful existence
was not the degree to which one served God, but the degree to
which one served his or her fellow human beings.

By the late nineteenth century, members of the Anglo-
Jewish elite no longer saw themselves as part of an exclusive
social community. Social contacts with non-Jews were frequently made and close friendships often developed. Many,
like Henrietta Franklin, Lily Montagu's sister, had predominately non-Jewish friends.[9] Some, like Edwin Montagu, Lily's
older brother, maintained that despite "certain undefined
Jewish feelings" they felt no sense of fellowship with the
Jewish people at all. A number of Jews were alarmed by the
rapid growth of intermarriage, but most accepted it as an oc-
currence concomitant with emancipation. While Judaism remained a source of religious identity, their strongest ties were
not necessarily with other Jews, but with men and women who,
like themselves, were citizens of Great Britain.

THE STRUCTURE OF THE RELIGIOUS INSTITUTIONS

The formation of the United Synagogue in 1870 pro-
vided--whether consciously or unconsciously--a Jewish coun-
terpart to the Church of England. It offered Orthodox congregations a financial framework as well as a unified administrative structure and, despite the fact that its religious
doctrines were grounded in traditional Jewish law, created an
"aura that was Anglican, even to the mock Gothic exterior of
its buildings."[10] Using as its cultural reference "anglicized
values, norms and patterns of behavior,"[11] the United Synagogue sought to transform organized Anglo-Jewish life into a
uniquely British institution.

All of the congregations incorporated in the United Synagogue previously had recognized the single authority of a
Chief Rabbi in matters concerning religious law and forms of
worship. Although the Chief Rabbinate was not an officially
created office, the native Ashkenazic congregations in London
acknowledged the primacy of the Great Synagogue, the first
Ashkenazic congregation formed after the Resettlement, and by
1802 accepted its spiritual leader as Chief Rabbi not just of
London but of England as well. This led to the institution of
"mono-rabbinism" within the Ashkenazic London community.
While, with the exception of the Great Synagogue, the other
city congregations still maintained their own religious leaders, they all helped to elect and financially support the
Chief Rabbi and placed under his control the religious direction and general superintendence of each of the constituent
congregations. In addition, he would determine questions of
religious observance, officiate at marriages, visit schools
and provincial congregations and supervise the ritual slaughter of animals in London and in the provinces.

When the United Synagogue was established, the office of
the Chief Rabbi gained formal recognition. The five "predominately middle class, native congregations" which formed the

Union agreed to maintain a Chief Rabbi to supervise their religious affairs. As Stephen Sharot points out, the concern of
the United Synagogue's wealthy, highly acculturated lay leaders was

> that Anglo-Jewry should have a religious leader who
> would occupy a position of authority somewhat par-
> allel to that of the Archbishop of Canterbury in
> the Anglican Church. [12]

However, while his religious jurisdiction gained some acceptance among native provincial and colonial congregations not
belonging to the Union, the London Sephardic and Reform Synagogues refused to acknowledge him and the United Synagogue
continued to provide for his financial support. Nevertheless, even without the successful creation of a single, Jewish ecclesiastical head, many native congregations recognized
the central religious authority of the Chief Rabbi and, by
the end of the nineteenth century, accepted the two-tiered
rabbinical hierarchy which had been established.

Below the office of Chief Rabbi was that of the minister. His role and appearance reflected the desire of native
congregations to anglicize Jewish institutional life. Ministers were clean shaven, wore canonicals and a silk scarf, instead of a traditional woolen prayer shawl, and like the Anglican and Nonconformist clergy, were expected to preach,
teach, engage in various charitable activities and serve as
administrators or secretaries of their congregations. [13] They
were neither required nor expected to possess a rabbinical
diploma and until the beginning of the twentieth century, had
to study abroad in order to obtain one. Although they did
study Jewish law, ministers were rarely asked to interpret
religious legal matters. As a consequence, this study was
considered important not as an end in itself, but as a means
of preaching better. [14]

While immigrant rabbis viewed these ministers with contempt, to the highly acculturated lay leaders of native Anglo-Jewry, it was important that their congregations have "a minister living like a Christian clergyman in the midst of his flock."[15] Yet because they were without either religious authority (what Stephen Sharot has identified as the "institutionalized charisma of the Anglican clergy") or the "scholarly status of the traditional rabbinate," the status of the Anglo-Jewish minister remained low.[16] Predominately from the lower middle class, they received relatively small salaries, did not take part in decisions concerning lay matters, preached but often did not lead the synagogue service and, in general, were under the control of the lay leadership. Thus, Anglo-Jewish ministers became English gentlemen, but their role within Jewish communal life was not highly valued.

Modifications which were made in the synagogue service also reflected the religious acculturation which had taken place within the native Jewish community. Changes were non-ideological and pragmatic. For example, English prayers were introduced, "special services" (corresponding to Confirmation) were held for children, and Hermann Adler, as Chief Rabbi, sanctioned choral weddings and, as part of the marriage ceremony, a question and answer form resembling that used by Christians.[17]

Constituent congregations of the United Synagogue consciously sought to model their worship services after those of the Church of England. Although the content of their services remained fairly traditional, the emphasis on decorum and form stood out in sharp contrast to the religious behavior within immigrant congregations. Unlike the immigrant services,

> the native services were orderly and decorous; the
> majority of worshippers did not participate; they
> could best be described as spectators of the highly

formalized rituals presented by the choir, *hazan*
[reader of the service], and minister. [18]

Women frequently attended these services. Following the
"church-going customs of the Victorian borgeoisie," they had
maids and governesses stay at home and look after the children. Subsequently, in newly-built Orthodox synagogues, the
ratio of seats provided for women and men was significantly
altered. Reflecting the acceptance of British ideas concerning the co-participation of women and men in public religious
life, the proportion of women's seats rose significantly and
in some cases "even achieved parity with [those] of men." [19]

In 1890, Simeon Singer, minister of the New West End
Synagogue, published an edition of the prayer book entitled
"The Authorized Daily Prayer Book of the United Hebrew Congregations of the British Empire." Containing an English
translation, it revealed both the centralized power of the
Chief Rabbi and the desire for a common Book of Prayer paral-
leling that used within the Church of England. Adopting words
such as vestry, overseer, Board, Ecclesiastical and even minister, the United Synagogue stressed its British character.
As Edward Jamilly maintains:

> With top-hatted officers, well-heeled congregants
> listening rather than praying, leaving the vocal
> work to cantor and choir, there can be no doubt
> that in its Victorian phase, the United Synagogue
> succeeded in establishing itself as the Church of
> the Anglican Jew. [20]

Congregations formed by the thousands of immigrants who
came to London in the latter decades of the nineteenth century adhered to more traditional dress, behavior and worship.
Yet the leaders of the Anglo-Jewish community actively attempted to absorb the immigrants into the native Jewish population. Their efforts included,

> . . . schemes to disperse the immigrants from the
> East End, supporting apprenticeships to draw Jews
> out of the "Jewish" trades, English language even-
> ing classes, youth clubs, the Jews' Free School,
> and the provision of Talmud Torahs to replace the
> hedarim [religious elementary schools] which were
> believed to perpetuate the immigrants' foreign
> culture.[21]

In addition, the United Synagogue planned to build a large
synagogue in the East End as a means of providing anglicized
services for foreign Jews. The so-called "East End Scheme"
eventually failed, but the attention devoted to it revealed
the importance attached to anglicization and the transformation of traditional Jewish life.

SECULARISM AND THE JEWISH COMMUNITY

As early as the mid-eighteenth century, the increasingly
secular nature of British society precipitated the growth of
religious indifference not only among Christians but also
among Jews. By the end of the nineteenth century, with secularism even more pervasive and almost all remaining barriers
between Jews and non-Jews removed, the Jewish community found
itself more subject than ever to the forces of secularization.

Expanded educational opportunities facilitated increased
social contact with non-Jews who were close to the intellectual currents of the day. Mandatory religious examinations and
oaths professing allegiance to the Church of England previously had prevented Jews, like other Dissenters, from taking
degrees and holding office in the universities. In 1854, however, the Oxford University Reform Act made lower degrees
open to Dissenters. Two years later, an act passed at Cambridge opened scholarships and all but theological degrees to

qualified individuals of any religious belief. Educational
gains were bolstered by an 1871 Parliamentary enactment which
permitted Dissenters to hold fellowships and take part in
university governance. With the exception of degrees and pro-
fessorships in Divinity, all offices were opened without regard to religious belief, and students were to be excused
from attending:

> . . . the public worship of any church, sect or de-
> nomination to which he does not belong, or any lec-
> ture to which he, if of full age, or, if he is un-
> der age, his parent or guardian shall object on re-
> ligious grounds.[22]

By the end of the nineteenth century, similar provisions
had been effected with regard to elementary and secondary education. For example, Jews (and other Dissenters) were exempt
from Anglican religious instruction in all schools which were
"public" or "endowed." Most of these schools excused Dissenters from attending worship services and Harrow, one of the
seven schools legally recognized as "public" by the Public
Schools Act of 1868, even provided its Jewish students with
instruction "in the tenets of their own religion."[23]

At the universities, Jews came into contact with ideas
which seriously challenged their traditional religious beliefs. Scientific theories and discoveries, Biblical criticism and the study of comparative religion brought their beliefs into question and created, for many, a seemingly irreconcilable conflict between science and faith. Old beliefs
were examined and often abandoned. Many began to formulate
new religious conceptions and returned to London with less
commitment to Jewish ceremonies, observances and laws.[24] Secularism, like agnosticism and religious skepticism, increased
and, like the young Beatrice Webb, many Jews attempted to unite "faith in the scientific method with the transference of
the emotion of self-sacrificing service from God to man."[25]

The *Memoirs* of Herbert Samuel, the first Jewish member of the British cabinet and later High Commissioner for Palestine under the British mandate, reveals the ways in which that which Beatrice Webb called the "mid-Victorian time-spirit" of doubt and inner struggle affected a good number of English Jews. Raised within an observant Jewish household (Lily Montagu was his first cousin and her father, Samuel Montagu, his guardian), Samuel learned Hebrew as a child, regularly attended services at the New West End Synagogue and conscientiously followed "the dietary laws and other requirements of the Jewish faith."[26]

Between 1889 and 1893, however, as an undergraduate at Oxford, he became an "active member" of the Balliol College debating society, the radical Russell Club, the Society for the Study of Social Ethics and the Social Science Club; formed "lasting friendships" with the leaders of the Fabian Society--Bernard Shaw, Graham Wallis, and Sidney (and later Beatrice) Webb; worked for social and political reform and helped organize public meetings. At Oxford, he read voraciously and, greatly influenced by John Morley's *Compromise*, grew increasingly dissatisfied with religious orthodoxy. By 1892, the tension created between his early education and family tradition on the one hand, and Biblical Higher Criticism and Darwin's theory of evolution on the other, had become acute. He found that he could not accept much that was "integral in the orthodox creed and ritual" and wrote to his mother that he could no longer confess any Jewish beliefs. While Herbert Samuel retained his synagogue membership, "though not attending the services, except on formal occasions," and rejected "the materialist philosophy which was then widely prevalent," he remained "in a very negative and critical frame of mind" for many years, "too busy" to develop new beliefs which could have meaning for him.[27]

Even those Jews who did not attend the universities became aware of the changes which were taking place in nineteenth century British thought. The steadily declining influence of the church, the confrontation between religion and
natural science, and the increasingly pervasive atmosphere of
secularism and skepticism found expression in popular essays,
novels, plays and poems. Moreover, as Owen Chadwick has observed, as defenders of religious toleration continued to
voice the conviction that liberty was an inalienable right,
"a good in itself, a quality of man and of society which enabled moral personality, moral development, [and] self realization," it became difficult if not impossible to defend the
"toleration of dissenting [religious] opinion" without de-
fending the "toleration of irreligious opinion" as well. [28] If
belief was to be a matter of private concern, there was nothing one could or ought to do to prevent the growth of secular thought.

Consequently, by the end of the nineteenth century,
while Jewish participation in such areas as business, indus-
try, medicine, law and architecture increased, synagogue attendance remained low, the intensity of religious practice
declined, and indifference to Jewish learning became widespread. Those individuals who had the money, time and inclin-
ation to play a major role in the public life of the community became the lay leaders of Anglo-Jewry. Yet most had little religious commitment and neither attended synagogue on a
regular basis nor "cared enough about ritual to concern themselves with proposed changes in the orthodox form of
service." [29]

Even those changes which were proposed reflected the
community's secular nature. For example, in 1879, a ritual
revision committee formed at the Central Synagogue, an Orthodox congregation largely composed of English-born, middle
class Jews, proposed that the prayer book omit selections

from the Talmud. Assigning a low value to religious knowledge, the committee maintained that:

> the Jewish man of business today . . . has no taste
> for those Talmudic studies . . . . He does not un-
> derstand the language of those Talmudic extracts.
> The time has gone by for the study of Talmudic lit-
> erature in the synagogue. The synagogue, as every-
> body knows, was once literally the *Shull*, the House
> of Study. It is now simply and solely the House of
> Prayer. Passages from the Talmud which were former-
> ly in their place in the prayer book are, conse-
> quently, out of place in it now. [30]

The committee also recommended that the repetition of the
Amidah prayer be omitted, the minister read the Ten Commandments during Sabbath day worship, and the service begin at a
later hour. These modifications, however, primarily affected
the form of the service and not its content. More radical
changes might have been made but, as Chaim Bermant has observed, the Anglo-Jewish elite was "sufficiently English to
revere antiquity, cherish tradition, and to take a proper
pride in ancestry and all that ancestors stood for."[31] What's
more, because most of its members were more interested in the
"outward appearance of religious life" than in religious life
itself,[32] those controversies that did arise were usually
adminstrative and personal rather than theological in nature.

The anglicized and secularized nature of the Anglo-
Jewish community greatly contributed to the entrance of Lily
Montagu into public religious life and to her later acceptance as a religious leader. By the end of the nineteenth century, as we already have seen, most of the lay leaders of the
Anglo-Jewish community, though identifying themselves as Orthodox, maintained little personal commitment to traditional
rabbinic law. While undoubtedly, then, Lily Montagu's attainment of religious leadership would have been more difficult

had she lived within a highly observant Jewish community,
within a community that no longer viewed either traditional
Judaism or religion as central to one's life, the establishment of the Jewish Religious Union was as inconsequential as
the fact that its founder was a woman.

THE ENTRANCE OF JEWISH WOMEN INTO PUBLIC RELIGIOUS LIFE

In founding the Jewish Religious Union, and later, func-
tioning as a lay minister and President of both the Union of
Liberal and Progressive Synagogues and the World Union for
Progressive Judaism, Lily Montagu had few if any role models
to follow. Throughout Jewish history, only a handful of women
achieved recognition as scholars, authorities in Jewish legal
matters and even more rarely, as the social-spiritual head of
a community. Most accepted their "preferred" roles as wives
and mothers.

Prior to the eighteenth century, Jewish women predominately were concerned with home-related duties. The public
sphere of Jewish religious life was considered to be a male
domain. While women were not explicitly prohibited from attaining positions of community leadership (although, according to Maimonides, all offices were to be held by men), their
legal, social and religious subordination made it psycholo-
gically difficult for them to do so. In marriage, divorce,
matters of inheritance and within the courts, women's rights
were severely limited and they were almost always dependent,
first on their fathers and later on their husbands. Moreover,
their responsibilities within the home exempted them from
many of the 613 commandments which Jews had to fulfill, including the obligation to study and to pray three times a
day. Within the synagogue, women were not counted as members
of the quorum required for public worship and could not be
called to recite a blessing before the reading of the Torah.

Their religious exemptions as well as their social exclusion
from public life precluded their serving as representatives
of the community in leading public prayer, while their physical separation from men during the worship service often
meant that they could hear and see little of what was taking
place, making them little more than non-participating
observers.

Within the medieval Jewish community, women essentially
were "enablers," i.e., by fulfilling their numerous household
and family obligations and providing a loving and supporting
atmosphere within the home, they enabled their husbands and
sons to occupy themselves in study and prayer. Consequently,
women realized their spiritual potential primarily through
the merits of their fathers or husbands rather than through
the development of their own spiritual nature. Yet, despite
women's exclusion from much of public religious life, Judaism's emphasis on the family, the celebration of many of its
holidays within the home, and the importance placed on fulfilling certain commandments (the majority of which extended
to women as well as men), provided many women with what was
undoubtedly a satisfying religious role.

By the eighteenth century, however, as Jews began to
participate in the social, economic and political life of
non-Jewish society, the traditional role of Jewish women was
seriously called into question. While secular learning
threatened men's total absorption in Torah study, providing
one's daughters with a secular education became a visible
symbol of Jewish adaptability. Thus, eighteenth century well-
to-do families encouraged their daughters "to learn the language of their neighbors and to acquire a familiarity with
foreign languages and literature." [33]

Yet as Jewish women increasingly recognized their capa-
city for knowledge, former justifications for their exclusion
from religious study and their unequal participation in

communal life and public worship could no longer be upheld.
Their traditional role appeared limited and circumscribed in
comparison with the greater opportunities available to middle
and upper class women in the "secular" world. Thus, once the
process of emancipation began, Jewish women began to seek
spiritual lives of their own. The stress on individualism,
dating back to the Renaissance and the Protestant Reforma-
tion, had a particularly strong effect, and led many Jewish
women to reevaluate their *own* religious identification. As we
have already seen, some, finding that Judaism offered only
limited means for exploring their spirituality, turned to a
romanticized form of Christianity which allowed for greater
"freedom, inner development and being true to oneself."[34] The
majority of women remained within the Jewish community, but
increasing numbers expressed dissatisfaction with the religious role which had been assigned to them.

By the end of the nineteenth century, women had begun to
demand greater access to Jewish public life. In England, as
efforts by the emerging women's movement helped create increased economic, social and political opportunities for single women, the Anglo-Jewish elite--all of whom sought to appear "British"--began to approve of an expanding role for
women within the Jewish community itself. In addition,
Christian associations were established, most of which encouraged women's participation. Consequently, Lily Montagu's
Jewish Religious Union received support among middle and upper class Jews who otherwise might have objected to a religious association founded and to a large extent led by a
woman. In order, then, to understand why Lily Montagu gained
acceptance as a Jewish religious leader, one needs to recognize not only the general impact of anglicization and secularization on the Anglo-Jewish community but also the specific impact of British feminism and the expanding role of
women within the church as well.

THE EMERGENCE OF THE "NEW WOMAN"

During the second half of the nineteenth century, the
so-called "woman's question" was much discussed and debated
throughout Great Britain. By the late 1850s, feminist agitation, previously fragmentary and sporadic, coalesced into a
movement which sought to improve the legal position of women,
increase their educational and economic opportunities, and
alleviate the harsh conditions in which working class women
were forced to live. These efforts, as Martha Vicinus has
noted, forced not only men but "women themselves - and particularly middle class women," to become "increasingly concerned with what their roles were and what they should be." [35]

By twentieth century standards, the goals and demands of
nineteenth century British feminism were conservative. Most
feminists accepted the Victorian notion that men and women
were different but complementary, that women were "by nature"
more intuitive, emotional and spiritual than men, possessing
the gift of influence as complement to the male gift of
power. Consequently, nineteenth century British feminism
failed to challenge the family-centered role of the middle
and upper class married woman, believing that it was her mission to create within the home an atmosphere infused with
female purity, righteousness and beauty.

At the same time, however, feminists like Barbara Leigh
Smith Bodichon, Harriet Martineau, Frances Power Cobbe, Jessie Boucherett, Anna Jameson and Josephine Butler actively
fought to uplift the social status of middle class single
women and to expand the number of careers open to them. They
argued that the special skills which women possessed regarding children, education, health care and domestic morality
should be extended beyond the family. Insisting that women be
released "from domestic idleness, confinement and impoverish-
ment and allowed to share in the productive work of the
world," they forced their contemporaries to think about

women's work in new terms.[36] By the end of the century, many
middle class single women had found employment as nurses,
clerical workers, printers, trained teachers and headmistres-
ses (gradually rendering governessing, formerly one of the
only occupations open to respectable, middle class unmarried
women, obsolete). A few became midwives and doctors; others
became writers. Wealthier single women often chose careers in
social work and philanthropy. As Janet Murray has observed,
some used their "organizational skills to set up woman-run
institutions that were meant to provide jobs and training for
other women."[37] At the beginning of the nineteenth century,
women were expected not to work unless to do so was financially necessary. By the end of the century, wealthy single
women had begun to explore new ways of being useful. The early Victorian image of the perfect lady, spending her time in
"elaborate idleness,"[38] began to give way to the image of the
perfect woman or the new woman who "worked, sought education
and fought for legal and political rights."[39]

While few lower class women gained immediate benefit
from the emergence of the new woman, feminists worked with
male reformers to gain improvements in the working conditions
of women laboring in factories and mines. Josephine Butler's
campaign against the Contagious Diseases Act was instrumental
in the repeal of an act that, in seeking to regulate prostitution, not only subjected prostitutes to public harassment
and humiliation but also made lower class women living in
garrison towns (believed to be the "resorts of prostitutes")
vulnerable to arrest, inspection and confinement.[40] Though
efforts on behalf of working class women were rooted in a domestic idealization of womanhood (hence, both middle class
feminists and their male supporters encouraged lower class
girls to enter into domestic service, that which helped cultivate their "womanly" talents), the image of the new woman
offered working class girls an ideal to which they could more

realistically aspire than that of the perfect lady. Most
working class girls undoubtedly realized the futility of such
aspirations. Yet a significant number of wealthy new women--
like Lily Montagu--continued to offer them classes in technical training, needlework, singing and other cultural re-
finements in the hope that they might gain greater means of
self-development and self-expression.

The philanthropic efforts of women like Lily Montagu reflected the new "more personally involved pattern of charitable activity" that had emerged by the middle of the
century.[41] Unlike earlier forms of benevolence,

> [it] committed the charitable not merely to some
> standing managerial and financial responsibility
> but to personal charitable activity; to the expend-
> iture of time and effort as well as, or even in
> stead of, money.[42]

While this new understanding of philanthropy was pursued by
both men and women, it particularly appealed to girls of the
upper classes, "new women," whose lives had been significantly altered by feminist agitation. By the 1890s, it was not
unusual for wealthy girls to visit the poor and provide them
with both secular and religious instruction. Occasionally,
cultural events were held for members of both the upper and
lower classes, encouraging greater social contact between
them. At the same time, however, upper class girls were admonished to keep their involvement within certain well-
defined limits of propriety. Thus, for example, many, such as
Lily Montagu and her sister Marian, could visit working class
families only if accompanied by a governess. In addition, it
was expected that their charitable activities not interfere
with their social obligations, including the numerous dances
and dinner parties at which wealthy girls might meet their
husbands-to-be. "The accepted life's programme for every girl
in my set," Lily Montagu wrote, "was that she should go out

as much as possible, know plenty of 'nice people,' and settle down in an early age in marriage."[43] Consequently, it was not until her "small beginning" as a social worker grew into a "practically whole-time service," that Lily Montagu met with parental anxiety and concern.

Yet Lily Montagu wasn't the only member of her "set" to turn aside thoughts of marriage and children. According to Anna Bronwell Jameson, writing in 1855, the 1851 census revealed that there were 104 women to every 100 men living in Great Britain, an excess female population of over half a million.[44] Thus, it seems, not all women *could* get married (unless they chose to emigrate, a suggestion that was at least raised if not seriously considered). As a result, increasing numbers of "surplus" or "redundant" middle class women found themselves financially forced to seek employment. Wealthier single women, like Lily Montagu, could have remained at home, but as the early notion of refinement, that which would have precluded their involvement in public activities, largely became discarded, many sought to "justify their existence by some form of useful effort."[45]

The demographic imbalance of men and women in nineteenth century Great Britain precipitated feminist demands for the re-evaluation and expansion of the concept of woman's work. As Jessie Boucherett argued in an essay written in 1869, redundant women would not be viewed as "superfluous," i.e., unnecessarily excessive, if they were given the opportunity to "engage freely in all occupations suited to their strengths."[46] Similarly, to a large extent, feminist concerns for women's education stemmed from the realization that greater and better schooling would provide middle class girls with new intellectual skills (and perhaps technical training) for jobs which, should they remain single, they might hold for much of their lives.

Throughout the second half of the nineteenth century,
the quality of women's education in Great Britain significantly improved. Steps were taken to upgrade the quality not
just of elementary schools but of secondary schools as well.
The Girls' Public Day School Company which, according to
Carol Dyhouse, may well have established the majority of

> girls' high schools founded in the last quarter of
> the nineteenth century . . . set out determined to
> contest any idea that girls were incapable of seri-
> ous academic study.

The schools which it founded thus offered courses in "classics, mathematics and later science: subjects conventionally
defined as inappropriate for the 'feminine mind.'"[47] A number
of large public schools for girls, also founded during the
late nineteenth century, similarly contested conventional notions of women's education as did the various Ladies Colleges
established as institutions of higher learning. Although some
of the Ladies Colleges (including Queens College which, in
1848, became the first such college to be established), in
actuality offered more of a "secondary" than a university-
level education, most of them, including Cheltenham Ladies
College, perhaps the most famous, did provide for the higher
education of women.

By the end of the century, both Cambridge and Oxford
(though not yet granting degrees) permitted women to take
their local examinations. In addition, a number of University
Colleges were opened, among them, Girton and Newnham at Cambridge and Lady Margaret Hall and Somerville College at Oxford. Other universities in London and the provinces not only
opened colleges for women but also granted them degrees.
While admittedly, these educational gains directly benefitted
only a small percentage of women (almost all of whom were
middle class), among upper class girls, as Lily Montagu later
reflected, newly acquired educational opportunities created a

dissatisfaction with those "small home duties which in another generation satisfied unmarried girls."[48]

The relationship between feminism and the education of
girls in late nineteenth century Great Britain is far too
complex to maintain that increased educational opportunities
were either caused by or strengthened feminist demands. As
Carol Dyhouse shows, in her study of *Girls Growing Up in Late
Victorian and Edwardian England,*

> the new girls' high schools and women's colleges
> were in some way conservative institutions: cer-
> tainly not seminaries of feminist consciousness
> committed to any comprehensive scheme of social
> change.

Rather than challenging Victorian notions about the sexual
division of labor, these institutions reinforced them, for
those that supported educational reforms for women insisted
that "women needed education not for revolutionary ends, but
in order to fit them to become better wives and mothers, better companions for men."[49] Nevertheless, as Dyhouse concludes
and as Lily Montagu's reflection implies, these institutions
did provide girls with a new--albeit limited--vision of independence and thus appeared, at least to some, as threatening
to the social order. Whether, then, one looks to demographic
factors (the need for "redundant" middle class women to earn
a living), the concern for education *in general* that clearly
emerged by the middle of the century (leading to the creation
of Inquiry Commissions which upgraded the education of boys
and girls) or to feminism itself as *most* responsible for
changes in female education, "formal education and academic
achievement gave women the confidence and the competence to
challenge the orthodoxies of the time."[50] In so doing, these
new schools and colleges, though not feminist institutions,
helped nurture and sustain what Carol Dyhouse has labelled
the "feminist tradition."

Within the Anglo-Jewish community, the emergence of the
"new woman" similarly led to a reevaluation of woman's work
and women's roles. Middle and upper class girls benefitted
from new educational and employment opportunities and wealthy
women, like their non-Jewish contemporaries, became increasingly involved in newly created philanthropic organizations.
In May of 1902, a Conference of Jewish Women was held in London. Its stated purpose was

> . . . to bring together Jewish women from all parts
> of the country to discuss matters concerning the
> social, moral and spiritual welfare of the Jewish
> community, and to interchange information and ex-
> perience as to various methods of communal work. [51]

A series of papers was delivered outlining the work of such
organizations as the Jewish Ladies' Visiting Association and
the Society of Jewish Maternity Nurses. While the speakers
made it clear that philanthropic activities were not to sup-
plant women's other obligations and, in fact, were to be done
only after "all one's home duties" had been completed, each
stressed the importance of social service as a means of making one's life more useful. Out of the Conference (attended
by over 800 women) grew a permanent Union of Jewish Women
created to "lay a network of Jewish women workers" throughout
Great Britain, promote "effectual cooperation" and communication among them, and provide information regarding available
educational and career training facilities. [52] A central leadership committee was formed and its members agreed to affili-
ate with the more general National Union of Women Workers
which had already been established.

By the 1890s, Jewish women began to serve as members of
a variety of communal organizations. They gained representation on the Jewish Board of Guardians (the major Anglo-Jewish
welfare association) and attended conferences aimed at im-
proving both the moral standards and the religious education

of British Jews. By the end of the century, it seems, the
participation of women within Jewish public life was widely
accepted, encouraging greater communal involvement among Jewish women and facilitating the rise of such exceptional women
as Lily Montagu to positions of public prominence.

As early as 1890, however, Lily Montagu began to assume
a position not just of communal leadership but of *religious*
leadership as well. At the encouragement of Simeon Singer,
minister of the New West End Synagogue, she began to function
as a "lay preacher," holding services for children on Sabbath
mornings. Her efforts received the approval of the Chief Rabbi, Hermann Adler, and other leading members of the Orthodox
community, including her father, Samuel Montagu, whose personal commitment to traditional belief and practice made him
among the more conservative of the community's leaders.

In order to understand why Lily Montagu was accepted,
first as a children's preacher and later as a formally recognized lay minister and founder of the Liberal Jewish movement, one needs to examine the changing role of women within
the Anglican and non-conformist churches throughout the Victorian era. As women began to play a greater and more meaningful role within the Anglican Church, and as women began to
assume more visible functions within British religious life
in general, so Jewish women began to assume new religious
roles as well. Though traditionally excluded from positions
of public religious leadership, Jewish women like Lily Montagu found the Anglo-Jewish elite, all of whom prided themselves on being "British," receptive to new ideas about
women's proper role within the Church and, more broadly,
within Victorian religion.

SISTERHOODS, DEACONESSES AND THE RELIGIOUS VOCATION OF WOMEN

The creation of religious sisterhoods and the revival of deaconesses within the Anglican Church provided many Victorian women with a vocation other than that of wife and mother. By the middle of the nineteenth century, demands by women for greater participation in the church were supported by those who recognized that the surplus of women necessitated the expansion of women's religious role. As sisters or as deaconesses, single middle class women could devote themselves to a life of service within the church, using their "moral influence" to bring others closer to God. As Michael Hill, in his study of Anglican religious orders, maintains,

> It is no accident that the revival of the religious
> life in the nineteenth-century Church of England
> should have been initiated by women's communities,
> [for] Victorian women, faced with a choice between
> a highly valued role of wife and mother and an in-
> determinate role as spinster, sought to make provi-
> sion for a greater range of laywomen's roles within
> a church which had previously allocated almost no
> roles at all to women. [53]

The Park Village Sisterhood, founded in 1845, was the first of a growing number of Anglican sisterhoods established during the nineteenth century. By 1878, there were 43 sisterhoods in existence; by 1912, "there were at least 1,300 professed sisters in the whole of the Church of England." [54] As communities of single women engaged in prayer or works of mercy, sisterhoods became an "influential section of the church." [55] Their activities included nursing (Florence Nightingale, for example, enlisted the help of Anglican sisters during the Crimean War) and various acts of charity. Though not receiving universal approval even within the Church (primarily, their support came from members of the High Church

Party), sisterhoods provided many single women with a meaningful and all-encompassing religious life.

The revival of the female diaconate, though less all-
encompassing, similarly provided single women with a new, religious vocation. Receiving their major support from the members of the Low Church Party, deaconesses worked within the
Church under the direct control and direction of men. Without
the independence of Anglican sisters, deaconesses thus did
little to challenge the existing social order (i.e., they
lacked what Michael Hill calls the "incipient feminism" of
the sisterhoods). Nevertheless, beginning with the formation
of the Mildmay Deaconesses by William Pennefather in 1860,
Anglican women who were either unable or unwilling to join a
sisterhood yet wanted to devote themselves to the Church,
found that the diaconate offered them "a share in her ministry" and an opportunity "for service wherever they were
needed."[56]

During the second half of the century, as missionary and
conversionist societies, philanthropic organizations and
groups applying new approaches to theology, Bible study and
the history of Christianity proliferated, women outside of
the Anglican Church found even greater opportunities for
religious self-expression. As Olive Anderson notes,

> . . . by about 1862 large numbers of women were
> working on a voluntary and part-time basis with
> both sexes in Sunday schools and Bible classes, and
> had formed their own ladies' prayer meetings, mis-
> sionary societies, maternal associations, temper-
> ance committees and sewing circles attached to
> their churches and chapels.[57]

Throughout Great Britain, paid, full-time and trained women
began to appear as Scripture readers, parish visitors and
so-called "mission ladies." Within the Methodist Church,
women could receive training as deaconesses and, among

evangelicals, women even gained acceptance as preachers.
While female preaching reached its peak during the 1860s (by
the 1870s and '80s many of these preachers had channeled
their activities into "more discreet forms"), women continued
to preach, most visibly within the Salvation Army. Founded by
Catherine and William Booth in the late 1860s, the Salvation
Army actively encouraged women not only to preach (Catherine
herself had been an evangelical preacher) but also to serve
as leaders (in fact, by 1878, forty-one of its ninety-one
officers were women).[58] Thus, it seems, by 1890, when Lily
Montagu first began to hold children's services at the New
West End, a variety of nontraditional activities had already
been assumed by women within both the Church of England and
dissenting congregations.

In light of Anglo-Jewry's desire to appear British, it
is not surprising that Lily Montagu eventually gained acceptance as a religious leader. None of the roles which she assumed exceeded those previously assumed by Christian women.
Had the Anglo-Jewish community been more traditional, (i.e.,
less secularized and acculturated), Lily Montagu's conducting
children's services and, perhaps even more so, her establishing of the Jewish Religious Union, would have been met with
great alarm. Yet even the opponents of the J.R.U. acknowledged the right of women (and especially single women) to
participate in public religious life. Consequently, they aimed their attacks solely at the Union's theological founda-
tions and not at the participation of women. Moreover, it
should be noted that within the Jewish Religious Union itself, Lily Montagu's emergence as a lay preacher came about
only gradually. During the earliest years of the Union's existence, her chief contributions were organizational and
hence acceptable not just to more traditional opponents of
the J.R.U. but to more traditional supporters as well. In addition, even when Lily Montagu did assume a position of

religious leadership, her functions were not those of a
"rabbi" but of an Anglo-Jewish minister. Her duties, which
included teaching, preaching, charitable activities and certain administrative work, were those which Lily Montagu had
already assumed through her involvement in the British social
work movement.

As early as the 1890s, at the Jewish Girls Club that she
and her sister Marian founded, Lily Montagu led services,
preached sermons, taught Bible classes and served as an administrator. By 1913, after the Jewish Religious Union had
declared itself to be an organization specifically committed
to the advancement of Liberal Judaism (and thus no longer ac-
countable to traditional members), Lily Montagu simply began
to assume, within the J.R.U., roles that she had already assumed within her club. Although, then, to a large degree,
Lily Montagu's own capability and drive enabled her to become
both a leading social worker and an important religious figure, Anglo-Jewry's willingness to accord women greater communal responsibility (and its willingness to make this res-'
ponsibility commensurate with that of women outside the Jewish community), clearly facilitated Lily Montagu's achievement of prominence within the public sphere of Jewish life.

II. Early Efforts at Reform

The emergence of Reform Judaism in nineteenth century Germany and America heralded the first of many major attempts at establishing a modern Jewish identity, one that sought to find a mid-way point between tradition on the one hand and the "spirit of the age" on the other. With its ideology formulated most clearly at a series of rabbinical conferences held in Germany during the 1840s (and crystallized further in America with the drafting of the Pittsburgh Platform of 1885), it rejected a number of traditional claims in favor of those that seemed more rational and hence more modern.

Among the traditional claims which the Reformers rejected was that of the Jews as a nation. Maintaining that Jewish nationality ceased with the destruction of the Second Temple and the dispersion of the Jewish people, they asserted that Jews were members of a specific "religious brotherhood," centering around a belief in the One, Universal God and the ethical teachings of His prophets. To be a Jew, the Reformers said, was to bear witness to God's reality, spreading His teachings throughout the world. To do so was to fulfill their mission as Jews--as God's "chosen people." Moreover, they continued, the fulfillment of this mission would help bring about a universal, messianic age of harmony and peace (replacing the traditional, more nationalistic concept of a messianic king, descending from the House of David). Thus, as Samuel Holdheim, a leader of the German Reform movement, maintained, it was to be the "messianic task of Israel to make the pure knowledge of God and the pure law of morality of Judaism the common possession and blessing" of humanity.[1]

In attempting to adapt Judaism to the spirit of the modern age, the Reformers sought to retain Judaism's essential
elements while eliminating those that they considered to be
inessential. Most of Judaism's traditional rituals and observances were subsequently discarded as inessential, only serving, they believed, to keep the Jew "aloof" from the modern
age. Deemed essential, however, were Judaism's more universal
teachings. In sifting and weighing these elements, the Reformers ultimately relied upon their conscience and the ability to reason, identifying this internal source of authority
as the Voice of God. Though not rejecting Jewish tradition,
they viewed the Talmud (Judaism's traditional source of authority) as one of many traditions, claiming that Judaism had
always adapted to the spirit of the age and thus, had always
continued to develop and grow.

One of the early concerns of the Reformers was the role
of women within Jewish religious life. Recognizing that
women's traditional status could not be defended on rational
grounds (and indeed, seemed entirely out of keeping with the
spirit of modernity), they demanded that the subordinate status of women be overthrown. As Abraham Geiger, the major
philosophical spokesman of German Reform, maintained, it was
incumbent upon the Reform movement to insure that whenever
possible women and men assume the same religious obligations,
that the ability of women to grasp the depths of religious
belief be acknowledged and acted upon, and that no worship
service either in form or content exclude women from
participation.[2]

By the 1840s, a committee of rabbis sympathetic to Geiger's religious views began to study the legal position of
Jewish women more closely. In 1846, at a rabbinical conference held in Breslau, it stated that the role of women within
Jewish religious life needed to be altered significantly before women could be emancipated, i.e., before they, like

Jewish men, could identify themselves as fully modern. Declaring "the equality of religious privileges and obligations of women in so far as this is possible," the committee stated that this position was in accordance with

> . . . our religious consciousness, which grants all
> humans an equal degree of natural holiness and for
> which the pertaining differentiations in the Holy
> Scripture have only relative and momentary valid-
> ity. It is a sacred duty to express most emphatic-
> ally the complete religious equality of the female
> sex.[3]

A number of steps to realize this equality subsequently were taken. Women were included in the prayer quorum, Jewish males no longer recited the benediction expressing thanks for not having been created a woman, formal religious instruction for girls was introduced, and in the Reform Temple in Berlin, women and men were seated on the same floor during the worship service. Moreover, confirmation as a ceremony replacing Bar Mitzvah gained widespread acceptance among progressive European congregations as that which recognized the entrance of both boys and girls into Jewish communal life.

In the United States, Jews who identified themselves as Reform made similar efforts to ensure the religious equality of women. In 1846, at his congregation in Albany, Isaac Mayer Wise admitted girls into the synagogue choir and in 1851 introduced family pews. He also encouraged women to attend the Hebrew Union College, the Reform rabbinical seminary which he had established in Cincinnati in 1875. While a number of women attended HUC, none of Wise's female students, it seems, ever sought ordination. Not atypical was the viewpoint expressed by Ray Frank, a popular preacher, lecturer and journalist who attended classes at HUC for one semester but did not enroll as a matriculating student. In a paper delivered at the Jewish Women's Congress held in Chicago in 1893, she

maintained that the ordination of women as rabbis was inconsequential so long as women recognized their capabilities for
holding such an office.[4]

Reform Judaism offered women, like Ray Frank and Lily
Montagu, a new means of becoming fully Jewish, one that did
not equate Judaism with Orthodoxy and that, at least in theory, held out for women the promise of complete equality.
What's more, it offered them a means of remaining fully modern by affirming only those religious beliefs which could be
harmonized with the spirit of the modern age. It is thus not
surprising that Lily Montagu found herself greatly attracted
to the Reform movement, whose success encouraged her to think
about ways of breathing a similar spirit of reform into the
Anglo-Jewish community.

In her autobiography, *The Faith of a Jewish Woman*, published in 1943, Lily Montagu established a direct connection
between her discovering that "both in Germany and in the
United States of America, over a hundred years ago, a new
presentment of Judaism had been given to the world"[5] and her
writing "The Spiritual Possibilities of Judaism Today" in
1899. While she failed to mention exactly how or when she
made this discovery, David Philipson's essay on "The Progress
of the Jewish Reform Movement in the United States," which
appeared in the *Jewish Quarterly Review* in October of 1897,
may well have been an important source of information.

Philipson's article traced the growth of Reform Judaism
in America. It described the external and theological reforms
which the movement had made and named some of its early leaders and congregations. It discussed the major components of
the Pittsburgh Platform which emerged from the Reform Rabbinical Conference of 1885 and made mention of both the Union of
American Hebrew Congregations, formed in 1871, and the Hebrew
Union College, established in 1875. In his essay, Philipson
portrayed Reform Judaism as an active and vital movement

which had "revivified Judaism" and thus led to the rebirth of
American Jewish life. Similarly, in *The Faith of a Jewish
Woman*, Lily Montagu described Reform Judaism as a strong
force within the American (and German) Jewish communities
which had deepened and preserved the religious loyalty of
"the children in the[ir] schools" by offering an understanding of Judaism which was new and "spiritually alive."[7]

While the indebtedness of Lily Montagu to David Philipson is conjectural, the significance of her having learned
about the existence of Reform Judaism in Germany and America
is clear. Having concluded that "Judaism was doomed, unless
it was a living influence in Jewish thought and conduct,"[8]
she previously had maintained that external changes in the
worship service were insufficient. Instead, she had insisted,
more radical theological changes needed to be made. These included belief in progressive revelation, stress on the universal mission of the Jewish people as witnesses to God's
reality, replacing belief in a personal Messiah with belief
in a future, messianic age, upholding the eternal nature of
Judaism's moral teachings, and presenting its ceremonial laws
as possible means towards holiness rather than as important
means in and of themselves. External reform, such as prayers
written in the vernacular, organ music played during the worship service, and family pews replacing traditional sex-
differentiated seating might well be introduced but their
primary significance, she had felt, would be as *reflections*
of the new theological stance which would be taken.

By the end of the nineteenth century, Lily Montagu discovered that these kinds of changes had already been instituted by Reform Jews in Germany and America. Moreover, she
learned, their efforts had proved to be highly successful and
the Reform movement as a whole was continuing to grow. Encouraged by this discovery, she began to act upon her own desire to offer the Anglo-Jewish community a new understanding

of Jewish religious faith. Her intent was not to form a
schismatic movement, as the American and German Reformers had
done, but rather to institute change from within the already
existing community structure. It was possible, she believed,
to engender the support of all religiously committed Jews in
a united effort aimed at a common goal. This goal, as she
perceived it, was to establish Liberal Judaism not as a potential rival to preexisting forms of Judaism, but instead as
a complement to it: one way among many, in which Jews could
express their religious identity within the modern world.

The growth of Reform Judaism outside of Great Britain
proved to Lily Montagu that Liberal Jewish ideas not only
could have but also *did* have significant appeal. It strengthened her resolve to form an association through which English
Jews who had already identified themselves as Liberal might
share their faith with others. In so doing, she believed,
those for whom traditional forms of Jewish belief held little
if any appeal might come to a new understanding and appreciation of Judaism as a spiritual inheritance. The stated purpose of the association, then, would not be to work for the
eventual triumph of Liberal Judaism, but rather to ensure the
future existence of a religiously committed Anglo-Jewish
community.

By establishing a set of broadly defined goals, Lily
Montagu also hoped to include non-Liberal Jews as members. In
part, this stemmed from a desire to placate her father--to
show him that her goal was not to establish a Liberal Jewish
movement, but simply to combat religious indifference. Yet,
in addition, Lily Montagu sincerely felt that an association
of "sympathizers" would be more effective than an association
of Liberal Jews. Reiterating the convictions of Joseph Mazzini (detailed more fully in Chapter IV), she maintained that
change could best be effected through a sustained and *united*
effort.

Thus, while her knowledge of Reform Jewish movements in Germany and America encouraged Lily Montagu, their existence did not inspire her to form a similar movement within England. Perhaps for this reason, Lily Montagu's later essays on the origins of the Jewish Religious Union make no mention of an indebtedness either to German or American Reform. In *The Jewish Religious Union and Its Beginnings*, published in 1927, "The History of Liberal Judaism in England," first delivered as an address in 1931, and "In The Beginning," published in 1950, she stated that the J.R.U. owed its

> . . . inception and development to the working of the Spirit of Religion in a small group of men and women . . . [who] were sincerely attached to the [Anglo-]Jewish Community.[9]

She acknowledged great indebtedness to those individuals who had supported and encouraged her early efforts (most notably her parents, Simeon Singer, Claude Montefiore and N. S. Joseph), and cited Mazzini as having helped her to establish the J.R.U.'s ideals and goals. Yet she discussed neither the development of Jewish Reform movements outside Great Britain nor the influence of those movements upon her. In so doing, Lily Montagu consciously declined to establish a direct relationship between the existence of German and American Reform and the creation of the Jewish Religious Union.

Nineteenth Century Reform in Great Britain

A more direct relationship can be discovered between the founding of the J.R.U. and the number of attempts made during the nineteenth century to introduce some measure of religious reform into the Anglo-Jewish community. While Lily Montagu either expanded upon or rejected many of their innovations, the initiators of such attempts helped form a core of individuals to whom she later could appeal for support. Having

declared themselves actively interested in the revivification
of Anglo-Jewry's religious life, they were obvious candidates
for membership within the Jewish Religious Union. Though not
all took an interest in the association which Lily Montagu
created, many of them (including the most prominent) not only
joined the J.R.U. but also helped constitute its initial
leadership committee.

The first self-proclaimed Reform congregation in London
was established as early as 1840. Formed by twenty-four men,
all of whom were members of the Anglo-Jewish elite, it sought
to introduce a number of moderate reforms into the worship
service by creating a revised, somewhat abbreviated Hebrew
liturgy, discontinuing the practice of calling up men to the
Torah, and including a weekly sermon to be delivered in English. In addition, it attempted to begin the service at a
more convenient hour, eliminated the observance of the second
day of the Jewish festivals, and minimized the Sephardic/Ash-
kenazic distinction between its members by identifying itself
simply as a congregation of "British Jews."

Despite these reforms, however, there is little indication that the major impulse behind the establishing of the
West London Synagogue was religious. The major difference between the revised liturgy of the West London Synagogue and
that of Orthodox Sephardic congregations was the omission in
the former of passages that were either repetitive or deemed
superfluous (e.g., psalms that unnecessarily lengthened the
worship service). Prayers for the coming of a personal messiah, the return of the Jews to Zion, the rebuilding of the
Temple, and the restoration of the sacrifical cult were all
retained. What's more, many of the innovations proposed by
the reformers were soon adopted by a number of Orthodox congregations, seemingly, then, making secession (and the founding of a "Reform" synagogue) unnecessary. For these reasons,

several scholars have suggested that the founding of the West London Synagogue was less theological than it was either social or political in nature.

According to Albert Hyamson, in his study of *The Sephardim of England*, it is likely that the West London Synagogue would never have come into being as an independent congregation had not the institution of a branch synagogue directly violated the provisions set up by the Spanish and Portuguese community. By 1840, many Jews had moved from the East End to the more prosperous West End of London and wanted to establish houses of worship geographically closer to them. When, in April of 1840, a petition presented to the governing body of the (Sephardic) Bevis Marks congregation asking permission for the establishment of a branch synagogue was denied, eighteen prominent members of the synagogue (along with six Ashkenazic Jews who similarly hoped to establish a synagogue in the West End) began to make plans for the creation of their own congregation.

Presumably, the Ashkenazic Jews in question were among those who in 1821, had requested that the (Ashkenazic) Great Synagogue make certain changes regarding decorum. While some of the changes were made, many of these self-styled reformers continued to push for alterations and modifications. Consequently, they were receptive to the kinds of innovations proposed by those pressing for change at Bevis Marks. This interpretation of the founding of the West London Synagogue suggests that certain Ashkenazic Jews (most notably Isaac Lyons Goldsmid and his son, Francis) were willing to join forces with their Sephardic counterparts because they too wanted to establish a house of worship in the West End of London which would reflect the kinds of (primarily liturgical) changes that they and the Sephardic reformers felt needed to be made.

While proponents of this view have argued that both theological and geographical considerations were behind the formation of the West London Synagogue, they have maintained
that the geographical motivations were of greater importance
than the theological. The changes initiated within the West
London Synagogue, they have insisted, were conservative in
nature. Although the decision to omit the second day of the
Jewish holy days, the creation of which was rabbinic, admittedly led the Chief Rabbi, Solomon Hirschell and the Sephardic Ab Beth Din, David Meldola, to issue a joint denuncia-
tion, the congregation (as Cecil Roth points out) never rejected "the Oral law as drastically as their critics al-
leged."[10] According to Roth, if the founders of the new synagogue were extreme, their extremism lay more in their actual
secession and subsequent abolition of the Ashkenazic/Sephard-
ic distinction than it did in their specific demands for
change. Thus, in a declaration issued on April 15, 1840, the
founders of what soon became identified as the West London
Synagogue claimed that while synagogue attendance had de-
creased significantly within the Anglo-Jewish community, this
was

> not owing to any want of a general conviction of
> the fundamental truths of our Religion, but . . .
> to the distance of the existing Synagogues from the
> places of our residence; the length and imperfec-
> tions of the order of service; to the inconvenient
> hours at which it is appointed; to the unimpressive
> manner in which it is performed and to the absence
> of religious instruction in our synagogue.[11]

Their intention, then, was not to inaugurate a movement
dedicated to religious reform, but simply to establish a synagogue that would be geographically closer to them. It seems
that this intention was later acknowledged by the rest of the
Anglo-Jewish community. In 1849, for example, the ban which

the head of the Sephardic community had issued against the
Spanish and Portuguese reformers was lifted, and by the end
of the century, their position within the Sephardic community
had considerably improved. Members of the West London Synagogue were permitted to give offerings and legacies to the
Bevis Marks congregation and support its charitable and educational institutions. They soon participated in communal associations, and in 1885 gained representation on the Board of
Deputies, the organization responsible for dealing with the
British government in matters concerning Jewish political interests. In 1892, representatives from all major Orthodox
synagogues in London were present at the special service held
for the congregation's fiftieth anniversary and in 1895, as a
final sign of reconciliation, the Bevis Marks and West London
Synagogues jointly purchased land for a cemetery which would
serve both congregations.

As Chaim Bermant notes, the influence of the West London
Synagogue in the nineteenth century was less religious than
social. Of the twenty-four men who had signed the Declaration
of 1840, three were Henriques, nine Montefiores, and of the
Ashkenazim, three were Goldsmids. The founders of the West
London congregation were thus from a limited number of
wealthy, socially prominent Jewish families. Consequently,
their synagogue was seen as a "point of [social] arrival and
became the Temple of the assimilated, prosperous Victorian
middle class."[12]

In an essay published in 1976, Robert Liberles offers an
alternative explanation for the founding of the West London
Synagogue. Focusing on the motivations of the six Ashkenazim
who helped constitute the original congregation, he maintains
that their efforts did not stem from geographical, social or
religious considerations but rather from the desire to establish a new political structure within the Jewish community
itself. More specifically, Liberles argues that the objective

of the Ashkenazic contingent (led by Francis Goldsmid) was to
challenge the Board of Deputies as "the only official medium
of communication with Government in matters concerning the
political interest of the British Jews," one of the clauses
contained in the Board's constitution.[13] As a member of the
Great Synagogue, one of six congregations affiliated with the
Board, Goldsmid had no choice but to comply with this clause.
As a member of the West London Synagogue, however, he and the
other Ashkenazim who left with him could appeal to the British government on their own, seeking nothing less than the
full emancipation of British Jewry. According to Liberles,
then,

> the controversy over the reform synagogue was . . .
> an extension of the controversy between the Gold-
> smids and the Board of Deputies over the Board's
> moderation in pursuing the fight for emancipation.[14]

The Sephardim who helped form the West London Synagogue were
sympathetic to the Goldsmids' position. In return for their
support, however, they insisted that certain reforms within
the worship service be made, reforms which they felt eventually would help them to gain political equality. Thus,

> What bound these two contingents together was their
> primary commitment to the struggle for political
> emancipation. The Goldsmids required a power base
> for their diplomatic activities. The Sephardim saw
> the introduction of reforms as the stepping-stone
> to political rights. The final product, the West
> London Synagogue, represented a merging of both
> views.[15]

What is important for our purposes is that the creation
of the West London Synagogue, though heralded by many historians as the beginning of the Jewish "Reform" movement in England, in fact established neither a new religious movement
nor an ideology to sustain it. Its significance, as we have

seen, was more social and political than religious. Yet many
of those who joined the West London Synagogue (later called
the Berkeley Street Synagogue) as well as those who served as
its ministers, *were* committed to reform, not as a political
stepping-stone but as a means of revitalizing Anglo-Jewry's
religious life. Recognizing that the congregation had failed
to become part of a movement "in any real sense of the word,"
neither training its own rabbis nor maintaining a specific
theological position with the exception of the anti-rabbinism
of its first minister, David Woolf Marks, and perhaps recognizing too that the congregation had "ceased to be an ener-
gizing liberal force" within Anglo-Jewish life, many were
sympathetic to the course of action which Lily Montagu later
proposed.[16] In 1899, seeking support for what would become
the Jewish Religious Union, Lily Montagu wrote to several
members of the West London Synagogue, asking them to join in
her efforts. Among those who responded favorably were Claude
Montefiore and Morris Joseph, minister of the congregation.

As early as 1890, Montefiore and Joseph had taken part
in another early attempt at reform. On February 22 of that
year, a group of men active in the formation of the (Orthodox) Hampstead Synagogue inaugurated a series of nontraditional Sabbath afternoon services. Held at the West
Hampstead Town Hall, they were led by Morris Joseph and were
based upon the revised order of service which Joseph had arranged. Prayers for the restoration of the sacrifical cult
were omitted from the traditional *mincha* (afternoon) service
and were replaced by the phrase: "Restore Thy worship to Thy
sanctuary and let the supplication and songs of Israel ever
be acceptable to Thee." There was a mixed choir, accompanied
by instrumental music; the Ten Commandments were read; and as
at the West London Synagogue, a prophetic reading in English
was included. In addition, prayers, hymns and psalms in English followed the Hebrew portion of the service, men and

women, while separated, were seated on the ground floor, and
preachers were given complete freedom in the style and content of their sermons.

The founders of the Hampstead Sabbath Afternoon Services, recognizing "that the appeal made by the liturgy of
the synagogue elicits but a feeble response from the intellect and emotions of the modern Jew," sought to reawaken interest in religious worship by combining "modern ideas and
aspirations" with those elements which were "distinctively
Jewish" in character.[17] According to the *Jewish Chronicle*,
two hundred people attended the group's first service, but
interest eventually declined. Despite the continuous objec-
tion of the Chief Rabbi, services continued for three years.
In 1893, with the failure of the Hampstead group, Morris
Joseph, its minister and "guiding spirit," replaced David
Woolf Marks as minister of the West London congregation. Nine
years later, Joseph, F. H. Samuel [Harvey-Samuel], its chairman, A. Lindo Henry, its secretary, and Claude Montefiore and
Israel Abrahams, who had served as occasional preachers, all
became leading members of the Jewish Religious Union.

Far more radical than the Hampstead Sabbath Afternoon
Services (and the J.R.U.) was the so-called Sunday Movement
initiated in 1899 by Oswald J. Simon. Its intent was not only
to awaken religious interest among British Jews, but also to
propagate Jewish faith actively among non-Jews. Maintaining
that there was "scarcely any difference"[18] between Christian
theists and "Reformed Jews" who, like himself, distinguished
between ritualism and spirituality, he claimed that a new
fellowship could be formed. Simon believed that those Englishmen who had rejected specific Christian doctrines still
needed a monotheistic and historical faith and therefore argued that Sunday morning services, based on a revised Jewish
liturgy, mainly in English and without most of the

traditional ceremonies or rites, could bring about the recognition of Judaism as the universalistic religion of the
future.

While sixty people, most of whom were not Jewish, attended Simon's first service, the movement failed to generate
sufficient support. Many Jews sympathized with Simon's desire
to establish a theistic "Church of Israel"[19] but either felt
that his theological position was too vague or believed that
present efforts to stem the tide of religious indifference
should be concentrated within the Anglo-Jewish community.
Although Simon's attempts to institute a universalistic Judaism proved to be unsuccessful, he continued to press for
changes which would make Judaism more relevant to modern
life. In 1902, he supported the establishment of the Jewish
Religious Union and soon became a member of its leadership
committee.

All of these attempts at reform helped convince Lily
Montagu that there were others who shared her vision of a religiously revitalized Anglo-Jewry. Recognizing, however, that
these attempts had failed, she sought to formulate a plan of
her own, one that would unite members of the West London Synagogue, the Hampstead Group and the Sunday Movement in a common effort. Though lacking self-confidence, she gained
strength from Montefiore's insistence that those who had a
vision of the future, even if it were a delusion, neede to
remain loyal to it, thus helping their "delusion" come to be.
Those who do so, he wrote,

> will not be the only men [sic] who have worked for
> a delusion, and have yet benefitted the world. For
> their devotion to the cause of an imaginary Judaism
> remains devotion to the cause of God.[20]

Throughout the 1890s, Claude Montefiore wrote that "the
existence of a liberal Judaism" must be assumed.[21] His conception of a liberal Judaism, however, did not necessitate

forming a separate religious movement. Like the members of
the Anglican Broad Church, Montefiore equated his liberal religious identity with the expression of particular theological beliefs. He openly defended the liberal Jewish stance tak-
en by himself, Oswald Simon and Israel Abrahams and maintained that it was possible to adhere personally to a non-
rabbinic form of Judaism without either separating oneself
from the Anglo-Jewish community or losing one's own sense of
Jewish identification.

Montefiore admitted that it was difficult for the liberal Jew to pray within any of the synagogues in London. Yet he
advised remaining within already existing congregations and
"reforming" them from within. Montefiore made it clear, however, that he was sympathetic to the concept of a separate,
Liberal Jewish movement, conceding that if at present Liberal
Judaism had no "organized expression or embodiment" in England, it was because many liberal Jews (presumably including
himself) felt that the time was inopportune, disliked "strife
and disunion," lacked the energy or desire to begin a new religious movement, and did not have a person willing to step
forward as the movement's leader. In 1900, in the July issue
of the *Jewish Quarterly Review*, Montefiore discussed the difficulties and duties of Liberal Judaism in England. Giving
expression to a hope that helped spur Lily Montagu to action,
he concluded:

> When the time may become propitious for any dis-
> tinct liberal movement or for any separate reli-
> gious organization, I will not here discuss. Some
> persons would say that it is not a question of the
> season, but of the man. If it be so, we can at all
> events, by faithful and quiet labour, prepare the
> way for his coming.[22]

III. The Literary Background

The self-identification of nineteenth century middle and upper class Jews as "British" was greatly precipitated, as we have seen, by social, political and economic changes that occurred during the second half of the nineteenth century, changes that helped complete the process of emancipation. Subsequently, both those Jews who came to reject Judaism (for social and/or religious reasons) as well as those who identified themselves as Englishmen of the *Jewish persuasion* became deeply influenced by British concerns and ideas. Much of this influence was informal, gained through friendships and acquaintances with non-Jews. Some, however, was imparted more deliberately, through school curricula that included the study of British history and thought. For a small, but growing number of Jewish men and women, those that received a university education, even greater opportunities were available not only for social contact but also for participation in the leading intellectual currents of the day. Yet equally, if not more important, were cultural influences, works of art, literature and theater that helped to shape what Walter Houghton has called the "Victorian frame of mind."

Like their non-Jewish contemporaries, Jews of the upper classes frequented the theater, read many of the great (and not so great) books of the day, and developed an appreciation for art (as evidenced by visits to art galleries and for some, including Samuel Montagu, through the amassing of impressive private collections). Lily Montagu herself asserted, in several of her sermons, that works of art could help one to form a better understanding of human relationships, nature and beauty. She also maintained that plays (and later she added movies) were significant reflections both of social reality and of contemporary expectations. Like other members of her generation and class, however, Lily Montagu attached even greater importance to what John Ruskin called "books of all time," works that were believed to impart eternal values. In his most popular book, *Sesame and Lilies*, first published in 1865, Ruskin contended that good books were like sesames, "that old enchanted Arab grain" which in legend opened doors. The difference, Ruskin wrote, was that the doors which good books opened were not "of robbers, but of Kings' Treasuries." In them, the wisest of men of the past, eager to share their knowledge, invited all those in the present to read their "studied, determined, chosen addresses . . . not merely to know from them what is true, but chiefly to feel with them what is just."[1]

Lily Montagu's understanding of "religion" was largely shaped by those literary sources with which she was familiar. Her formal education having ended at the age of fifteen, she spent the following two years studying at home with private tutors. Fearful of losing the educational opportunities enjoyed not only by her brothers but also by her sisters, who stayed at school until they were seventeen, she made a timetable for herself to which she adhered strictly. While it is not completely clear why Lily Montagu left school (the explanation she gives in *My Club and I* is that her parents thought "that with the fifth child it might be well to introduce some change in the routine of education"), she apparently was given a great deal of freedom both in choosing her studies and in deciding how much time she wanted to devote to them.[2] If we are to believe *My Club and I*, she actually spent as many hours studying at home as she had when she was at school.

Lily Montagu never described the specific content of these studies. In *The Faith of a Jewish Woman*, however, she

maintains that after leaving school she spent much of her
time reading "books on social philosophy and all sorts of papers and pamphlets." Moreover, between the ages of fifteen
and nineteen (presumably, then, even after her private studies ended), she "collected any amount of intellectual food
and suffered acutely from mental indigestion." "It was the
best reading period," she writes, "I have ever had in my
life."[3] During this period, there were two books which seemed
to make a particularly deep impression upon her: Buckle's
History of Civilisation and *Robert Elsmere*, a popular novel
by Mrs. Humphrey Ward. "I remember," she reveals,

> being terribly shocked by reading in Buckle that it
> could be computed how many people were likely to
> make the same mistakes every year, how many would
> stick on stamps the wrong way up, and how many
> babies would be born, how many women die in child-
> birth. My world, my beautiful, human world, lighted
> up by the flame of God in its midst, was then only
> a thing evolved in a mathematician's brain, and
> moving mechanically from one stage to the next.[4]

Robert Elsmere, it seems, similarly disturbed her. First published in 1888, its title character is a young Anglican minister who finds that he can no longer accept the intellectual
and dogmatic framework of the Church. Recognizing that faith
"does not depend . . . upon anything external, but upon the
living voice of the Eternal in the soul of man," he renounces
his ministry, much to the dismay of his pietistic wife, Catherine. Elsmere tries to explain to her that Christianity, as
he now understands it, is not false but "only an imperfect
human reflection of a part of truth," since "truth has never
been, can never be contained in any one creed or system."
Catherine insists, however, that his religious struggles represent the triumph of Satan. By the end of the novel, the two
are reconciled and Elsmere opens up a Workingman's Club in

London revolving around a "New Brotherhood in Christ," based
not on miracles but on Jesus' humanity. Catherine still
clings to the old faith but she comes to acknowledge the validity of Elsmere's faith as well, now realizing that "God has
not one language but many."[5] Interestingly, in describing the
effect of this book upon her, Lily Montagu does not mention
that the book is essentially a plea for religious toleration.
Rather she points to the "intolerance and silly prejudices"
of those around Elsmere as attitudes which she found to be
depressing.[6]

One needs to turn to Lily Montagu's Club letters and
sermons to discover some of the other works that not only affected her emotionally but also, and more importantly, actually shaped the development of her religious thought. An examination of her letters and sermons reveals the extent to
which Lily Montagu drew upon literary sources, most of which
continued, throughout her lifetime, to exert an influence
upon her. The vast majority of these sources were British;
almost none of them were Jewish. Having received only a minimal Jewish education, one that seems to have been limited to
Bible lessons, Lily Montagu formed a conception of "true religion" that had more in common with Robert Elsmere's than it
did with that of her father. One might argue, of course, that
Lily Montagu could have turned to Jewish literary sources on
her own, that even without an extensive formal Jewish education she might have learned Hebrew (it seems that she could
read the letters but knew little of the language) and might
have attempted, at least, to tackle traditional Jewish texts.
Yet although, as we shall see in chapter four, she later read
the works of liberal Jewish thinkers, those who shared her
own, already formulated, understanding of true religion,
there is no evidence that Lily Montagu ever tried to compen-
sate for her inadequate Jewish education. In part, perhaps,
this was due to her own lack of self-confidence, a fear that

such studies would be too difficult for her to undertake. Accepting the prevailing view that girls were less intellectual than boys, she remained content with reading material that was deemed appropriate for women. Popular guides of the day admonished girls to "read historical and serious books which would neither inflame their sensibilities nor make them overly learned."[7] Lily Montagu, it seems, followed their advice.

Yet lack of self-confidence and an acceptance of the Victorian double standard of education and the pursuit of knowledge does not explain why Lily Montagu either ignored or developed little interest in the novels and poems of contemporary British Jews. Linda Gertner Zatlin, in her study of *The Nineteenth Century Anglo-Jewish Novel*, identifies forty-two Anglo-Jewish novelists, fifteen of whom wrote (though not exclusively) about Jewish life and culture in Great Britain. Many of them, including Grace Aguilar and Israel Zangwill, not only wrote novels and essays but also poetry, the literary form to which Lily Montagu was most attracted. Lily Montagu may have been familiar with their works, but if so, they apparently made little impression upon her. According to Zatlin, a number of novelists, especially those writing at the end of the century, attempted to "define for themselves what being Jewish means and how to live in a Christian society."[8] Although these questions were of major concern to Lily Montagu, none of these novels seems to have merited her serious attention. It is curious that while Lily Montagu often referred to such writers as Charles Dickens, William Makepeace Thackeray, George Eliot, Elizabeth Gaskell, Charlotte Bronte and Victor Hugo, even assessing their works, she made virtually no reference either to Jewish novelists or novels. An examination of well over one hundred sermons and addresses and over two hundred sermonettes sent to members of the West Central Club (the so-called Club Letters), reveals that the

only Jewish novelist whom she discussed was Edna Ferber. In a
Club Letter focusing not on Ferber's novels but on her autobiography, dated June 1944 (when Lily Montagu was over the
age of seventy!), she maintains that while Ferber was "Jewish
in outlook and in behaviour and intellectual interests," she
possessed too little feeling for the Jews as a religious
group. Clearly, the reference here is not meant to show the
possible influence of Edna Ferber on Lily Montagu's religious
thought but is intended as a chastisement of Jews who, like
Ferber, fail to share in Judaism's "activities and responsibilities and [to] live collectively in contact with the
unseen."[9]

It may well be that Lily Montagu's apparent lack of interest in Jewish literature stemmed from her own internaliza-
tion of the criteria established by Ruskin for judging "good
books." The Jewish works to which she had access, i.e., contemporary poems and novels, may have achieved popularity but
they were not necessarily well written. Neither did they necessarily contain the kind of breadth and uniqueness of vision
which, for Ruskin, was an essential component of "books for
all time." The works to which Lily Montagu referred most
often--the essays of Thomas Carlyle, the novels of George
Eliot and the poems of Robert Browning--were, she maintained,
timeless. Thus, for well over half a century, she continued
to quote from their writings and to find new meaning in their
works.

It is no coincidence that the writers whom Lily Montagu
identified as immortal were among the most respected authors
of the day. While her attempt to harmonize their thoughts
with that which she considered to be Jewish was "new," the
high regard in which she held not only Carlyle, Eliot and
Browning but also Lord Tennyson and Matthew Arnold, reveals
the degree to which Lily Montagu assimilated Victorian notions of beauty and taste. Like other members of the Jewish

upper classes, her self-identity as an "Englishman [sic]" extended far beyond a sense of national pride. Her taste in literature, in "good books," was one she shared with cultured men and women both within and outside of the Jewish community. The great extent to which wealthy Jews, like Lily Montagu, saw British literature as "theirs," testifies to their acculturation. Similarly, one can point to their familiarity with other non-Jewish literary classics as "proof" of their adaptation to British society and, more generally, to the modern world. For some, this familiarity was also a sign of secularization. Many of those who turned to Tennyson and Browning rather than to the Talmud in searching for values did so out of the conviction that the Talmud, indeed Judaism altogether, no longer spoke to them or to their generation. Others, like Samuel Montagu, for whom traditional Jewish values remained important, may have turned to British literature for enjoyment and/or edification, finding the moral overtones of Carlyle, Arnold and others to be uplifting.

I would argue, however, that for many Jewish women, like Lily Montagu, these works provided far more than either enjoyment or edification. Those who felt that they were religious yet had little understanding of what religion was (and little if any opportunity to turn to traditional Jewish texts), saw the works of Carlyle, Arnold et al. as sources of religious vision. While Lily Montagu may have been the first to identify their visions as "Jewish," the Victorian association of womanhood with spirituality and moral influence may well have led Jewish women, especially those from the so-called leisured classes, to search for religious truth. Not even attempting this search would mean ignoring their female "mission." As Lily Montagu wrote in an essay published in 1904, it was the responsibility of women to exert their influence of "purity, temperance, righteousness and peace" over men.[10] Yet to exert this influence, women needed to recognize

their spiritual nature and the power of religion in the
world. It is clear that Lily Montagu discovered both not
through Jewish literature (with the exception of the Bible,
that which was the common possession of Christians and Jews),
but through those literary achievements which her contemporaries acknowledged to be great. An examination of some of
these works, and the visions that Lily Montagu discovered in
them, not only illuminates her understanding of the religious
but also reveals the extent to which emancipation afforded
Jewish women the opportunity for new, albeit untraditional,
religious study.

ARNOLD'S "POWER NOT OURSELVES, THAT MAKES FOR RIGHTEOUSNESS"

Lily Montagu's understanding of the Divine stemmed from
Matthew Arnold's definition of God as a "Power not ourselves,
that makes for righteousness." As a young child, she saw God
as powerful but not righteous. He appeared as an absolute
monarch, demanding that His laws be followed and His words
obeyed. In her autobiography, Lily Montagu describes the
great lengths to which she and her siblings were expected to
go in order to keep God's commandments. Convinced by her
father that laxity led to sin, Lily Montagu attempted to follow the path of "undeviating obedience," though it seems that
most of the traditional observances appeared, even then, to
be little more than "small regulations which, in the name of
Judaism, restricted [her] liberty."[11] Her early religious behavior was apparently motivated both by fear and by a willingness to obey her father. If at times she became enthusiastic over the preservation of traditional religious symbols,
it was not because these symbols stimulated any kind of personal spiritual experience. Rather, as she later maintained,
her enthusiasm stemmed from the belief that their preservation was actually *required by God*.

Yet despite these moments of enthusiasm, the concept of God as Powerful Monarch failed to satisfy Lily Montagu's own spiritual longings. She became dissatisfied with the notion of obedience as an end in and of itself. Why, she wanted to know, do we obey God, or, as she later entitled one of her sermons, "Why do we bother?" In the writings of Matthew Arnold, Lily Montagu began to find an answer. We bother, Arnold wrote, because it is God who makes us righteous, God who helps us to become all that we can be. In *Literature and Dogma*, Arnold identified this power as morality touched by emotion. Basing his understanding of religion on personal spiritual experience, he maintained that religiosity is measured not by obedience but by holiness, i.e., the attempt to sanctify life through everyday, moral action. While for Arnold, it was Jesus' example of inwardness and self-renunciation that best exemplified righteousness, he acknowledged that Jesus' understanding of God and the importance of holiness were "Hebrew" ideas. Jesus may have revived them but, as Arnold writes, the Jews "deserve their great place in the world's regard" for their original perceptions of God as enduring power and righteousness as life's foundation.[12]

Arnold's maintaining that his understanding of God derived from the "Hebrews" undoubtedly helped Lily Montagu incorporate his thought into her own. While acknowledging that Arnold was "not a Jew" (yet ignoring his explicit defense of Christianity), she insisted that it was Arnold who discovered the "real germ of religious consciousness" out of which Israel's name for God emerged.[13] Experiencing the Divine as a "power not ourselves that makes for righteousness," the Jewish people, she concluded, recognized that when we surrender to God and humble ourselves before Him, we feel a reality, a Divine power, that stimulates greater effort and helps to make us holy.

CARLYLE'S GOSPEL OF WORK AND DUTY

In recognizing the centrality of religion and the way in
which spiritual values do or at least should shape our lives,
Lily Montagu was very much indebted to Thomas Carlyle. His
ideas, she said, were "alive in the world," his idealism true
and honest. Though it's unclear how many of Carlyle's works
Lily Montagu actually read, she acknowledged his "stimulating
influence" upon her.[14] Through Carlyle, Lily Montagu began to
believe that observance did not make one religious. Rather,
as Carlyle maintained, one became religious through work and
duty, through recognizing and responding to a Divine Call.

"Perhaps better than any other writer," Lily Montagu
once said, Thomas Carlyle "taught that work alone justifies
existence and develops character."[15] Honest work, as viewed
by Carlyle, helps us to overcome pessimism and affirm the
"Everlasting Yea," the source of blessedness and love (rather
than happiness and pleasure). To Carlyle, one draws nearer
the Divine not by faith but by action. Thus, as he wrote in
Sartor Resartus, "Produce! Were it but the pitifullest infin-
itesimal fraction of a Product, produce it, in God's name,"
for to produce (even order out of chaos) one needs to utilize
"the utmost thou hast in thee."[16]

The notion that what God demands is not a specific code
of behavior but a giving of oneself had tremendous appeal to
Lily Montagu. Though she never detailed why she found this
notion so appealing, perhaps its appeal stemmed from its val-
idating all of her activities as religious. Sensing that observance did not make one righteous (an insight which, as we
have seen, she gleaned from Matthew Arnold) yet wanting to
attain righteousness, Lily Montagu needed a new path, one
that would stimulate the kind of effort and sense of holiness
that Arnold had described. Work became for her not only a
possible means of achieving righteousness but also, given her
commitment to "useful effort," something that she was

actually engaged in doing. As a wealthy single woman, Lily
Montagu had already begun to devote herself to a life of
"service." Through Carlyle, she began to recognize that in
serving others she was also serving God.

Carlyle's notion of duty gave further validation to Lily
Montagu's activities. Maintaining that one should "do the
duty which lies nearest to thee, which thou knowest to be a
duty," he emphasized the intuitive aspect of recognizing that
which one ought to do. In founding the West Central Jewish
Girls' Club (despite her lack of training as a social worker)
and in establishing the Jewish Religious Union (though she
had neither the experience nor the confidence to become a
communal leader) Lily Montagu seemed to be following Carlyle's advice. It is not surprising, then, that she credited
Carlyle with having helped her to grapple with doubt. His understanding of duty gave her a self-confidence that she previously had lacked, an assurance to act on what she inwardly
sensed to be right. Though as a young child, she unhesitat-
ingly followed the dictates of her father, Carlyle convinced
her that "the beginning of all wisdom is to look fixedly on
clothes, or even with aimed insight, till they become *trans-
parent*," that is, to look through the garments, the symbols,
even the truths, with which we have been presented. Carlyle
thus encouraged her to question her father's understanding of
religion and to begin to discover, for herself and her generation, the ways in which *they* could see the "living garment
of God."

Lily Montagu's personal growth and recognition of her
own religious nature was stimulated not only by Carlyle's notions of work and duty but also by his concept of the hero.
Many Victorians (including Lily Montagu) readily accepted
Carlyle's vision of history as the biographies of great men.
Acknowledging the force of personality, they accepted their
heroes as superior beings, those whom, as Carlyle said, we

may call "poet, prophet, God." Yet Carlyle also maintained
that all human beings, even the "noble, silent men, scattered
here and there, each in his department," have the potential
to become heroes. Though they may not possess the genius of
those who are "great" (i.e., the objects of hero worship),
they are nonetheless worthy of admiration. If to be a hero is
to be sincere, to search for the truth and to recognize our
potential, then, Carlyle rhetorically asked, "may not every
one of us be a hero?"[18]

Rejecting Carlyle's admiration of force (the idea of
might is right), Lily Montagu saw the hero as one who can influence others through the sheer strength of his or her personality. Though Carlyle insisted that only great heroes be
vocal, Lily Montagu maintained that all heroes, great and
small, have a duty to speak out and to share their visions.
One sees this conviction most clearly in her book, *God Revealed*, where the religious beliefs of "ordinary people"
(housewives, teachers and others whom she knew) are inter-
mingled with those of great Jewish thinkers, past and present. I would further suggest that it was this conviction
that led Lily Montagu to establish not only the Jewish Religious Union but also the World Union for Progressive Judaism.

As a role model (or, as she saw it, a "small hero"),
Lily Montagu encouraged others to follow her example, to
seek--as she had sought--to serve others and to be all that
they could be. While Carlyle himself emphasized renunciation
as an important aspect of the religious life, Lily Montagu
minimized the significance of self-sacrifice. Perhaps she
found it difficult to reconcile her becoming a hero (a coming
to self) with renunciation. Perhaps too, as we shall see in
chapter seven, the concept of renunciation diminished in importance as late Victorians, like Lily Montagu, began to accept the idea of an "ambitious calling," a calling that demanded self development rather than sacrifice of self.

GEORGE ELIOT AND THE RELIGION OF HUMANITY

Lily Montagu found many of Carlyle's ideas echoed in the writings of George Eliot. Like Carlyle, Eliot believed in the dignity of work. She also believed in the importance of duty. As she wrote in a letter to J. W. Cross (contained in a compilation of her letters and journals which Lily Montagu, as is apparent from one of her sermons, seems to have read):

> It must remain true that the highest lot is to have definite beliefs about you which you feel that "necessity is laid upon you" to declare them, as something better which you are bound to try and give to those who have the worse.[19]

Moreover, like Carlyle, Eliot believed that work and duty made one religious. True religion, she maintained, was not to be found in liturgies or creeds but in a life of service.

While George Eliot refrained from discussions of hero worship, Lily Montagu discovered in her writings a concept of the hero that closely mirrored her own. In "Oh May I Join the Choir Invisible," Eliot speaks of joining the choir "of those immortal dead who live again in minds made better by their presence." Their music is "the gladness of the world" for they "urge man's search to vaster issues." Their immortality, then, is rooted in their power of influence, their ability to broaden the vision of others. This notion of greatness helped reinforce Lily Montagu's own belief in the "power of personality." Viewing the idea of merging one's personality in the multitude as detestable, she maintained that the value of personality was "infinitely above that of material possessions."[20]

Eliot, like Carlyle, spoke of renunciation, but she believed that one best served others not through selfless dedication but through sacrifice *based* on self-affirmation. For Eliot, a life of service necessitated recognizing one's potential, attempting to fulfill it, and *then* giving of one's

time and effort. One was called, in other words, to give of
oneself but not to negate that which made one unique. In her
poem "Stradivarius" (often quoted by Lily Montagu), Eliot
stressed the importance of self-actualization not just as a
means of serving humanity but as a means of serving God.
Though Eliot herself identified the will of God with the will
of men [sic], her poem contains a traditional description of
God as creator, He who has given Stradivarius the talent and
skill to make his violin. Yet without Stradivarius' efforts,
God's power is ineffectual for He and Stradivarius are partners. God, as envisioned by Eliot, is powerful, but He is not
an Absolute Monarch whose commands must be obeyed. Rather, He
is a deity who works *with* humanity, enabling men and women to
do more and be more, yet *needing* them to enact creation. If,
in reading the works of Matthew Arnold, Lily Montagu was able
to answer the question "Why do we bother?" in reading the
works of Eliot she found an answer to her question "How much
do I count?" All of us, she concluded, count a great deal,
for "God has given each of us our undeveloped personality. He
trusts us with it [and] He asks us to use it in His
service."[21]

Though both Eliot and Carlyle stressed the importance of
personal development, it was Eliot's religion of humanity
that helped Lily Montagu understand the intrinsic connection
between individualism and community. Unlike Carlyle, who often let his admiration of force blind him to human suffering,
Eliot attached great importance to what she called the "truth
of feeling," that which formed a "universal bond of union"
between all women and men. As she wrote in a letter to
Charles Bray dated November 15, 1857, she was convinced that
"moral progress may be measured by the degree in which we
sympathize with individual suffering and individual joy."[22]
Sympathy, then, became for Eliot, as important as self-
development. Indeed, she believed that self-development could

not be achieved fully without love and concern for others, for to Eliot, it was emotion rather than intellect that truly made one human.

As Eliot came to reject the evangelism of her youth, her understanding of religion began to change. No longer believing that the spiritual life was one marked by obedience to the will of a supernatural God, she began to view sympathy, human goodness and moral action as the hallmarks of true religion. Writing to Harriet Beecher Stowe in May of 1869, she maintained that

a religion more perfect than any yet prevalent . . . must express . . . [a] deeply awing sense of responsibility to man, springing from sympathy with that which of all things is most certainly known to us, the difficulty of the human lot.[23]

In *Scenes of Clerical Life* (a work which Lily Montagu greatly admired), none of the three clergymen on whom Eliot focuses are identified as religious out of adherence to Christian doctrine or concern for ritual and prayer. Rather it is their human qualities--Gilfil's love for the sickly Tina, Tryan's sympathy for the invalid Sally Martin and Barton's taking in the Countess Czerlaski as a house guest despite his own poverty--that makes each of them religious. While Gilfil smokes long pipes and preaches short and disorganized sermons, he is noble, brave, faithful and tender. Tryan, though preaching fire and brimstone, learns that "there is a transcendent value in human pain," and Barton, though "superlatively middling, the quintessential extract of mediocrity," who may have "failed to touch the spring of goodness by his sermons," nevertheless touches it "effectually by his sorrows."[24]

Eliot explicitly universalized this notion of human sympathy in her last novel, *Daniel Deronda*. Describing Deronda, her Jewish protagonist, as kind and compassionate, an

admirable figure amidst a number of other, equally admirable
Jewish men and women, she took great effort not to stereo-
type these emotions. Linda Zatlin credits *Daniel Deronda* with
being "the only nineteenth-century [British] novel which
treats Jews, at least the minor characters, as complex human
beings."[25] Though Zatlin admits that Eliot was not entirely
successful in this endeavor, Eliot's description of Jews as
inheritors of a religious trust and her defense of Zionism
reflected the belief that a religion of humanity--by defini-
tion--needed to be based on sympathy for the sufferings and
dreams of *all* human beings. As Eliot wrote to Harriet Beecher
Stowe, her hope was that *Daniel Deronda* would "rouse the
imagination of men and women to a vision of human claims in
those races of their fellowmen who most differ from them" in
beliefs and customs.[26] Though Lily Montagu never adopted
Eliot's religion of humanity, Eliot's spiritual vision helped
humanize Lily Montagu's own, supernaturally based understanding of religion. Recognizing the truth of feeling, she came
to believe that one best acknowledged both the "Fatherhood of
God" and the "Brotherhood of Man" through sympathy and concern for others.

POETRY AND THE IMPACT OF ROBERT BROWNING

While Lily Montagu clearly enjoyed reading novels, plays
and essays, it was poetry that she enjoyed reading best. One
finds in her sermons and Club letters constant reference to
those poets whose words seemed not merely to reflect but to
crystallize her own understanding of religion. Though she admired the Romantic poets (especially Shelley, Coleridge and
Wordsworth) for their visions of natural beauty, Victorian
poets like Arnold, Eliot, Tennyson, Swinburne and especially
Robert Browning, lay closest to her heart. She used their

images and words to express her religious thoughts, simply
ignoring those that failed to accord with her own.

One sees this most clearly in Lily Montagu's use of Tennyson. Maintaining that he had given her the courage to
struggle against religious doubt, she carefully minimized
Tennyson's own lack of confidence in the existence and power
of God. In Club Letter 175, for example, she quotes (from
Tennyson's "In Memoriam A.H.H."): "Upon the great world's al-
tar stairs that slope through darkness up to God" as teaching
that to achieve faith (and to feel God's undeniable power)
one must struggle against doubt and negation. Yet in reading
the stanza from which these lines are taken, one finds Tennyson faltering and falling "with his weight of cares" as he
ascends. Similarly, in the next stanza, Tennyson stretches
"lame hands of faith" and gropes as he calls out to what he
feels is "Lord of all," "faintly trust[ing] the larger hope"
that the God to whom he calls is real. Later in the poem,
Tennyson maintains that "there lives more faith in honest
doubt, believe me, than in half the creeds." In a sermon dated March 1934, Lily Montagu takes Tennyson's line to justify
the use of Biblical criticism. Glossing over Tennyson's contention that one can have faith even with perplexities and
doubts, she narrows the stanza's focus, asserting that it is
a religious duty to ask questions, to honestly doubt traditional interpretations of the Bible. God, she insists, does
not ask us to worship Him blindly but to "use our brains in
the service of our faith."[27] While Tennyson also wrote poems
on womanhood (viewing woman as the lesser man) and in celebration of the Empire and military glory, it is significant
that Lily Montagu made no reference to them. It seems that
her intention was not to mold her ideas to fit those of the
poets whom she admired but to use some of their thoughts as
springboards for exploring--and verbalizing--her own.

Of all those poets to whom Lily Montagu was indebted, it was Robert Browning who touched her most deeply. Though Browning may have discovered God's love through the incarnation of Jesus, Lily Montagu found that his *understanding*, not only of God but also of true religion, closely mirrored her own. As Lily Montagu's faith grew, Browning became more than a source of inspiration. He became a kindred spirit, possessed, as she was, by an "intense, unswerving, unquestioning faith" based upon an inner experience of the Divine.[28]

Lily Montagu quoted Browning more frequently (and more extensively) than she did any other writer. Though her enthusiasm for Browning was shared by many other late Victorians (by 1868 he apparently had become "the fashion"[29]), her enthusiasm lasted for well over seventy years. Finding that Browning's poetry gave clear expression to her own religious thoughts, she repeatedly used *his* phrases to describe her *own* convictions. Thus, for example, she found her belief in God's beneficence eloquently described by Browning in his poem, "Pippa Passes." When the young Pippa begins to realize that God extends His love to all human beings and that all deeds are "useful to men and dear to God," she sings out that "God's in His heaven, all's right with the world!" As Lily Montagu maintained in a Club letter written as late as 1961, one who serves God can never feel alone for as Browning's poem reveals, God is everywhere, influencing our activities and helping us choose that which is right.

In emphasizing the presence of the "Divine Spirit" in all things, Lily Montagu often quoted from Browning's "Abt Vogler" and "Fra Lippo Lippi." She took verses from "Paracelsus" to describe the recognition of this presence as an emergence from darkness to light. Finding a sense of confidence in Browning that Tennyson clearly lacked, Lily Montagu used Browning's images of the "finger of God . . . existence behind all laws" and "the high that proved too high" (both from

"Abt Vogler") to convey her own assurance not only that God exists but also that we can commune with Him.

Through Browning's influence, Lily Montagu's sense of optimism flourished. As she maintained in one of her sermons, Browning helped her to discover goodness in all things and convinced her that "the best is yet to be." Quoting from "Rabbi ben Ezra," Lily Montagu insisted that one who trusts in God cannot be afraid. Because God *is*, she wrote, we can believe that there is always opportunity for us to create goodness, to seek God's guidance and "to introduce God's thoughts into the thoughts of men."[30]

Browning's universalism both influenced and echoed Lily Montagu's notion of true religion. As she asserted in her sermon on "Immortality in Literature," his doctrine of love as interchangeable with religion helped her to realize that in loving other people, one came to love God. Moreover, Browning's contention that since love is eternal, death is but a turning point (that which Lily Montagu later described as of no greater consequence than hanging up one's coat), increased her faith in the immortality of the soul and perhaps more importantly, led her to accept death without fear. As Browning maintained in "Prospice," addressing his beloved, death is but a "peace out of pain, then a light, then thy breast." Thus, "I shall clasp thee again, and with God be the rest!"

By the time Lily Montagu was nineteen (the year in which she and her sister, Marian, founded the West Central Jewish Girls Club), her concept of religion was clearly formulated. The literary sources to which we have referred helped give her vague spiritual longings greater shape and self-expression. Identifying God as a power not ourselves that makes for righteousness, she came to identify righteousness with holiness and morality. The religious life, she asserted, was one of work and duty, of serving God through serving others. What

remained, however, was a means of reconciling this view with
Judaism, that which, as defined by her father, maintained
that good deeds made one a good person, but only observance
made one a good Jew. During the 1890s, she read the works of
Claude Montefiore, Israel Abrahams and other self-professed
Liberal Jews whose understanding of Judaism helped validate
her own thoughts as Jewish. As we shall see, it was they (as
well as Joseph Mazzini and possibly Benjamin Jowett) who encouraged her to formulate a plan through which she could
share these thoughts with others, enabling them to discover,
as she had, that Judaism was not antithetical to the "true"
religious life.

IV. Intellectual Background

Lily Montagu's intellectual growth was stimulated by a number of essays, books and sermons that she read during the 1890s. Although by the time she was fifteen she already had begun to think about religion in a new, more meaningful way, her understanding of "real" or "true" religion seemed antithetical to Judaism as she understood it. Equating Judaism with Orthodoxy, she came to believe that its emphasis upon the observance of externally imposed commandments could not be reconciled with real religion as the outward expression of an internal, *personal experience* of the Divine. What mattered most was not obedience to God's will but hearing God's voice or, as she often said, opening oneself up to God's eternal presence. Consequently, she insisted that ethical behavior took on greatest significance only when it emerged out of this Divine-human encounter, thus serving as a sign of faith rather than of mere loyalty to a particular religious tradition.

By the turn of the century, however, Lily Montagu succeeded in discovering a way of reconciling Judaism with real religion. Through the writings of Claude Montefiore and a number of other self-professed Liberal Jews, she began to realize that Orthodoxy was only one of many equally legitimate forms of Jewish self-identity. Though for her Orthodoxy might never become a real religion, it was possible, she saw, to find within the kind of Judaism articulated by Montefiore and others a means of awakening her own spiritual nature. Subsequently, she began to envision a Judaism that could be

identified as personal (or real) religion, one that stressed
inner piety, a striving for righteousness, and communion with
God.

Through the writings of Joseph Mazzini and Benjamin Jowett, Lily Montagu subsequently became determined to share her
vision with others. Jowett's conception of a Broad Church
that unified all Anglicans helped Lily Montagu (and Claude
Montefiore) formulate a broad notion of Judaism, one that
transcended sectarian or denominational claims. A few years
later, the Italian patriot and writer, Joseph Mazzini, helped
Lily Montagu transform this vision into reality, for, maintaining that "God has created us not for contemplation, but
for action," he convinced her that it was through association, i.e., the united effort of men and women working towards a common goal, that human progress might best be
served.[1] In forming the Jewish Religious Union (that which
Mazzini would have identified as a "special association"),
Lily Montagu consciously sought to carry out his plan. Her
stated intent was to help Anglo-Jewry progress by revitalizing the religious life of the community. To do so, she
attempted to unite, in Mazzini's words, the "individual means
and strengths" of all those who sympathized with her
intentions.

JUDAISM AS PERSONAL RELIGION

As we have seen, Lily Montagu's initial concept of true
religion was based primarily if not exclusively upon non-
Jewish sources. She therefore had little reason to believe
(or hope) that Judaism and "real religion" could be reconciled with one another. The writings of Claude Montefiore,
however, offered Lily Montagu a new understanding of Judaism
as personal religion based, not upon rabbinic law, but upon a
relationship established between the individual Jew and God.

Montefiore identified this vision as Liberal Judaism. As he
later wrote, it acknowledged, in a way which he felt Orthodoxy did not, that "actual, living religion is not the written page, but the person - as he thinks, wills and feels." To
Montefiore, the "essence of religion" consisted in the "influence of the divine Spirit without upon the human spirit
within." His aim was to demonstrate, through his works, the
ways in which Judaism in its "liberal presentation" both recognized and gave expression to this "essence."[2]

Well respected as a scholar by Christians and Jews, Montefiore claimed that his concept of Liberal Judaism was rooted in his own understanding of Judaism as a "living historical religion that belongs to the present as well as to the
past, and, it perhaps may be, to the future as well as to the
present."[3] As such, it neither conflicted with science or
rested on antiquated beliefs, but was capable of absorbing
external influences and developing from one age to the next.
Making a distinction between Judaism's essential ethical laws
and its inessential ceremonies and observances, Montefiore
claimed that the justification for a modern Judaism lay not
within dogmatic faith, but within moral action. He therefore
envisioned Judaism as an inspirational force within modern
life, recognizing that just as the Unity of God implies the
Brotherhood of Man, so one serves God best by serving other
human beings.

Montefiore's ethical monotheism placed great value on
the relationship between the individual and God. Believing
that the moral life was possible only through "the direct,
close and immediate relation of the soul of man to God," he
attempted to describe the ways in which this communion could
be attained. Significantly, he rejected reason and knowledge
as means through which God could be experienced, and instead
maintained that one could approach the Divine through "righteousness in action and truthfulness of the heart." While

he favored retaining those traditional ceremonies and rites
which led to a deeper understanding of religious truth,
prayer, self-sacrifice and a sense of vocation were of greater interest to him. Although he admitted that within Biblical
religion the importance of the community superseded that of
the individual, Montefiore's emphasis on personal religion
was not meant as a denial of Biblical faith, but rather as a
higher understanding of the Will of God. [4]

Montefiore identified his interpretation of Judaism as
"liberal," for unlike the "rigid orthodoxy" of many within
the Anglo-Jewish community, it allowed, he insisted, for both
spiritual growth and individual expression. Moreover, in representing personal integrity, openness and greater freedom in
approaching Jewish literature and law, it sought to reexamine
religious history in light of contemporary knowledge and
truth. In 1891, Montefiore was invited to deliver the presti-
gious Hibbert Lectures at Oxford. Speaking on the "Origin and
Growth of Religion as Illustrated by the Ancient Hebrews," he
maintained that while the acceptance of Biblical criticism
and the questions which it raised in regard to authorship and
dates undermined any literal acceptance of Biblical law as
Divine, other ideas expressed by the ancient Hebrews remained
immune to critical inquiry. These included the connection between religion and morality, first taught by Moses and later
expanded upon by the prophets; the nature and unity of the
Divine; and the relationship between God and humanity. He
also defended the concept of election but maintained that
Israel's election implied a special duty, not a special privilege. Such particularism, he explained, was necessary as
long as the religious task to which the Jews had been elected
remained unfulfilled. Specifically, this "Jewish mission" was
to spread Judaism's concepts of God throughout the world.
While such concepts lacked any particular Jewish content,
representing, instead, ideas of God in their purest and most

universal form, they had developed within Jewish sources and reflected Judaism's present stage of historical growth and therefore could be seen as "Jewish" and not merely as "theistic."[5]

Having rejected the Mosaic authorship of the Torah, the historicity of miracles, concepts of a personal Messiah, the return of the Jews to Palestine and the restoration of the Temple, and the importance of observing all of Biblical and rabbinic law, Montefiore based his identity upon the necessity of fulfilling the task for which the Jews, as a religious community, had been chosen.[6] Once this mission was completed, however, a prophetic Judaism, "as spiritual as the religion of Jesus, and even more universal than the religion of Paul," would be created, representing a "world-wide Theism" which would "proclaim the truth of man's kinship and communion with the Father of all."[7]

In formulating his universal religious vision, Montefiore freely quoted from both Jewish and non-Jewish sources. Though true religion, he believed, was rooted in the teachings of the Hebrew prophets, "the religion of the Jews in its essence and fundamentals was too great and universal to be confined to the limits of a single person." Thus, discovering in the writings of many non-Jews religious sentiments that seemed to echo his own, Montefiore maintained that "we may find truth, consolation and enlightenment wherever we can."[8] In order to illustrate this belief, he made frequent reference to the teachings of English poets and novelists, to the religious ideas of contemporary Christian thinkers like Matthew Arnold and Benjamin Jowett, and even to the sayings of Jesus and to the writings of St. Paul.

This appropriation of non-Jewish sources figures prominently in Montefiore's *The Bible for Home Reading*, published in two volumes in 1896 and 1899. Intended for Jewish and Christian parents as well as for older children, it sought to

make the Hebrew Bible more readable primarily through para-
phrasing and simple exegesis of the Biblical text. In this
work, Montefiore quoted from Robert Browning, Alfred Lord
Tennyson, George Eliot, William Wordsworth, Milton, Shake-
speare and other non-Jewish authors. Without trying to label
their thoughts as Jewish (a temptation to which Lily Montagu
occasionally succumbed), he asserted that their words expressed, as clearly as any, the meaning of the Biblical writer. While one might argue that Montefiore's use of non-Jewish
source material here is understandable in light of the fact
that *The Bible for Home Reading* was not written solely for
Jews (and that Montefiore therefore wanted to include those
sources with which the majority of his readers would be familiar), the frequency with which Montefiore drew upon non-
Jewish material, even in sermons intended for specifically
Jewish audiences, leads one to conclude that quotes from
Browning, Tennyson, et al., were intended not as general
points of reference but as sources which Montefiore felt
clearly conveyed the universal spirit of the Hebrew Bible.

     In numerous sermons written for the Jewish Religious
Union (and published in a series entitled *Papers for Jewish
People*), Montefiore explicitly defended the use of non-Jewish
authors to help convey the meaning of Jewish ideals. In one
such sermon, "Liberal Judaism and Nationalism," he stated
that there were "Jews who owe much to Tennyson, Browning,
Ruskin [and] Carlyle." He admitted that all of these thinkers
were impregnated with Christian teachings. Yet since much of
Christian culture, he argued, is congruent to or essentially
Jewish, Judaism becomes "all the richer and truer" as it as-
similates these ideas.[9] In *Truth in Religion and Other Sermons*, a collection of sermons first delivered at worship services held by the J.R.U., Montefiore once again expressed indebtedness to a number of non-Jewish thinkers. Quoting from
Wordsworth and Elizabeth Barrett Browning, he maintained that

there was a close relationship between religious awe and love
of nature and, echoing the words of Matthew Arnold, described
religion as "righteousness touched by emotion." Montefiore
pointed to George Eliot's *Romola* as revealing the importance
of self-sacrifice and in a sermon entitled "The Lessons of
Death" credited Eliot with having helped him to understand
that death can be a stimulus to a noble life.

Montefiore expressed particular gratitude to Benjamin
Jowett whom he had known from his days at Oxford. In an essay
on Jowett's religious teachings, published in the *Jewish
Quarterly Review* in January of 1900, Montefiore argued that
while Jowett's religion was a "Christian theism," it nevertheless "partly belonged to a sphere where the purer Judaism
and the purer Christianity fade into each other." Jowett, he
continued,

> would have smiled if I had ventured to tell him
> that his teaching was Jewish, but I think he would
> not have been wholly displeased. To agree about the
> essentials of religion, he would have said, is far
> more important than to agree by what names we shall
> call them.

Montefiore thus went on to translate Jowett's thoughts into
Jewish terms, openly conjecturing as to what a "Jewish Jowett" might say. Were Jowett Jewish, wrote Montefiore, he
would state that

> a Jew is not he who believes or disbelieves that
> Moses wrote the Pentateuch, but he who loves God
> and loves men . . . not he who observes or neglects
> this ceremony or that ritual, but he who loves
> righteousness and loving-kindness, and walks humbly
> before his God.

Urging his readers to follow these teachings, Montefiore
maintained that Jowett's thoughts were important in pointing
the way towards an enlightened and progressive Judaism. As

Jews, he concluded, we still have much work to do in moving
Judaism "from the letter to the spirit, from the national and
the historical to the ideal." From Jowett, he suggested, we
can learn how to place Judaism on a firmer footing, helping
to create a "more comprehensive religion of the future,
which, under whatever name or label, may include an increasing number of seekers after God."[10]

Montefiore's appropriation of non-Jewish sources, perhaps more than anything, convinced Lily Montagu that her own
understanding of true religion was in fact Jewish. It may
have been sheer coincidence that Montefiore and Montagu favored the same non-Jewish authors (certainly, there were many
Victorians who could claim, as they did, that Robert Browning
was their favorite poet and George Eliot their favorite novelist). Yet had Lily Montagu ever commented on this "coincidence," she undoubtedly would have said that if she and Montefiore found meaning in similar literary works it was because they were kindred spirits, united by a common vision of
both humanity and God. Discovering that Montefiore identified
this vision as Jewish, Lily Montagu began to reexamine the
significance of her own religious tradition. No longer equating Judaism with Orthodoxy, she began to believe that it was
possible to find the truths expressed by Browning, Eliot and
Arnold within Judaism itself. Moreover, the fact that Montefiore, a far greater scholar that she ever could hope to be,
often turned to popular non-Jewish literature in expressing
his vision, encouraged Lily Montagu to express her own.
Through the influence of Montefiore, then, Lily Montagu began
to feel not only that she could harmonize Judaism with real
religion but also that in expressing this conviction, she
could draw upon those authors whose writings she loved best.

During the 1890s, Montefiore wasn't the only individual
to describe what a "liberal presentation" of Judaism might
be. Israel Abrahams, co-editor with Montefiore of the *Jewish*

Quarterly Review, shared Montefiore's vision of a Judaism based not on the teachings of the rabbis but on inner religious experience. In *Aspects of Judaism*, a collection of sermons by Montefiore and Abrahams published in 1895, Abrahams called for a conception of Judaism that transcended "narrow sectarian boundaries." It would be a mistake, he cautioned, to close Judaism off to new possibilities for development and growth, for while "tradition is a chain of many links," some of these are of pure gold, others of inferior metal. Thus, "if we remove the latter, the chain will still hold, so long as we weld the remaining links honestly and add links of durable and genuine metal."[11]

Abrahams' words were later echoed by N. S. Joseph (the man credited with having first encouraged Lily Montagu to form the Jewish Religious Union) and Israel Mattuck, an American rabbi who became spiritual leader of the Liberal Jewish Synagogue in 1912. Abrahams, Joseph and Mattuck, like Montefiore, contributed written sermons to the J.R.U.'s series of *Papers for Jewish People*. In them, they helped clarify and expand upon the concept of a Liberal Judaism. It was Mattuck, in fact, who convinced Lily Montagu that women were qualified not only to serve as religious organizers but also as religious leaders. While in the early days of the Union she believed that women should not preach or lead the worship services (for fear of "shocking the community"), Mattuck brought her to a new understanding of the role of women in religious life. At his insistence, in 1918, she preached her first sermon at the Liberal Jewish Synagogue. Though retaining the notion that women and men were meant to complement one another, she came to understand, again through Mattuck, that complementarity did not imply separate spheres of activity. Rather, he said, it was the distinct way in which men and women approached these activities that made their contributions unique. In letters to Mattuck, in sermons and in her

autobiography, Lily Montagu attached a great deal of importance to what became the first of many sermons that she delivered at constituent congregations of the J.R.U. With an un-
characteristic lack of modesty, she maintained that the reason why her sermon was later printed was because it "represented a development in the story of Liberal Jewish progress."[12] At the very least, it represented a new stage in
Lily Montagu's own intellectual growth.

Throughout her lifetime, Lily Montagu continued to gain
intellectual stimulation from sermons that she heard or read.
As Amy Cruse observes in her study of *The Victorians and
Their Reading*, many Victorians regarded the sermon not just
as an emotional and spiritual exercise but as an intellectual
exercise as well. Thus, she notes,

> no right minded Victorian thought his Sunday prop-
> erly spent unless he heard at least one sermon.
> Many made a practice of hearing two, and there were
> some who often heard three.[13]

Similarly, Lily Montagu made a point of listening to Liberal
Jewish sermons (and particularly those of Montefiore and Mattuck) whenever she could. Often, after hearing Montefiore and
Mattuck preach, she would write to them, either to discuss
ideas contained in their sermons or to tell them how much
their sermons meant. In one letter to Mattuck, dated May 13,
1918, Lily Montagu maintained that she couldn't go to bed
without thanking him for the address that he had given that
afternoon. "I do thank God," she wrote, "that we have you as
our minister and I pray that you may . . . give your message
to a larger and larger Congregation."[14]

Although, beginning in the late 1920s, Lily Montagu's
official responsibilities as lay minister of the West Central
Liberal Jewish· Congregation occasionally prevented her from
attending other services, she often spent Sabbath mornings
attending worship services at the Liberal Jewish Synagogue

(or another constituent congregation of the J.R.U.) before going to the West Central to lead a service of her own. Some who knew her, in fact, have suggested that Lily Montagu continued to hold Saturday afternoon services at the West Central after other Liberal Jewish congregations had shifted their services to the morning (a shift that took place in the 1920s) so that she could hear Montefiore, Mattuck and others preach without sacrificing her own leadership role. While both Montefiore and Mattuck died before Lily Montagu (indeed, she outlived Mattuck by almost ten years, Montefiore by twenty-five), she never tired of reading their printed sermons. Neither, it seems, did she tire of reading the sermons of Israel Abrahams, N. S. Joseph and other Liberal Jews whose words (by her own admission) continued to give her not just spiritual nourishment but intellectual nourishment as well.

FROM BROAD CHURCH TO BROAD SYNAGOGUE

In "Kinship With God," the first sermon that Lily Montagu delivered at the Liberal Jewish Synagogue, she quoted Benjamin Jowett's description of God as a spirit above the world who has an affinity within it. Jowett, she said, rightly recognized that human holiness is attainable because God has created us to be like Him. Thus, in acknowledging our kinship with the Divine we acknowledge the possibility of humanity's "ultimate perfectability." "Kinship With God" was only one of several sermons in which Lily Montagu expressed her indebtedness to Jowett's thoughts. It was Jowett, she wrote elsewhere, who led her to believe in progressive revelation, to understand that although the truths of God always existed, we only become conscious of them gradually, over a long period of time.

While Lily Montagu may have come to an appreciation of Jowett through Claude Montefiore who, as we have seen,

admired Jowett greatly, she may well have discovered Jowett's
works during the years following the completion of her formal
study. His "On the Interpretation of Scriptures" included in
Essays and Reviews (first published in 1860) was widely read
and debated throughout Great Britain. Though its authors were
Christian, many of the religious problems which they presented, particularly the apparent conflict between religion and
science, were of equal interest to Jews. Montefiore, however,
helped validate her interest in Jowett, just as he helped
validate her interest in Browning, Eliot and other non-Jews.
Certainly, Montefiore's essay on "The Religious Teachings of
Jowett" to which we already have referred, not only brought
Lily Montagu to believe that Jowett's teachings were compatible with Judaism, but also convinced her that Judaism would
benefit from following Jowett's lead. His notion of a Broad
Church, capable of uniting all Anglicans, helped her to conceive of a Judaism in which all Jews similarly would be united. While Lily Montagu never referred to the Jewish Religious
Union as a Broad Synagogue, her vision of a revitalized
Anglo-Jewish community consciously or unconsciously owed a
great deal to Jowett's religious thought.

Jowett's vision of a Broad Church enabled him and other
liberals to affirm a universal religion of humanity while at
the same time identifying themselves as members of the Anglican Church. Broadening their understanding of Anglicanism to
include their universal vision, they aimed at a more inclusive definition of Anglicanism based upon morality and the
love of one's neighbor. In formulating her own liberal understanding of Judaism, Lily Montagu reiterated Jowett's belief
that one could unite opposing factions by arriving at a common denominator of thought. While Jowett's was morality in
imitation of Christ, Lily Montagu's was morality in response
to God's commandment to be holy. Reducing Judaism to ethical
monotheism, she thus began to believe that it was possible to

arrive at a unified vision of Judaism's "essence," one that would validate her religious vision as Jewish and receive the approval of Orthodox Jews like her father.

The notion of a Broad Church, as articulated by Jowett, provided Lily Montagu with a new sense of religious optimism. Jowett's vision led her to believe that Liberal and Orthodox Jews could coexist as members of a single Anglo-Jewish community, united by their belief in the significance of God's moral teachings. Despite the rigid orthodoxy of her father and her mother's more passive but equally committed acceptance of Orthodoxy as an all-encompassing way of life, Lily Montagu found, through Jowett, a means of retaining her family ties and loyalty. Though articulating a vision of Judaism that seemed antithetical to their own, Lily Montagu began to believe that she and her family were united by a common religious vision, one that transcended—and ultimately rendered insignificant—the many differences between them. Jowett, then, exerted an important influence over Lily Montagu, for he helped convince her that her own liberal understanding of Judaism was not antithetical to that of her parents but simply gave expression (in a different but no less valid way) to a commonly held Jewish "essence."

ACTION THROUGH ASSOCIATION: THE INFLUENCE OF JOSEPH MAZZINI

While Claude Montefiore remained content with what similarly became for him a vision of a broadly defined Judaism, uniting the Anglo-Jewish community if not in reality at least in thought, Lily Montagu began to entertain ways of actively sharing this vision with others. In 1901, she wrote to N. S. Joseph, telling him that she hoped to offer the Anglo-Jewish community a new understanding of Judaism's religious principles, one that would give expression to her own more broadly conceived notion of Jewish faith. Her intent, she

insisted, was not to form a schismatic movement, but to create an association of all those who sympathized with her vision of a religious reinvigorated Anglo-Jewry. Though the aim
of the association would be to promote Liberal Jewish ideas,
membership would not identify one as a Liberal Jew. Rather
membership, as she envisioned it, would indicate a recognition of Liberal Judaism as capable of bringing previously apathetic Jews back to Judaism, thus acknowledging the legitimacy of Liberal Judaism as one of the many valid forms of
Jewish self-expression.

Lily Montagu's belief in the need for such an association stemmed from a familiarity with and acceptance of the
political and religious thought of the Italian patriot, Joseph Mazzini. Like Mazzini, Lily Montagu viewed the world as
a collective whole created by God. She too felt that all men
and women had an obligation to strive towards the common good
and advance the progress of humanity by directing their faculties "to the development of the faculties" of others and
contributing

> . . . some portion to that collective work of im-
> provement and that discovery of the truth which the
> generations slowly but continuously carry on.[15]

While Mazzini, in seeking to establish a united, independent
and Republican Italy, devoted much of his life to political
and social goals, he, like Lily Montagu, viewed all such effort as religious. Even social revolutions, he insisted,
needed to be animated by the Divine spirit and hallowed
through the love of God and one's fellow human beings. Yet he
too believed that society could not be revived and transformed until men and women were shaken out of their state of
inertia and induced into action.

Mazzini offered Lily Montagu more than an eloquent
articulation of her own sentiments and ideals. His works
convinced her that change could best be effected through

"fraternal cooperation towards a common aim." Association, he maintained, multiplied individual strength. In uniting the ideas and capabilities of its members, it joined them "in one single faith, under one single law and for one single purpose." A peaceful, public association, he continued, helped men and women better realize the collective nature of humanity. Though it would employ persuasion rather than compulsion, the "wider, the more intimate and comprehensive" the association became, the further could it advance the "path of individual progress."[16]

To be successful, he stated, an association needed to develop a new philosophy of life. Dead or dying creeds had to be replaced with a "positive, ruling principle" and the spirit of self-sacrifice awakened. While eventually these principles would be transformed into actions, it was the Word of God, he insisted, that would "raise the standard of Humanity in the midst of the nations of the earth."[17] For Mazzini, such efforts represented the incarnation of Christ's moral teachings. Through them, he felt, one became an apostle, a preacher of the doctrine of Humanity which Christ had come to reveal.

While Lily Montagu did not wish to become a herald of Christian faith, she attached great significance to Mazzini's message. She too wanted to bring God's moral teachings to those around her and instill in others a sense of human kinship and love for the Divine. Moreover, not wanting to cut herself off from family and friends, she found that Mazzini's concept of associated labor held greater personal appeal than did the notion of a schismatic movement of Liberal Jews alone. Thus using his ideas to meet her own situation, she sought to create an organization which, generated by the principles of religious reexamination and reform, would deepen the religious life of the Anglo-Jewish community by uniting its members in a common struggle.

One sees the influence of Mazzini most clearly in the
numerous sermons and addresses in which Lily Montagu referred
to Mazzini and his ideas. Repeatedly, she stressed the importance of association as helping the world to progress and exhorted others to recognize, as Mazzini did, the connection
between faith and conduct. It was not enough, she maintained,
to have a specific vision. One needed to translate that vision into action, displaying, as Mazzini had, aspiration, devotion and singleness of purpose. Both before and after the
founding of the J.R.U., Lily Montagu insisted that Mazzini's
idea of association had great importance for the Anglo-Jewish
community. In the "Spiritual Possibilities of Judaism," published in 1899, the article which Lily Montagu once said
started the Liberal Jewish movement in England, she pointed
to Mazzini's attempts to unite the Italian people in the service of God and their country, suggesting that British Jews
might similarly come together in united effort. Years later,
in a letter written to members of the West Central Club, she
asserted that in founding the J.R.U. she and her supporters
were asking young people to find what Mazzini called "the
spiritual formula of their generation."

Mazzini, it seems, became an inspiration for Lily Montagu. Though his efforts produced few tangible results--his attempts to free Italy were futile, his followers abandoned
him, and he died a "lonely exile" in London--she nevertheless
maintained that his goals, his sense of duty and his love of
God made him an exciting and stimulating figure. At the very
least, she wrote, Mazzini was a "noble failure," for, despite
his misfortunes, the personal qualities which he displayed,
the religious faith which he upheld, and the call for action
which he issued all remained worthy of emulation.[18]

Thus, through the influences of Montefiore, Mattuck and
other Liberal Jews, the Broad Church vision of Benjamin Jowett and Mazzini's notion of associated labor, Lily Montagu

began to view her own understanding of religion not only as
Jewish but also as that which was capable of uniting all
British Jews through a common effort. These ideas, together
with the successful development of Reform Judaism in Germany
and America and the moderate success of liberalizing Jewish
efforts initiated during the nineteenth century in London,
eventually led Lily Montagu to believe that it might be
possible to infuse the Anglo-Jewish community with a
far-reaching spirit of reform.

PART TWO

LILY MONTAGU: A PERSONAL AND SOCIAL BIOGRAPHY

V. The Making of a Religious Leader

Lily Montagu was born on December 22, 1873, the sixth child of Samuel Montagu (later, First Lord Swaythling) and Ellen Montagu, nee Cohen. The daughter of a self-made millionaire, she was constantly surrounded by wealth. Her family owned two homes, their London residence in Kensington Palace Gardens and their country estate, South Stoneham House in Swaythling, Hampshire, and her father became a noted collector of both art and silver. While according to her nephew, Eric Conrad, the Montagu children were brought up strictly and "were not allowed to acquire a sense of wealth or luxury," with their pocket money "austerely rationed and even their mother's household allowance severely controlled," inevitably their home was infused with an atmosphere of comfort and leisure. Consequently, as Conrad concludes,

> If anything in it helped to develop Lily Montagu's
> particular inclination [towards social service] -
> which her parents, worried about her health, and
> the extremes to which she went in utter disregard
> of her own person, soon tried to discourage - it
> was the discrepancy between the comfort in which
> she was brought up and the social misery and lack
> of security at large against which her inborn sense
> of justice rebelled.[1]

By the age of seventeen, Lily Montagu began to devote an increasing amount of time to social service. At first, she and her sister, Marian, helped tutor working class girls living in the East End of London, later she and Marian formed the West Central Jewish Girls Club to share with those less

fortunate than they that which they valued most, namely education, faith and friendship. By 1914, the Montagu sisters
had also founded a Day Settlement for Jewish Girls and in
1926, established the Maude Nathan Home for Little Children,
where Jewish and non-Jewish children could be sent "when difficulties at home resulting from illness, the birth of a new
baby or the death of a parent occurred."[2]

Yet, unlike her sister Marian, Lily also became immersed
in religious activities. As her thoughts turned more and more
to God, she sought a means of bringing others to a similar
awareness of the Divine eternal presence. As we shall see, it
was this desire that propelled Lily Montagu into a role of
religious leadership, not just within the Anglo-Jewish community but outside of England as well. Founding the Jewish
Religious Union in 1902, she later became lay minister of her
own congregation, President of the Union of Liberal and Progressive Synagogues in Great Britain (the renamed J.R.U.),
and of the World Union for Progressive Judaism, an organization which she conceived and helped establish. In recognition
of her achievements, she received, in 1929, an honorary
D.H.L. (Doctor of Hebrew Law) degree from Hebrew Union College in Cincinnati, and twenty-six years later had the title
of C.B.E. conferred upon her by the British crown (an honor
which succeeded an earlier O.B.E. for her efforts as a social
worker and magistrate). In February of 1963, one month after
Lily Montagu's death, the *Liberal Jewish Monthly* published a
memorial supplement in her honor. Included were a series of
tributes written by those who knew her. Each sought to cap-
ture the "essence" of Lily Montagu's personality by describing a particular aspect of her life's work. Leslie Edgar,
then Senior Minister of the Liberal Jewish Synagogue, discussed her contribution to the Liberal Jewish movement in
England. He noted her remarkable "spirit of devotion and
service" as well as the "youthful vision . . . [which she]

maintained to the end." Lily Montagu, he wrote, was a "woman
of religious genius," for

> she lived throughout her life by her faith, by her
> sense of the nearness and presence of God, by her
> faith in and love of Judaism, and of her fellow
> creatures.[3]

The establishment of the Jewish Religious Union was an expression of this faith. Yet shy and, contrary to the descriptions of others, lacking in self-confidence, Lily Montagu
would never have undertaken such an endeavor were it not for
the recognition afforded to her as Samuel and Ellen Montagu's
daughter and for the constant encouragement and assistance of
both family and friends.

FAMILY BACKGROUND: THE MONTAGUS AND THE COHENS

Samuel Montagu, Lily's father, was a prominent member of
both the Anglo-Jewish community and upper class British society. Born in Liverpool on December 21, 1832, he came from a
lower middle class family and was the youngest of seven children. At birth, he was named Montagu Samuel, but his parents
later reversed it to Samuel Montagu, apparently because
"there were so many Samuels in Liverpool."[4] When Montagu was
fourteen, he left school and, in order to supplement his family's income, worked for a firm of foreign exchange mer-
chants. Soon after, he left for London and became the London
agent for a small Paris bank. In 1853, Montagu decided to set
up a foreign exchange business of his own. Borrowing £3000
from his father, he opened an office in Leadenhall Street.
Within a short period of time, Samuel Montagu and Co. had
become one of the major private banks in the city and, as a
result, Montagu acquired a great deal of personal wealth.

As a self-made millionaire, Montagu purchased a large
home at 12 Kensington Palace Gardens, bought a 1200 acre

estate at Swaythling, near Southamptom, and, as we have
noted, became a distinguished collector of art and silver.
His reputation as a financier whose "business life was guided
by certain ethical principles to which he gave absolute and
rigid obedience" enhanced the esteem in which he was held,
and his advice was sought both by Liberal and Conservative
Chancellors of the Exchequer.[5] From 1887, Montagu served as a
member of the Gold and Silver Commission. He also published
articles on the dangers of depreciation and means of prevent-
ing it and fought in Parliament for the acceptance of international bi-metallism and the decimalization of currency.

Within British society, Montagu achieved fame not only
as a businessman, but also as a politician. A devoted admirer
of William Gladstone, he decided to stand for election in
1885, and from 1885 to 1900, served in Parliament as a Liberal M.P. for Whitechapel. Both during and after Gladstone's
tenure as Prime Minister, Montagu attained recognition as a
radical member of his party. As Lily Montagu recounts in her
biography of her father, he vigorously supported a number of
progressive measures. Among them were free education and the
improvement of technical training, better state care for
neglected children and those under the guardianship of the
state, proportional representation in Parliament, improved
land and emigration laws, legal aid to the poor against
"usurious landlords," and tax reform as a means of "equalis-
ing the burdens" among the upper and lower classes.[6]

Montagu also took great interest in philanthropic activity and served as a member of the governing committee of the
London Hospital and as Director of the 4 Percent Industrial
Company which sought to improve housing conditions in London's East End. He continually worked to strengthen the organized, institutional life of the late nineteenth century
Anglo-Jewish community and at one time belonged to forty synagogues. What's more, he regularly contributed towards the

maintenance of Talmud Torahs and Synagogue Schools and helped
establish small, independent congregations for those Eastern
European immigrants to whom the United Synagogue's anglicized
form of worship held little appeal.

Although Montagu's social involvement with the immigrant
community was limited, he became their chief patron and bene-
factor. In 1870, he formed the Jewish Working Men's Club as a
social and educational center for Jewish immigrants and in
1885, he and Hermann Landau reopened the Poor Jews Temporary
Shelter, an establishment which supplied newly arrived immigrants with bed and board for two weeks. As a firm supporter
of trade unionism, he founded a Jewish Tailors Machinist Society and in 1889, successfully served as arbitrator in the
Jewish Tailors Strike. Later, he created a Jewish Dispersion
Committee which helped immigrants resettle outside of London's congested East End.

In 1887, Samuel Montagu formed the Federation of Synagogues, a voluntary association of immigrant congregations
aimed at removing "insanitary places of worship" while preserving the separate "corporate communal life" of the immigrant population.[7] It sought to maintain the high standard of
religious observance to which a large proportion of the immigrants were accustomed and worked to provide financial and
organizational assistance through shared resources and leadership. A highly observant Jew who identified with the religious convictions of the immigrants far more than with those
of the majority of United Synagogue members, Montagu took a
personal interest in the Federation's success and, until his
death, remained its Active President and assumed major responsibility for its financial support.

During the 1890s, Samuel Montagu's reputation within the
Anglo-Jewish community grew. He traveled to Russia, Palestine, Canada and the United States as its representative,
served as an active member of both the Jewish Board of

Guardians and the Board of Deputies, and aided the Russo-
Jewish Committee in its efforts to bring Russian Jews to England. Believing in the "important influence of the dietary
laws on the Jewish Community as a whole,"[8] Montagu devoted
much time and effort to the work of the Shechita Board (the
association which supervised the ritual slaughter of animals)
and in 1905 was chosen as its President.

He also became Treasurer of the Hovevei Zion (the Lovers
of Zion), an early Zionist organization which established
colonies in Palestine primarily for persecuted Eastern European Jews. In 1895, he met with Theodor Herzl to discuss ne-
gotiations with the Turkish government as well as ways of en-
listing additional Anglo-Jewish support.[9] Montagu promised
Herzl both financial and political assistance. Several months
later, Herzl attempted to convince a group of Jewish bankers
to accompany him on his next trip to Turkey. His intention
was to offer the Sultan an annual tribute of one million
pounds in return for the creation of a Jewish principality in
Palestine. Though Herzl apparently considered Samuel Montagu
to be the "key figure in the scheme," Montagu, who by then
had become less enthusiastic about Herzl's plans, offered him
only

> . . . lukewarm support . . . conditional on the
> participation of Edmond de Rothschild who had al-
> ready intimated that he regarded Herzl as a danger-
> ous adventurer.[10]

Subsequently, Herzl found himself unable to gain sufficient
approval and soon abandoned his scheme completely.

Montagu's achievements as a financier, politician, philanthropist and communal worker were recognized by the crown
and in 1894 he was made a baronet. Thirteen years later he
was raised to the peerage and in 1907, as First Baron Swaythling, took his seat in the House of Lords. Lily Montagu,
then, did not enter Jewish public life as an unknown, but as

Samuel Montagu's daughter. As such, she possessed a certain
amount of respect and recognition both within and outside of
the Jewish community.

This recognition was similarly rooted in Lily Montagu's
maternal relationship to the Cohen family--a family which ri-
valled Samuel Montagu in wealth and distinction. Levi Barent
Cohen, Ellen Montagu's great-grandfather, was an Amsterdam
merchant who migrated to England in 1770, established himself
as a successful financier and, through the marriages of his
children, became the progenitor of almost every eminent Jewish family in Great Britain.[11] Ellen Montagu's father, Louis,
was a wealthy banker and stockbroker who founded the firm of
Louis Cohen and Co. and, from 1819 until his death in 1882,
served as a member of the British stock exchange. A well-
known philanthropist, Louis Cohen supported most of the leading charities in London and, as a highly regarded botanical
scholar, became a Fellow of the Royal Botanical Society.
Within the Anglo-Jewish community he attained equal prominence. He convinced the London Ashkenazic synagogues to ap-
point one joint Chief Rabbi and after the subsequent creation
of the United Synagogue served as a member of its council. In
addition, he was a warden of the Great Synagogue, a member of
the Board of Deputies, Vice-President of the Jews' Free
School and President of the Shechita Board.[12]

Two of his sons, Benjamin and Lionel, similarly became
prominent community leaders. Like their father, both were
members of the British stock exchange (and partners in their
father's firm) and involved themselves in a variety of philanthropic activities. In 1859, at the age of twenty-seven,
Lionel co-founded the Jewish Board of Guardians. The leading
spirit of the Board and, according to V. D. Lipman, "perhaps
the greatest Jewish communal administrator of all,"[13] he became its President in 1869. In 1870, Lionel took a leading
role in the formation of the United Synagogue and served as

one of its Vice-Presidents. In 1879 he helped establish a
Jewish house at Clifton College, one of England's major public schools. Six years later, he was elected to Parliament
and later became Vice-President of the National Union of Conservative Associations.

Like his brother, Benjamin was politically conservative.
He served as a Tory M.P. from 1892 until 1906 and in 1905,
four years before his death, was made a baronet. Benjamin also took an active role within Anglo-Jewish affairs. He served
as a Vice-President of the United Synagogue and in 1887, after the premature death of his brother Lionel, became President of the Board of Guardians. Thirteen years later, due to
ill health, Benjamin was forced to resign. However, he was
succeeded by Lionel's son, Leonard, who served as President
of the Board for twenty years.

Lily Montagu, then, inherited not only wealth but also
membership into the "Cousinhood," an elite group of men and
women connected by blood and money, from whom most of the
community's leadership was selected. Were Lily Montagu not a
member of this group, it is doubtful whether she would have
been accepted within the Jewish community as a religious
leader. Yet membership within the Cousinhood offered Lily
Montagu more than public recognition and potential access to
power. It also enabled her to turn to some of the most prominent members of the Anglo-Jewish community for support. Some
were friends of the family. Others (indeed most) were relatives, all of whom encouraged Lily Montagu to take a more active role within Anglo-Jewry's communal life.

ENCOURAGEMENT AND SUPPORT

It was Simeon Singer, Lily Montagu later wrote, who
first led her to realize "the need for thinking about religion."[14] It was Singer too who first provided Lily Montagu

with the opportunity to assume a role of leadership (albeit a
limited one) within the Anglo-Jewish community. As tutor to
both Lily and her sister Marian, Singer stressed the ideals
of the Hebrew prophets, helping Lily and Marian discover the
connection between Judaism and "social service of all kinds."
In addition, he encouraged them to ask even the most elementary questions about Judaism, thus helping Lily Montagu, apparently for the first time, gain an understanding and appreciation of Judaism as a religious tradition. In 1890, Singer
encouraged Lily Montagu to establish special children's services at the New West End. Although as minister of the congregation, he could have supervised the services closely, he
gave her complete freedom. In so doing, as Lily Montagu later
observed, he provided her with the opportunity to explore
ways of "awakening a spirit of worship" in others while, at
the same time, helping her to recognize her own leadership
potential.[15] The services which Lily Montagu developed were
based primarily on an English liturgy. She varied its order
of worship from week to week and included informal talks instead of sermons. The services were well-attended not only by
children but also by women and, as a result, Lily Montagu began to envision ways of instituting similar services specifically for adults.

Both of her parents approved of the children's services
which she continued to lead at the New West End until 1909.
Ellen Montagu, in fact, regularly attended and apparently always spoke of the services with great enthusiasm. Lily Montagu recognized that her mother's participation stemmed solely
out of an interest in her daughter's work, viewing each as
"an extra Sabbath experience" rather than as "a substitute
for the 'proper' service."[16] Yet this support and "loving understanding" meant a great deal to Lily Montagu and she later
wrote that much of her success in winning the confidence of
others was derived from having had as a model,

. . . [a] mother who throughout her life had no
greater pleasure than that of sharing her children's interests, and whose faith in God was expressed in every detail of her life.[17]

By the age of nineteen, Lily Montagu had begun to broad-
en the scope of her activities. Through her cousin, Beatrice
Franklin (later the wife of Herbert Samuel), she met Emily
Harris, a social worker who conducted Sabbath classes for
Jewish working girls. At Miss Harris's request, Lily and Beatrice initiated Sunday afternoon get-togethers for class members. These meetings proved to be so successful that, shortly
after, Lily decided to join the participants into a more permanent educational and social group.

Consequently, in 1893, Lily Montagu established the West
Central Jewish Girls Club. She did so with the personal and
financial help of family members and friends. Shy and self-
conscious and lacking confidence in her own leadership capabilities, she often turned to them for advice and assistance,
and frequently remarked that without this she might neither
have recognized nor developed her own leadership potential.

Occasionally, this assistance consisted of little more
than moral support. In *My Club and I*, for example, Lily Montagu maintained that her uncle and aunt (Mr. and Mrs.
Nathaniel Cohen) provided her with insights "into the greatness of life" by giving her "the opportunity for long private
talks on all the big questions of Jewish and general interest." To the young girl's great joy, they seemed interested
in her thoughts and, most importantly, "encouraged her to develop ideas which were truly her own."[18]

Lily Montagu received similar assistance from her
parents. Having led "strong, purposeful lives" themselves,
they apparently were "convinced that it was desirable and
altogether right and proper for young girls to have some
outlet in social service."[19] Even when Lily's increasing

preoccupation with her work became a matter of concern, they continued to support and encourage her "Club career." In 1897, four years after the West Central Girls Club was established, Ellen Montagu became Club President. She retained the position until her death in 1918, consistently maintaining an active role in the Club's affairs. Samuel Montagu also lent his assistance. In 1897, he helped an undenominational committee of Club leaders purchase a small house in Littlehampton, Sussex. Hundreds of working class girls (including members of the West Central Club) were thus able to spend their yearly vacations at what was called The Green Lady Hostel.

While some family members remained critical of the West Central Club, many took an active interest in its organization. The Ladies' Committee, formed to assist in the Club's management, was composed primarily of relatives or friends of the Montagu family and classes were led by a number of such relatives, including Lily's cousin, Herbert Samuel, who in 1897 instituted a class in debating. Early in the Club's existence, Mrs. Ellis Franklin, Lily's aunt, helped find a suitable--albeit temporary--location for the West Central Club. Her display of "kindness" meant a great deal to Lily Montagu who, at that time, was "not allowed to go to London" and "look for rooms" herself.[20]

In the preface to her book, *My Club and I*, Lily Montagu thanks each of her five sisters for their involvement. Marian, Lily's "alter-ego" and "constant companion," helped found the Club and later became its Treasurer and Vice-President. Henrietta (Franklin), an active member of the Parents National Educational Union, assisted the Club in developing an educational curriculum and served as hostess to Club members at get-togethers annually held at her home. Florence (Waley) served as Club Treasurer and head of its Finance Committee, while Ethel (Hart) and Elsie (Myer), whom Lily Montagu thanks for their "gentle sympathy" and "down-right sincerity,"[21]

similarly participated in Club affairs. So did her sisters-
in-law, Florence and Gladys Montagu, and later a number of
her nieces and nephews.

The additional encouragement which Lily Montagu received
from friends (both within and outside of the Cousinhood) bolstered her self-confidence and precipitated her involvement
in Jewish communal affairs. Within the West Central Club, she
was surrounded by a number of dedicated workers and, within
the Anglo-Jewish community as a whole, she found that her religious concerns were viewed with great sympathy and respect.
Many of those who became workers in the West Central Club began as members. Dora Isaacs (a teacher at the Club and secretary of its Day Settlement), Nellie Levy (its Leader and Organizer from 1920 until 1956) and Hannah Feldman (a trustee,
member of the executive committee and founder of the Montagu
Circle, a social group for older members) were only three of
the many Club girls who devoted much of their lives to both
the Club and "Miss Lily." Others, like Olga Lazarus, whom the
Club employed as a Settlement Worker from 1913 until 1962,
provided Lily Montagu with similar support. She gave to the
Club a selfless and "consecrated devotion,"[22] and like Dora
Isaacs, Nellie Levy and Hannah Feldman, was considered to be
more than a colleague. Like them, she became one of Lily
Montagu's closest friends.

One early Club worker to whom Lily and Marian Montagu
became especially close was Constance Lewis. In 1903, Lewis
founded and became Director of an Employment Bureau for Club
members. She also established and led a Flower Guild which
encouraged members to learn about and care for plants. Until
her death in 1952, Constance Lewis "assisted in almost every
activity" of the Club.[23] In addition, she lived with Marian
and Lily Montagu at the "Red Lodge" in Bayswater and maintained the household for them. During the thirty-three years
in which they lived together, Constance Lewis, Lily Montagu

and Marian Montagu were affectionately known as the Red Lodge Trio. The "happy, peaceful" atmosphere which Constance Lewis created, and the interest which she took in all that they did, meant a great deal to Marian and Lily Montagu. Without her, as Lily Montagu later noted, they could not have given themselves so completely to a life of social service.

Viewing her efforts as a means of self-expression, Lily Montagu approached her work with enthusiasm and absolute devotion. Like Joan, the heroine of her novel *Broken Stalks*, she felt that every woman instinctually yearned to "give herself out in something"[24] and leave a mark on the times in which she lived. Women, she said, possessed both maternal love and a creative spirit. Those who married were given the best opportunity to fulfill these "passions." They could teach their children to pray, exert a moral influence upon their families, and more generally ensure the sanctification of their homes. Yet, she continued, those women who were not in love or whose love was unrequited, needed to explore different ways of channeling their energies and emotions. Rather than enter into a loveless relationship, they were to choose that which was "second best to a happy marriage": a useful, single life of dedication, self-sacrifice and service.[25]

While still in her teens, Lily Montagu became indifferent to dances and other "such suitable interests" and spent an increasing number of hours engaged in charitable, educational and religious endeavors. Lacking the "special love of an individual man," she put aside all thoughts of marriage and, again like her fictional heroine Joan, found the "general love which is about us everywhere and in everybody."[26] As her involvement within the Anglo-Jewish community grew, however, the focus of her work narrowed. Gradually, Lily Montagu found her life's purpose in the revitalization of Judaism and the advancement of the Liberal Jewish "cause."

In 1899, when she began to envision the creation of a
movement aimed at the revitalization of Anglo-Jewish life,
she once again enlisted the support of her family and
friends. A letter, expressing interest in formulating a program which would stress "such vital elements of Judaism as
are consistent with Truth and with modern standards of morality" was sent to leading members of the community.[27] Carbon
copies of the letter and a handwritten list of recipients reveal that most if not all were relatives and/or friends of
the Montagus. While some, like Claude Montefiore, Israel
Abrahams and Oswald Simon, had previously expressed a desire
to formulate such a program, many (perhaps the majority) had
not. These included her sister, Henrietta, Mrs. Nathaniel
Cohen (her aunt), and Sylvie d'Avigdor and Isidore Spielman
(her cousins), as well as Laurie Magnus and Philip Hartog
(leading members of the West London Synagogue, friends of the
Montagus, and relatives through marriage,[28]) and Simeon Singer and N. S. Joseph (both prominent members of the Orthodox
community and two of Samuel Montagu's closest friends).[29]

Lily Montagu believed that these men and women would
sympathize with, if not actively support, her proposal and
indicated as much in her letter. Yet, despite the significant
few who, as we have seen, had participated in earlier efforts
at reform, Lily Montagu's conviction that her proposal would
receive support stemmed less from the previous activities and
public statements of the recipients than from Lily Montagu's
acquaintance with the recipients themselves. Most of the men
and women to whom she appealed were not Liberal Jews and
therefore would have refused to participate in a specifically
Liberal Jewish movement. However, Lily Montagu, as a friend
or relative of the recipients, knew of their alarm over the
growing religious indifference within the Jewish community
and thus felt that they *would* be willing to assist in
strengthening the religious life within their midst. The

purpose of her letter, then, was twofold: 1) to elicit ideas
for a new, reformulated Judaism aimed at attracting those for
whom the traditional formulation held little appeal; and 2)
to ascertain whether there was a real interest among the community leaders in such a reformulation. If so, Lily Montagu
hoped to form a "sympathetic association." As we have noted,
members would not be united by common religious ideas, but
rather by *sympathy* with the belief that a revitalized Judaism
was one which held, or at least could hold, meaning for all
Jews. Lily Montagu wrote to those friends and relatives whom
she felt shared her religious concerns. Those who later joined the Jewish Religious Union did so with the firm belief
that Lily Montagu's stated desire to strengthen rather than
weaken and divide the Jewish community was honest and
sincere.

Neither Samuel nor Ellen Montagu took part in the activities of the Jewish Religious Union. Lily, however, felt
that her mother viewed the J.R.U. sympathetically and, were
it not for her "complete wifely devotion" to her husband,
might have given it explicit approval. Samuel Montagu, on the
other hand, was adamantly opposed to the Union and became one
of its most hostile critics. Yet Lily Montagu, unable to accept her father's rejection, convinced herself that even he
might eventually have approved of her involvement.[30] From
1909 (when the J.R.U. declared itself to be a specifically
Liberal Jewish organization) until his death in 1911, Samuel
Montagu barely spoke to his daughter, but Lily Montagu
staunchly maintained that "beneath the strain occasioned by
the different point of view between [them] . . . was essential sympathy and deep understanding love."[31] Shortly after
her father's death, Lily Montagu had a vision. Although Montagu's will clearly prohibited the use of his money for Liberal Jewish causes, Lily became convinced that the religious

work which she had undertaken had received his approval. "I
saw him in a dream," she wrote,

> . . . and he gave me a document. I am not psychical
> and have not had another experience of this kind
> before or since. But with the presentation of that
> document I felt a revival of trust, and with it
> an absolute certainty that he approved of my
> efforts. [32]

The significance of this vision seems clear. While there
is no evidence to suggest that Samuel Montagu ever possessed
an "essential sympathy" for his daughter's religious work,
Lily Montagu needed to believe that her father approved of
her efforts. Lacking his support during his lifetime, she
succeeded, after his death, in convincing herself that she
had his approval, that he understood (though again, Lily Montagu's later relationship with her father belied this) that
her efforts would not weaken Judaism but rather ensure its
survival.

Lily Montagu needed no such vision to form a relationship of "essential sympathy" between herself and any of her
five sisters. Among them, she remained closest to two--
Henrietta and Marian. Henrietta completely sympathized with
her sister's liberal religious views. She shared her desire
to form a movement aimed at revitalizing Anglo-Jewish life
and held the J.R.U.'s first official meeting at her home. She
became a member of the Union's initial Leadership Committee
and, during the Union's earliest years, conducted Bible classes for children. Later, she served, along with Lily, as an
honorary member of the Liberal Jewish Synagogue Council and
occasionally assisted in synagogue services. Although Henrietta got married when Lily was only twelve, she retained a
keen interest in her sister's work and from the very beginning provided Lily with constant encouragement and support.

Yet without her sister, Marian, to whom Lily felt "bound by the ties of the closest and deepest friendship,"[33] it is doubtful whether she would even have attempted to become a religious leader. Although quiet and often content to remain a silent spectator, Marian Montagu shared all of her younger sister's experiences and ideals. Believing in the importance of her sister's "cause," she devoted her life to seeing that Lily Montagu's dream of a living Judaism was fulfilled. Marian supported the formation of the Jewish Religious Union, the Liberal Jewish Synagogue, and the World Union for Progressive Judaism. She assisted Lily in all of her organizational tasks and assumed responsibility for her business affairs.

Though Lily Montagu never had the feeling of being wealthy, her father, and later the executors of his will, provided her with a sufficient income. The will stipulated that Lily and Marian were to receive whatever funds they deemed necessary as long as this money was not used to promote Liberal Judaism. In a letter written to her eldest brother, Louis, on March 8, 1911, Lily Montagu proposed that she and Marian receive a small legacy which they could spend freely rather than be subject to the will's conditions.[34] This offer, however, was rejected and Lily and Marian continued to live on their generous, but restricted, inheritance.

While Lily and Marian Montagu spent little on personal amenities, they unstintingly assisted various social service organizations (including the West Central Girls Club), offered loans to those in need, and frequently served as private benefactors. A letter written to Marian on September 2, 1919, for example, refers to Mary Bonin and Maurice Isaacs. In the letter, Lily requested that in the event of her death, Marian continue to support Mary while she studied to become a singer and Maurice while he trained for the navy.[35] During the 1930s and 1940s, German Jewish refugees received similar aid. Lily

and Marian helped them settle in England, often found them
jobs, and provided many with housing, loans and educational
support.

The two sisters were inseparable. They went everywhere
together and, after the death of their mother in 1919, moved
to Palace Court (and the Red Lodge) where they shared a home
(and even a bedroom) for over forty years. The more practical
of the two, Marian was also emotionally stronger. Lily, who
hated to be alone, greatly feared their parting. But she
tried to overcome this fear and in a letter dated September
1, 1939 (to be opened upon her death), wrote to Marian:

> I think we shall join one another somewhere and
> somehow because we love each other so deeply and
> God could not have given us the power to love like
> this if it was not a love which should go on
> forever.[36]

Throughout her lifetime, Lily relied on her sister, Marian,
not only for friendship and love, but also for daily support,
comfort and strength. As she herself admitted, Marian did not
simply share in her achievements; she helped her to attain
them.

Lily Montagu's reliance on others, including her strong
emotional ties to both Marian and her father, is understandable in light of her lack of training either as a social
worker or as a religious leader. Moreover, with few if any
female role models to follow, she must have entered Jewish
public life with great trepidation. Had she been less shy and
more self-confident, her growing involvement within the
Anglo-Jewish community might have seemed more natural. As it
was, she found herself forced to overcome her own fears concerning her ability to assume a role of communal leadership.
As we have seen, the encouragement and support of family and
friends, as well as her access to the Anglo-Jewish elite as a

fellow member of the Cousinhood, helped bolster her self-confidence and provided her with a much needed network of people to whom she could turn. Yet equally important, perhaps, were Lily Montagu's own early achievements as a social worker, writer and leader of children's services. These achievements not only bolstered her self-confidence further but also facilitated her later acceptance as founder (and eventually President) of the J.R.U. and lay minister of her own congregation.

VI. Early Achievements and Opportunities for Self-Expression

By the beginning of the twentieth century, Lily Montagu had attained a good deal of recognition and respect within the Anglo-Jewish community. Her pioneering efforts within the British Club movement as well as numerous published works afforded her both visibility and credibility, facilitating her involvement within the religious life of the community and her later acceptance as a lay minister and spiritual head of the West Central Liberal Congregation. In addition, available time and financial resources enabled Lily Montagu to immerse herself in her work. They made it possible for her to devote her life to that which she identified as Liberal Judaism.

Reputation as a Club Leader

Lily Montagu's earliest involvement within the Anglo-Jewish community lay within the field of social service. Although her West Central Club was not the first educational and social club formed in England, it was the first founded specifically for Jewish girls of the working classes. In 1893, when the Club was established, the British Club movement was still in its infancy. Social workers received no educational or practical training. There were no courses offered either on theories of social work, types of Club management, or forms of social organization. For the most part, Club leaders were amateurs who tried to develop (often through trial and error) ways in which the intellectual and cultural needs of the working classes, at least as they understood them, could best be met.

According to Eric Conrad, Lily Montagu's unique reputation within the British Club movement stemmed from the West
Central's "distinctive quality" and "rare spirit."[1] Though
Lily Montagu's own portrayal of the Club (particularly in her
book, *My Club and I*) reveals that she never completely freed
herself of the "spirit of patronage" that she abhorred, she
attempted to establish the West Central Club in a spirit of
"friendship and mutual understanding." She thus insisted that
each worker "not attempt to foist her standards" on Club members but rather "study their standards, and exchange her
points of view with them."[2] Within her own social set, Lily
Montagu was accused of drawing the girls away from their
homes and rebuked for mixing freely with them. However, she
ignored such criticism and maintained that the needs of "her"
girls could only be met through personal friendship. "My approach to them," she later wrote, "was so simple." It was
"just the kind of friendliness given by one girl to others
like herself, and they gave me affection in generous measure."[3] Even when the Club was small, Lily refused to lump
the members together into a specific "Club girl" type. Consequently, she sought to create a program which fostered
self-expression and growth.[4]

Yet, at the same time, Lily Montagu believed that the
success of the Club would not rest with the variety or at-
tractiveness of its programs. Rather, she asserted, girls
would join only if they felt that Club workers cared for them
and wanted to be part of their lives. She therefore insisted
that teaching commitments be taken seriously and placed great
emphasis on teacher-student relationships. She urged workers
to visit members outside of the Club and encouraged them to
invite members to their homes. What's more, she organized social events, outings, and country holidays for both workers
and members which, again, helped promote friendship and
understanding.

Members gained a sense of responsibility and self-worth by governing the Club themselves. At first, the West Central was run by a Management Committee composed of Club workers. Members were free to make suggestions, but final decisions rested with the Committee. Within a short period of time, however, a more democratic form of government was adopted. Although some feared that such a measure would undermine the workers' authority, Lily Montagu maintained that "the only authority worth having is based on affection and respect"-- something which each worker had to earn for herself.[5] Subsequently, a Club members' subcommittee was established. It was given representation on the "Main [Governing] Committee" made up of workers. Yet the notion of two separate committees was soon abandoned and a single Executive Committee--of workers and members--was created.

The Executive Committee was divided into a workers and members section. Representation on each was determined by all members through regularly held elections. Later, the Committee was composed almost entirely of Club members, for

> . . . gradually, it came about that nearly all of the workers were actual members, or girls who after many years of membership only came to the Club to assist in the management.[6]

A council, made up of elected representatives from each of the Club's classes, was also established. It was able to bring "special matters" to the Executive's attention and thus served as a link between the Executive and the membership body.

Lily Montagu became the Club's official Leader. As such, she assumed major responsibility for its activities and events. Since she could not always be present, a superintendent was hired to look after the girls' "happiness and welfare" in her absence. While most of the women whom she employed were kind and hard-working, she believed them to lack

sufficient sympathy and understanding. Subsequently, after
"frequent changes and several disasters," Lily Montagu and
her co-workers agreed to run the Club without a superintendent and rotated supervisory responsibilities among themselves. In addition, "Miss Lily" (as she was known within the
Club) prepared Club letters which listed classes and special
activities as well as "messages to girls, teachers and other
workers." These letters were returned to her with appropriate
comments and each received careful consideration.[7]

The education of Jewish working girls became one of the
Club's primary concerns. As membership increased, so did the
number of classes. By the turn of the century, there were
over one hundred members and classes were offered in drill,
singing, needlework, Bible, drama and English language
instruction. Within ten years members had reached several
hundred, and there were classes in physical training, domestic science, art (including metalwork, drawing and design),
music and drama, languages (French, German, Hebrew and English), arithmetic, economics, literature, dressmaking, model-
ing, first aid, millinery, commercial letters, nature study
and shorthand.[8] In planning the Club's curriculum, Lily Montagu looked to the girls themselves. Without abandoning
either her cultural or spiritual concerns, she recognized
that there was little advantage in offering courses in which
Club members had no interest. Thus, in expanding the curriculum, she waited until a certain subject was requested by the
members themselves. Gradually, the Club's educational program
came to include formal classes, hobby groups and recreational
facilities. Its stated goal was to provide intellectual
training, opportunities for alternative trades, preparation
for "satisfactory home keeping" and physical, emotional,
spiritual and creative growth. Lily Montagu also believed
that the program stimulated character development. For

example, she maintained, "quick physical movements stir the power of hopefulness," while

> creative work strengthens self-respect, especially for those who are part of the great machine in which all industrial processes are minutely self-divided.[9]

Lily Montagu made every effort to attract Jewish working girls to the Club. She obtained lists of girls about to leave school and attempted to contact them and, within the Club, insisted that a high quality of instruction be maintained. Most of the early members were tailoresses who worked in domestic workshops from eight in the morning until eight at night. Lily Montagu realized that, after a long day's work, the girls were tired and would only attend classes that were taught in an interesting and effective way. The achievements of the Club were recognized by the London Board of Education. Only a few years after the West Central had been established, the Board awarded it with a long-term grant, apparently making it the first Club in England to receive such assistance.[10] This, as well as the "Annual Displays" of members' work, social events and home visitations gave the Club greater visibility and enhanced Lily Montagu's reputation as well.

Most of the Club's members were religiously indifferent and, from the beginning, Lily Montagu realized that efforts to "interest the average member in institutional Judaism" would fail.[11] However, she firmly believed that a few *could* become interested if Judaism were presented in a new, more meaningful way. This "presentment"--which Lily Montagu identified as Liberal Judaism--minimized the importance of ceremonies and observances and placed greatest emphasis on faith and its relationship to everyday life. Through prayer, discussion and personal example, Lily Montagu attempted to awaken within "her" girls a spirit of worship and tried to

convince them that the God of Beauty, Truth and Love was
ready to enter their souls if only they would receive Him.

Lily Montagu maintained that faith could best be stimulated through prayer. She therefore created special services
which she hoped might appeal to Club members. She felt that
those who had turned away from the synagogue had done so because its services were long and boring. The girls had little
if any Hebrew knowledge and thus found the traditional liturgy unintelligible. The sermons were dry and did not speak to
them directly. Moreover, as women, their participation in the
synagogue was limited and appeared to be unimportant, and
many questioned whether it was necessary even to attend.

The Sabbath services instituted by Lily Montagu were
held in the afternoon.   This was because most of the Club
members worked until one o'clock. The services were relatively brief, in English, and "brightened by congregational singing."[12] Lily Montagu attempted to deliver sermons on subjects
which were of "vital" interest to the girls and only those
traditional prayers which she felt had "meaning for modern
Jews and Jewesses in the actual circumstances of their lives"
were retained.[13] In *My Club and I*, Lily Montagu admitted that
the services failed to attract the majority of Club members.
However, a few, she wrote, "responded with zeal and enthusiasm and moulded their lives accordingly,"[14] and by 1913 the
Sabbath services--as well as the High Holy Day services which
she prepared--gained formal recognition as the West Central
Section of the Jewish Religious Union.

In encouraging Club members to observe the Sabbath, Lily
Montagu presented them with a nonlegalistic interpretation of
sanctification. The Law, she stated, was not an end in itself
but rather a vehicle towards holiness. Thus, one desecrated
the Sabbath by going to a concert on Friday evening even if
no specific law was broken (i.e., even if one did not pay for
the tickets and walked instead of rode to the theater). She

stressed the beauty of Friday evening observances within the
home and urged "her" girls to discover God's word and try to
live by it. Those who did so, she maintained, could worship
God all day long in

> . . . whatever they were doing, and not only at
> Sabbath services. Moreover, they could hallow any
> day and every day through prayer and could use for
> worship any part of the recognised Sabbath which
> was at their disposal.[15]

In 1895, Lily Montagu wrote a small booklet entitled
Prayers for Jewish Working Girls. Dedicated to the members of
the West Central Club, it offered a variety of prayers, all
of which she wrote, to be said on different days, at different times, and at different life stages. Each prayer emphasized the significance of faith and the obligation of every
Jew to share that faith with others. Those written for particular days of the week also stressed moral virtues such as
courage, strength, loyalty, trust and righteousness and asked
for God's guidance in becoming a better human being. In addition to special Sabbath prayers and meditations, she included
a "Prayer for Those Who Are Unavoidably Prevented from Keeping the Sabbath." Intended for girls who had to work on Sat-
urdays, it asked God for forgiveness and stated that the worshipper would strive to improve her position so that she
could observe the Sabbath in the future.

Lily Montagu hoped that her booklet would awaken within
her girls a spirit of devotion and eventually lead them to
create prayers of their own. A number of prayers focused on
those aspects of life which were especially meaningful to
Club members and each attempted to show how those aspects
could be used to their best advantage. Prayers on entering
and completing one's apprenticeship as well as "A Prayer for
Girls Entering Domestic Service" stressed the importance of
labor as a means of being useful, attaining self-respect,

strengthening one's sense of duty and serving the Universal
God. One prayer, in celebrating the worshipper's youth, asked
God to "Help me to use my youth in such a way as to prepare
me for my life hereafter," while another, thanking God for
the worshipper's womanhood, added:

> Help me to develop all its powers, so that I may
> become gentle, truthful, brave, loving, and honour-
> able, and be able to influence all around me for
> good.[16]

To further impress upon her girls the power of worship,
Lily Montagu concluded each "Club evening" with a brief religious service. It included an extempore prayer by her and the
recitation of the *Shema* by all present. On Club holidays,
prayers would be said each morning and evening, and on the
Sabbath open air services were held. Thus, Lily Montagu made
prayer an important part of Club life and in so doing imbued
her Club with a distinctively religious character.

Lily Montagu also encouraged Club members to reflect
about religion. Recognizing that most only paid lip service
to Judaism's teachings, she led talks and discussions in
which even the "frankest questioning" was welcome. She gave
frequent addresses on various religious themes and on Club
holidays organized nightly "talks under the tree," again, on
the subject of religion. Moreover, through personal example,
Lily Montagu tried to show the connection between faith and
everyday conduct and appealed to co-workers to "try to induce
members to regard their religion as a potent influence in
their lives and in their search after righteousness."[17]

Through her Club work, Lily Montagu gained a good deal
of recognition within the Anglo-Jewish community and British
society as well. In 1910, she became Secretary of the Women's
Industrial Council and soon after helped found the National
Association of Girls' Clubs. As its first Honorary Secretary
and later as Chairman and President, Lily Montagu became a

well-known figure within British Club life and, within her
own Club, was seen not only as a social worker and educational pioneer but also as a religious leader.[18]

LILY MONTAGU'S EARLY PUBLISHED WORKS: 1895-1907

As early as 1895, at the age of twenty-one, Lily Montagu
began to publish articles and books of Jewish and general interest. These works provided her with public recognition and
further enhanced her reputation with the Anglo-Jewish community. In 1895, as we have noted, she wrote *Prayers for Jewish
Working Girls*. A year later, she wrote an article entitled
"The Condition of the Individual in a Socialist State" that
appeared in the *Westminster Review*. Defining socialism as

. . . a system, by which a perfect equalisation of
opportunity will be effected principally through
the State-ownership of land, and the State-control
of the production necessary to the maintenance of
human life, ...[19]

she argued that only within such a system could individuals
realize their intellectual, physical and moral potential.

Although in theory equal opportunity could exist within
the individualistic state, in reality, she claimed, only the
few succeed at the expense of the many. Those who are involved in a constant struggle for existence cannot simply choose
the work for which they feel best fitted, and even the ambi-
tions of the wealthy are "generally cramped and thwarted by
class or sex prejudices." Within a socialist state, however,
the condition of the individual would improve. The misery of
the proletariat and the "vicious luxury" of the rich would
disappear, and men and women would be encouraged to find a
useful and honorable means of employment. Unmarried women
would be "induced to work their utmost" in order to achieve a
sense of self-reliance and growth while, during the first

years of motherhood, married women "in every rank of life"
would be free to devote themselves to their families and
homes. Thus, through the creation of a socialist state, even
those "whose powers are at present wasted would . . . [be
free to] accomplish their share in the progress of humanity."[20] For this reason alone, she concluded, such a state
deserved consideration and support.

In 1901, Lily Montagu wrote an essay on Joseph Mazzini,
the Italian writer and patriot whose notion of associated
labor, as we have seen, had a profound influence upon her.
The essay was published in a monthly review called *Present
Day Papers* and attempted to show the significance of Mazzini's life and thought. In her article, Lily Montagu described
Mazzini as a man of faith, whose concepts of mission and duty
were rooted in his understanding of God as a power directing
the world towards perfection. Mazzini, she wrote, felt that
human beings had an obligation to assist in the moral advance
of humanity and believed that this could best be achieved
through communal effort. He insisted that individuals recognize their responsibilities towards their country, their families and themselves, and in a spirit of self-sacrifice and
truth, serve God by serving one another.

Like most of her essays, Lily Montagu's study of Mazzini
emphasized the importance of faith. In fact, the majority of
her published works (before and after 1907) focused on themes
that were specifically religious. In "The Spiritual Possibilities of Judaism Today," published in 1899 (an article that
we will discuss at greater length in Chapter Eight), she contended that "Judaism has been allowed by the timid and the
indifferent to lose much of its inspiring force"[21] and suggested ways in which it could be reanimated. In 1904, she
contributed a chapter to E. J. Urwick's *Studies of Boy Life
in Our Cities* that emphasized the importance of developing
the spiritual nature of the "Girl in the Background" and in

1907, in an article called "The Relation of Faith to Conduct
in Jewish Life," established a direct connection between belief in God and "active, practical well doing," i.e., bearing
testimony to God's reality through "devotion to truth" and
righteousness. [22]

In *Prayers, Psalms, and Hymns for Jewish Children*, co-
edited with Theodora Davis in 1901, Lily Montagu attempted to
show the ways in which Sabbath services could be adapted for
children. Based on the order of worship that she had created
for her own children's services at the New West End Synagogue, it combined elements of the traditional Sabbath service (e.g., the *Adom Olam*, part of the *Amidah*, the *Shema* and
the Benedictions, and the *Alenu*) with the recitation of the
Ten Commandments, a Bible discussion, a brief address, an extempore prayer by the leader, and English hymns and psalms to
be sung by the congregation. [23] Lily Montagu hoped that these
additions would give the service greater appeal and help
awaken within Jewish children a spirit of prayer. Their in-
clusion reflected her conviction that it was not the form of
Jewish worship--in and of itself--that was important, but
rather its ability to bring the worshipper closer to the
Divine. She thus believed that changes in the worship service
were justified and often necessary. As she later maintained:

> The ideal of congregational life can only be ap-
> proached when each individual member becomes con-
> scious of his religious life, or, in other words,
> of his "kinship with God." [24]

The publication of this work gave Lily Montagu's efforts
at the New West End Synagogue greater recognition. With its
publication, it became clear that her interests and talents
lay beyond social service. While there is no evidence to suggest that the publication of *Prayers, Psalms, and Hymns for
Jewish Children* led to an increase in attendance at the services which Lily Montagu led, it may well have reassured a

number of Orthodox Jews (several of whom later joined the
Jewish Religious Union) that Lily Montagu's commitment lay
not only to reform but also to Jewish tradition.

In *Thoughts on Judaism*, published in 1904, Lily Montagu
presented, more fully than she had before, her own understanding of Judaism and the significance of religious faith.
Theologically, it owed a great deal to the writings and personal influence of Claude Montefiore. We have already noted
the influence of Montefiore's work upon Lily Montagu, an influence that began in the early 1890s (when she was in her
late teens) and lasted throughout her lifetime. Yet equally
important was their personal relationship, one that had its
beginning at a social gathering held by Lily Montagu's aunt
and uncle, Mr. and Mrs. Nathaniel Cohen. Montefiore, having
heard of the newly established West Central Club, apparently
was as interested in Lily Montagu as she was in him and, according to her, they easily engaged in conversation. She
later recalled that from this first meeting, Montefiore offered her guidance and encouragement, made her feel that her
work had real value, and suggested ways in which this work
could be expanded.

In *Thoughts on Judaism*, Lily Montagu reiterated many of
Montefiore's religious teachings. She shared his belief in
the Unity of God, the Brotherhood of humanity, the power of
worship, the connection between faith and moral conduct, and
the universal mission of the Jewish people. Yet she revealed
a greater appreciation than Montefiore for traditional ceremonies and observances as "aids to holiness," "reminders of
God's goodness," "the most helpful of educational instruments," and the "best possible links for binding" Jews together.[25] While Montefiore felt that the Liberal Jew's adherence to traditional observance was simply a matter of "individual sentimentalities and idiosyncrasies,"[26] Montagu advo-
cated retention of all those which could be given ethical

meaning. Every section of the Jewish community, she stated, should "assuredly make use of all the aids to righteousness" which are found in the Bible, for as reminders of God's presence, they stimulate prayer, aspiration and the sanctification of life. [27]

Thoughts on Judaism was not intended to be a major theological work and Lily Montagu herself acknowledged its indebtedness to Montefiore's essay "Liberal Judaism," published a year before. Instead, it was to be a personal account of her own "conception of Judaism as a living religion." She therefore omitted most of Montefiore's critical and historical references and made no claims to objectivity. "The beauty of Judaism," Montagu wrote, "is useless unless we can consciously assimilate it in our lives." Others can teach us *about* God, but experience alone convinces us of His existence. With this as the book's underlying theme, Lily Montagu described her personal struggle. In so doing, she hoped to encourage her readers to begin a struggle of their own. [28]

In 1901 and 1902, Lily Montagu published two novels: *Naomi's Exodus* and *Broken Stalks*. They received generally good reviews (and the popularity of *Naomi's Exodus* led to a second edition) but both were weak on plot and characterization and primarily served as expressions of Lily Montagu's religious development and thought. Her first novel traced the spiritual growth of a young Jewish girl named Naomi. Raised by her "rigidly orthodox" aunt, Mrs. Saul, Naomi lived in accordance with rabbinic laws and customs. Although she failed to understand their religious significance and had little sense of God's presence, Naomi unquestioningly accepted them as essential. Shortly before her twentieth birthday, Naomi met an old woman--a Christian--named Mrs. Finch, who told the young girl of her belief in the Divine and her effort to

share God's teachings with others. Following their conversation, Naomi began to think about God and the meaning of
religion.

She contrasted her aunt's identification of faith and
external observance with the love of God and humanity displayed by Mrs. Finch. While her aunt "complacently" maintained that observance made one righteous, Mrs. Finch, whose life
had been one of self-sacrifice and service, still doubted
that she was "good." This comparison inexplicably disturbed
Naomi and she became increasingly unhappy. She felt distant
from her aunt and her fiance, Jacob, and looked to Mrs. Finch
for guidance and support. Under the influence of Mrs. Finch,
Naomi became aware of her own "spiritual yearnings" and for
the first time turned towards God in prayer. Mrs. Saul,
learning of her niece's new friendship, accused her of having
converted to Christianity. This accusation pained and angered
Naomi but made her realize that to resolve her religious
struggle she would have to leave home.

Naomi became a servant at a club for working class girls
and was befriended by Miss Miles, the Club's Leader. She
helped Naomi discover the cause of her unhappiness and gave
her assurance that eventually she would find contentment and
peace. With the encouragement of Miss Miles and Clement Marks
(a Liberal Jewish social worker with whom she falls in love),
Naomi gradually recognized that religious laws were worthless
unless they served as vehicles towards holiness. She came to
understand that one did not become pious or good through observance alone, but rather through serving others. Although
later rejected by Clement, Naomi was grateful for the feelings of love which he had awakened and for the new understanding of Judaism which he had revealed. A year after her
spiritual and physical exodus had begun, she returned to her
aunt. No longer a child, but a "wise and gentle woman," Naomi
promised that she would never leave her.[29]

Broken Stalks, published in 1902, lacked the simplicity of Lily Montagu's earlier novel. Although, like *Naomi's Exodus*, it described the spiritual journey of a young English girl, the introduction of numerous minor characters and subplots detracted from its central theme. Joan Carey, the book's heroine, lived with her parents at the home of Eric Frankland, a family friend. Frankland had to leave England, and asked the Careys to manage his estate and care for his daughter, Millicent, in his absence. Years later, however, Frankland suddenly reappeared—dishevelled and drunk. Mr. Carey, fearing that Millie's fiance, Harold, would not marry her if he knew that Eric Frankland was an alcoholic, decided to keep the stranger's identity a secret. But his wife, jealous of Millicent's beauty, revealed the truth, and Millie, aware of Harold's vow not to marry the daughter of an alcoholic, ended their engagement.

Frankland's reappearance troubled Joan. She feared that Millicent's future happiness was endangered yet could think of no way to help her. Looking for guidance, she went to visit Nana, an old woman who lived nearby. Arriving there, she saw Molly, Nana's grand-niece, attempting to put a rootless geranium back into the ground. Joan explained to the little girl that without its root the stalk could not grow. Molly replied that although she knew that, perhaps God would *make* the plant grow, if only the stalk were straight. Joan laughed at her answer, but Molly, whose faith was unshaken, continued to play with the stalk's shrivelled pieces.

She then went to Nana and asked the old woman for advice. Nana responded that if Millie truly loved Harold, God would make sure that all worked out for the best. Still not certain of what to do, however, Joan turned to her father. Like Molly and Nana, Mr. Carey answered with an affirmation of faith. While he lacked Nana's confidence and Molly's belief in miracles, he assured Joan that "God in His Wisdom and

Love" would help her make the right decision. It was not the
outcome of that decision that mattered most, he said, but
rather the joy in experiencing God's presence. The inner
peace which Nana, Molly and her father seemed to have discovered deeply impressed Joan, and slowly she too became aware
of God's guiding power. Consequently, she attached a new significance to Frankland's return. Urging Millicent to take
care of him, she added that perhaps God "means you to mend
your father's broken life with your love." Harold eventually
recognized that, without Millie, his life was also "broken,"
and once more asked her to marry him. Supported by Joan, who
maintained that God would ensure her future happiness, Millie
accepted his proposal.

Joan's decision to become a painter and, later, the wife
of Richard Ellis, a social worker and temperance leader, similarly were influenced by faith, human sympathy and love.
Through these emotions, she learned to "stand straight" and
look to God for direction. God then took the pieces of Joan's
life, cemented them together, and made her whole. Thus, like
the geranium of Molly's imagination, Joan was no longer
"broken" and, having been healed, could once again grow and
flourish.

Through the literary sentimentalism of both *Naomi's Exodus* and *Broken Stalks*, Montagu sought to impress upon her
readers the beauty and inspirational force of true religious
faith. She presented her characters sympathetically and her
heroines as "living sermons" whose actions revealed their understanding of God. Like many other Victorian middle and upper middle class women who expressed themselves through fiction, Lily Montagu's primary concern lay with the books'
deeper meanings. Using her characters as spokespersons for
her own liberal religious ideas, she thus did little to dis-
guise the didactic nature of her novels.

Naomi's Exodus and *Broken Stalks* were essentially "introspective autobiographies"[30] which traced Lily Montagu's own spiritual awakening and growth. The resemblance between Montagu and her two fictional heroines is apparent. Like Naomi, Lily Montagu was raised in a strictly Orthodox home. Through the influence of others, she too began to suspect that the observance of externally-imposed laws did not automatically make one righteous and eventually concluded, as did Naomi, that "Judaism" and "real religion" were not necessarily identical.

Joan, the heroine of *Broken Stalks*, experienced a similar religious transformation. At first, she rarely thought about religion and lacked an awareness of God's living presence. Gradually, however, she too came to feel God's regenerative power and, like Naomi and Lily Montagu, attempted to share this newly-found faith with others. Significantly, the content of her faith was universal. Although described as Christian, Joan maintained--as did Lily Montagu and Naomi-- that real religion was based on the Oneness of God and the Brotherhood of humanity.

In creating the characters for her novels, Lily Montagu often used familiar Victorian literary types. Molly, for example, like Harriet Beecher Stowe's Little Eva, personified "the sanctity of the childish heart";[31] Mrs. Finch and Nana, the wise and saintly woman; and Harold and Eric Frankland, the materialistic male brought closer to God by the spiritually superior female. Some of the characters, however, were based upon family members and friends. For example, the rigidly Orthodox Mrs. Saul clearly was patterned after the equally rigid Samuel Montagu (one might even note the similarity of their names) while Richard Ellis and Clement Marks, both highly intellectual, wealthy men who involved themselves in social service, bore a striking resemblance to Claude Montefiore (in fact, Clement Marks and Claude Montefiore even

shared the same initials!). Yet even these characters were
superficially portrayed and were significant primarily because of the personality types which they represented. Thus,
like many other sentimentalized domestic novels of the day,
Naomi's Exodus and *Broken Stalks* were important, not as major
literary achievements, but rather as sermons set in the
framework of fiction. Consequently, Lily Montagu, like other
Victorian literary women, "inevitably confused theology with
religiosity, religiosity with literature and literature with
self-justification."[32]

Unlike most of these women, however, Lily Montagu expressed herself through a number of literary media. In addition to her novels, she wrote, as we have noted, theological
tracts, prayer manuals, biographical and political essays,
and papers like "The Relation of Faith to Conduct," which
were little more than printed sermons. In so doing, Lily Montagu attempted to reach as wide an audience as possible.
Thus, for example, "The Spiritual Possibilities of Judaism
Today" appeared in a Jewish periodical, while "The Condition
of the Individual in a Socialist State" was published in the
Westminster Review and her essay on Mazzini in *Present Day
Papers*, "a monthly review for the discussion of modern
thought and its application to Christian faith and practice."[33] Similarly, *Naomi's Exodus* and *Broken Stalks* were
aimed at a female, Jewish and non-Jewish audience, while
Thoughts on Judaism was written for Jewish women and men.

A scrapbook of press notices assembled by Marian Montagu
attests to the favorable reviews which these early writings
(especially *Naomi's Exodus, Broken Stalks* and *Thoughts on
Judaism*) received.[34] Though it is uncertain how widely read
they became, their appearance alone at least provided Lily
Montagu with greater visibility both within and outside of
the Jewish community. Moreover, they helped her move beyond
the British Club movement, gradually establishing herself not

only as a social worker but also as a religious leader. Thus, for example, *Prayers, Psalms and Hymns* highlighted her activities as a leader of children's services, *Thoughts on Judaism* revealed her interest in theology, and "The Spiritual Possibilities of Judaism Today" showed her desire to form an association that would help revitalize Anglo-Jewry's religious life. In addition, it may well be that in writing about religion (and in "reliving" her spiritual journey through her heroines, Naomi and Joan), Lily Montagu began to realize how important "real religion" was to her and how much she wanted, if not needed, to share this understanding with others.

Thus, in attempting to discover why Lily Montagu was able to assume a role of religious leadership within the Anglo-Jewish community, one needs to take into account a variety of factors. Certainly, Lily Montagu's membership within the Cousinhood, the number of men and women to whom she could turn for support, as well as Anglo-Jewry's willingness to accept women within communal roles facilitated her entrance into Jewish public life. Equally important, however, was the recognition that Lily Montagu had already gained, through her work at the West Central Club, her worship services at the New West End Synagogue, and her own literary endeavors. All of these gave Lily Montagu an identity beyond that of Samuel and Ellen Montagu's daughter. By the time she began contemplating the formation of the Jewish Religious Union, her interest in Judaism as well as her energy, enthusiasm, seriousness and sense of dedication was known and admired, even among her critics. Consequently, many individuals--including Claude Montefiore--found it difficult, if not impossible, to refuse her requests. Perhaps this helps to explain why, in 1902, the then twenty-eight-year old Lily Montagu was able to gather sufficient support to establish the J.R.U., an organization whose creation marked the beginnings of the Liberal Jewish movement in England.

VII. The Spiritual Awakening of Lily Montagu

In establishing the Jewish Religious Union, Lily Montagu revealed her own understanding of society and the concept of human obligation. It was not enough, she believed, to possess religious faith; one needed to share that faith with others. In part, her desire to form the J.R.U. reflected this concern for those around her, indicative of a growing sense of liberalism within the Anglo-Jewish community. Yet her determination to revitalize Anglo-Jewry's religious life was also rooted in the conviction that God had called her. She maintained that it was her duty, not just as an individual but as a member of the Jewish "brotherhood," to testify to God's reality and to bring other men and women to Him.

By the end of the nineteenth century, increasing numbers of wealthy men and women within the Jewish community, like their non-Jewish counterparts, began to identify their own self-interest with that of others. Measuring progress by the degree to which all citizens prospered, they began to develop a greater sense of social responsibility and concern for humanity as a whole. Freedom, it was argued, meant more than lack of restraint. It also meant the opportunity to develop oneself fully. Thus, many individuals began to lend their assistance, not merely by giving charity but by helping others recognize and fulfill their potential.[1]

Lily Montagu's activities reflected this new liberal spirit. As we have seen, she founded the West Central Club in order to enrich the lives of Jewish working class girls, hoping that through classes, religious services, concerts, outings and other special events, she might encourage their

educational, spiritual and social development. Similarly, in
her early essays, she focused upon educational, religious and
social conditions, suggesting ways in which the quality of
human life could be improved. Through each of these writings,
Lily Montagu sought to spark change. In so doing, she hoped
to be of use to her fellow human beings.

The Jewish Religious Union, established to strengthen
the religious life of the Anglo-Jewish community, best revealed Lily Montagu's sense of communal responsibility. She
saw it as the first major challenge to the Jewish community's
earlier "policy" of laissez-faire.[2] Believing that spiritual
growth was an important aspect of self development, she
sought to help other Jews acknowledge the potentiality of
their spiritual inheritance. To do so, she attempted to adapt
Judaism to the progressive needs and demands of the modern
age. The children's services which she led at the New West
End Synagogue represented one such effort. The J.R.U., as she
envisioned it, would continue and expand upon this attempt.

SPIRITUAL AWARENESS AND GROWTH

While Lily Montagu's sense of communal responsibility
(given greater direction by Mazzini's notion of associated
labor) led her to think of ways in which the Anglo-Jewish
community might be rescued from its growing state of religious indifference, her decision to form the J.R.U. was rooted in something more than either communal responsibility or
the influence of Joseph Mazzini. Though she never discussed
her reasons for founding the J.R.U. at length, scattered references reveal that behind her decision lay the conviction
that she had received a call from God. Her *desire*, then, to
establish an association of religiously committed Jews may
have stemmed from her perception of the Anglo-Jewish
community as secularized and religiously apathetic, but her

decision to form the Union was based upon the belief that God had called upon her to do so.

To Lily Montagu, the most important aspect of religious life was the individual's experiencing of the Divine. Like William James, she viewed such "apprehension of the Unseen Reality"[3] as *synonymous* with the word religion. Yet although she had always identified herself as Jewish, Lily Montagu's earliest identification had not been rooted in faith, but, as we have seen, in a sense of tradition, family loyalty and obedience to the "dictate" of her father. Judaism, she later wrote in her autobiography, had been only an external aspect of her life. She had observed the rabbinic commandments without understanding their spiritual significance and regularly attended synagogue without engaging in prayer. Instead, she "sat through the services, quite unimpressed, but pleased with the familiarity of everything around her."[4]

Gradually, however, she found her sense of Jewishness to be inadequate. She questioned the "utility" of observances which were performed either for the "pleasure of having carried them out in good company" or for the satisfaction of having "done what was expected" of her.[5] Lily Montagu wanted Judaism to be more than one among many aspects of life. Instead, she wanted it to provide her with a framework in which all of life could be experienced. Yet to do so, she realized, Judaism would have to be imbued with new meaning. It would have to become a *religion*, i.e., that which stimulated personal religious faith, rather than that which was external to her spiritual needs and desires. While before the age of fifteen Lily Montagu rarely thought about the connection between "Judaism" and "religion," she later became convinced that unless such a connection were established, Judaism would be incapable of commanding either self-sacrifice or genuine commitment. Subsequently, she began to search for

ways of redefining Judaism so as to awaken within her a
spirit of devotion and faith.

In order to do so, Lily Montagu attempted to differentiate between Judaism's essential and inessential elements.
Those ceremonies and observances which did not stimulate a
sense of inner devotion were to be discarded while those
which did were to be retained. Moreover, she believed, the
significance of religious observances could be tested on the
basis of their ethical value. Those which were capable of
deepening one's moral nature were to be recognized as most
important, while those lacking any "moral lesson applicable
to modern life" necessarily had to be rejected. Though she
admitted that past devotion to Jewish ceremonies and observances served to make them "more lovable in our eyes, . . .
the beauty of Judaism is useless, unless we can consciously
assimilate it in our lives." Judaism, she insisted, must become a personal religion, whose vital principles are to be
grasped through the "voice of God within man" rather than
through externally imposed commandments. Thus, to Lily Montagu, Judaism was not the faith of either a people or a nation,
but simply the faith of those individuals who, inspired by
Judaism's teachings, sought to discover the presence and influence of God.[6]

Lily Montagu arrived at this redefinition after a con-
siderable period of reflection. At first, as she herself admitted, she found Judaism incapable of cultivating inner,
spiritual growth. Nevertheless, she remained "quite content
to be interested in it as something outside" of herself.[7] At
the age of fifteen, however, once her formal education came
to a close and she began to determine her own course of
study, she read a number of books which, as we have seen,
both shocked and depressed her. Those (like Buckle's *History
of Civilisation* and Mrs. Ward's *Robert Elsmere*, referred to
in chapter three) that depicted a world in which spirituality

was viewed with disdain greatly upset her and subsequently, as she later wrote, she "[began] to lose . . . her sense of security" and her "normal belief that life was full of glorious possibility."[8]

As a result of both "mental strain" and "spiritual anxiety,"[9] Lily Montagu began to suffer from what was, at best, a serious nervous condition. Although the medical attention which she received helped precipitate her recovery, a number of other factors were also responsible. First, in order to verbalize her feelings of self-doubt and confusion, she began to write stories. Undoubtedly, these early attempts either inspired or became the basis for her later novels, *Naomi's Exodus* and *Broken Stalks*, both of which, as we noted in chapter six, were spiritual autobiographies written in novel form. Second, with the help of Simeon Singer, Montagu became increasingly aware of God's presence. Singer, it seems, gave her a prayer to recite in which she asked God to teach her to pray and to make her "grateful for the opportunities . . . to serve . . . [Him] with . . . [her] whole heart."[10] Consequently, as she later wrote, she began to turn to social service as a means of enabling God's justice and righteousness to flourish. This new orientation to the world gave Montagu a much-needed sense of purpose and direction. As her nephew Eric Conrad later suggested, "at an age when for others religion is no more than a school discipline," Lily Montagu discovered that religion "was the moving factor in her life."[11]

Gradually, through the influence of Claude Montefiore, Montagu began to recognize that it was possible to harmonize "Jewish" with "religious" faith. It was Montefiore, as we saw in chapter four, who gave her both the means and the confidence to redefine Judaism so as to allow for personal expression and growth. With his encouragement and guidance, she began to examine traditional ceremonies and observances, retaining only those which she felt might lead to an awareness

of the Divine, and began to form new images of God until she
no longer saw him as a stern lawgiver, but rather as the
source of all goodness, love and truth. While not denying the
validity of her father's faith, Lily Montagu realized that
she could not worship with her father's heart. Neither, she
believed, could she define Judaism as he had defined it.

Several years later, in her *Thoughts on Judaism*, Lily
Montagu acknowledged the "painful anxiety" which accompanied
this process of redefinition. She recognized that

> . . . when we do refuse to stifle our conscientious
> questionings, and to profess a creed to which we
> are really indifferent, the change must cause much
> pain and sorrow to ourselves . . . . Perhaps we al-
> so cause pain to those we love, and would give our
> lives to please.[12]

Nevertheless, she wrote, "the search for truth is God's work"
and therefore "must be accomplished in the teeth of every
conflicting consideration," for

> . . . it is only when we are embarked on this
> search, when we have rejected that which appears
> false to our intellectual conceptions, and have re-
> fused to conform outwardly, when our spirit is un-
> moved, it is only then, that we can feel at one
> with our God.[13]

HER AWAKENING AS REFLECTIVE OF WOMEN'S SPIRITUAL QUEST

On the surface at least Lily Montagu seemed to have undergone a kind of religious conversion. Before the age of
fifteen, she rarely thought about religion. Later, it became
the moving force of her life. Similarly, while at first she
identified Judaism simply as the faith of her ancestors, she
later felt it to be her own faith as well. Before her illness, Lily Montagu apparently was nervous and shy. Later,

after her recovery, she felt new strength, vigor and self-confidence.[14] As she began to recognize her spiritual needs and emotions, she became increasingly aware of God's continual and loving presence. Surrendering herself to the Divine, she perceived new truths and new solutions. She felt a sense of inner peace and contentment and, in a spirit of what William James labelled a "healthy minded optimism,"[15] maintained that ultimately God's goodness would prevail.

Religious conversion, as described by James in his *Varieties of Religious Experience*, involves a movement from one state of being to another. This experience, he writes, is a kind of rebirth, for the individual begins to view both him/herself and the world in a very different way. Thus, the materialist who discovers God begins to see the profane as sacred, and the natural as supernaturally directed. God becomes his/her ultimate source of authority and his/her "true end" becomes the attainment of a harmonious relationship or union with the Divine.[16]

Although Lily Montagu's "thinking about religion" radically and irrevocably changed her life, she herself denied having undergone an experience of conversion. As she maintained in her (undated) sermon "The Peace of God," she became aware of God gradually, through a great deal of sustained effort. She contrasted this process with the kind of sudden "emotional experience known as conversion" through which, for example, the individual "is suddenly turned from evil to good by the realisation of the hatefulness of sin."[17] Lily Montagu's orientation towards the world may have altered, but she remained a woman, a British subject, and a Jew. Lily Montagu did not become a different person. Rather, over a period of years she became increasingly aware of her spiritual needs and potential.

Carol Christ has described this kind of reorientation as an "awakening." While it involves "a transition in

consciousness and a new perception of reality," it does not
involve a change of being. An awakening, Christ writes, is
simply a "coming to self," a "grounding of selfhood in the
powers of being." Christ identifies these "powers" with that
which is "really real." More traditionally, one might identify these powers with God. An awakening, she writes, is a process of enlightenment through which the individual begins to
recognize that "the ability to see or to know is within the
self." Within the context of women's spiritual quest, it is a
"new affirmation of selfhood, power, and responsibility." Unlike conversion, which is a process of self-negation, it is a
process of self-assertion, often leading to greater self-
confidence and awareness. It is that through which women
learn to value their own thoughts and feelings and is "followed by a *new naming* of self and reality" and articulates
this new orientation to both one's self and the world.[18]

Women's awakening, Christ writes, is often preceded by
an experience of nothingness or emptiness. While she acknowledges that men are also vulnerable to "feelings of inferiori-
ty and self-hatred," women's experiences of nothingness, she
maintains, "are more far-reaching." Beginning at birth and
continuing "throughout their lives," women

> . . . learn to doubt the value of their thoughts,
> their feelings and their creativity. They concede
> that the   things women do are not valuable . . . .
> And they believe that men's work, whether it is
> fixing cars, working on a factory line, building a
> house, or running a business, is more important
> than what women do.[19]

Yet because of these feelings, Christ continues, women may be
more open to mystical experiences than are men. While it may
be difficult for men to reject "conventional power and ego
gratification" for the sake of opening themselves to the
powers of being,

. . . women need only to strip away the ideology of
patriarchy that tells them they are fulfilled as
wives and mothers in order to come face to face
with the nothingness they know as lack of self,
lack of power, and lack of value for women in a
male-centered world. To open their eyes to the emptiness of their lives requires great courage . . .
but it may be easier for women since they have less
to lose.[20]

Christ's analysis of women's spiritual quest helps make
Lily Montagu's own process of awakening more intelligible.
Lily Montagu was raised within an Orthodox Jewish home. Up
until she was fifteen, she never thought to question the Divine origin of Judaism's 613 *mitzvot*, even though, as she
herself admitted, they failed to stimulate a sense of devotion within her. While her brothers received a "complete Jewish education,"[21] she and her sisters had to remain content
with "Bible and religion lessons" given by private tutors.[22]
Moreover, they learned only a minimal amount of Hebrew since,
with their religious role largely confined to the home, their
parents decided that a more solid Hebrew background would be
of "no use" to them.[23] At the New West End Synagogue, Lily
Montagu had to sit upstairs in the women's gallery, unable to
take full part in the worship service. She subsequently felt
that women had no real place within the synagogue and believed that her position within the Jewish community was inferior
to that of her brothers.[24]

Later, however, as she began to think about religion,
she came to realize that, despite their superior education
and their "feelings of contemptuous condescension,"[25] her
brothers had no greater sense of Judaism *as a religious faith*
than she had. What's more, they showed little interest in
making it one. In her autobiography, Lily Montagu describes
annual Passover seders during which her father solemnly read

through the Haggadah while many of the family joked, laughed
and sang "without even the slightest reverence." After one
such seder, she ran up to her eldest brother, Louis, and confided that she was ashamed at the behavior of many of those
present.

> How dare they think they are praying? If that is
> religion, I hate it and would rather take the reli-
> gion of _____ (mentioning a rigid Christian
> of my acquaintance).

Louis responded that it was she who didn't understand. It was
their bank holiday and therefore they *should* "be jolly." "But
why pretend to pray?" she asked him. As Louis laughed at her
question, her cheeks became hot and red and, for the first
time, Lily Montagu "began to wonder about the funny religion
which permitted such crass irreverence."[26]

Similarly, on one Yom Kippur, she observed people walking in and out of the synagogue, lounging in their seats,
seemingly unaffected by the prayers. At the end of the day,
she saw the "pious" men of the community throwing down their
prayer shawls and rushing home to break the fast. How, she
wondered, could piety "be *finished* so suddenly? . . . Why
didn't it get inside you and change you a little?"[27]

Both of these incidents apparently occurred before Lily
Montagu reached the age of fifteen. Thus, it seems, even before she consciously began to think about religion, she began
to realize that outward observance did not necessarily make
one religious. Later, when she read the works of Matthew Arnold, Robert Browning, Thomas Carlyle, Joseph Mazzini, and
others, she found expressed that which she had been afraid to
articulate. Each seemed to understand that religious faith
involved a stirring of the soul, an inner longing for the
Divine. Religion, they maintained, was not a matter of the
head, but of the heart. She found similar teachings in the
writings of the Hebrew prophets. God, she discovered, did *not*

require that his people be "observant." Rather, He required
that they be just, merciful and loving, and continually aware
of His presence.

Gradually, Lily Montagu began to recognize her spiritual
needs and desires. She longed to become closer to God, yet
found herself unable to do so. How could she pray in a language that she barely understood? How could she feel part of
a worshipping congregation which did not count her as a member? How could she continue to be observant when observance
meant so little to her? In short, how could she be both Orthodox and religious? Perhaps, at least in part, her nervous
condition was caused by an inability to answer these questions. Her father, she knew, believed that one could only be
a good Jew if one were observant. Yet, much as she loved and
respected him, she had begun to suspect that he was wrong. A
good Jew, she felt, was a good individual, whose religious
faith directly affected the conduct of his or her life. But
could she ever convince her father that this view was as valid as his own?

While she feared that Samuel Montagu would never understand her rejecting Orthodoxy, gradually she became convinced
that such a rejection was inevitable. As she began to share
her thoughts with others (although, significantly, not with
her father), she came to realize that for her Orthodoxy could
never be a "living religion." The observances which regulated
her life were not spiritual vehicles but rather externally
imposed commandments which had to be obeyed. Moreover, the
religious role to which she had been assigned seemed limiting
and inferior. Although she had been "cherished and protect-
ed,"[28] she had been given little opportunity to develop her
spiritual nature.

In voicing these feelings, Lily Montagu began to acknowledge the emptiness which she had long felt. Yet through
this acknowledgement she became increasingly aware of her own

"spiritual yearnings."[29] She felt an inner creative energy
which seemed to lead her towards God, and slowly began to
sense that the Divine existed both within the world and within every human being. With the help of Simeon Singer and the
prayer which he had taught her, she began to experience God's
presence. With new-found strength and courage, she maintained
that God had revealed Himself to her. God, she believed, had
called her to serve Him, not through ceremonies and observances but rather through serving others. This "mystical insight"[30] became the basis for Lily Montagu's reformulation of
that which she identified as Judaism's vital principles. It
also became the basis for her later redefinition of Jewish
self-identity. To be a Jew, she asserted, is to be a witness
to the reality of God, bearing testimony not only through
words but also through actions. While the verbal testimony of
all Jews may be the same, the actions which are performed
necessarily differ. Ultimately, she believed, they are to be
rooted in one's experience of the Divine. Although, to a
large extent, one's actions depend upon ability, opportunity
and desire, God, she insisted, calls each of us to serve Him
in a particular and uniquely different way.

One one level, Lily Montagu felt that she had been called by an external power of Being. God, she believed, was the
creator and ruler of the universe, the source of all justice,
truth and beauty. He was omnipotent and omnipresent and His
nature eternally "one." Yet, on another level, she felt that
God existed within her as a kind of creative energy through
which her spiritual nature had been awakened. He had also,
she realized, helped her to "care for the right things"[31] for
He had given her absolute standards by which her own human
conceptions could be measured. In so doing, she maintained,
He had revealed her essential kinship with the Divine and
thus enabled her to strive towards perfection.

Through this revelation, Lily Montagu gained a new sense of dignity and self-worth. She believed that it was possible to commune with both God the indwelling spirit of holiness and God the "Universal Father."[32] Gradually, she became convinced that both had called her. "My own experience of a living God," she later wrote,

> . . . impels me to the work of redemption. . . .
> We have to save the good, and overcome the evil; we
> have to combat, rather than to endure evil condi-
> tions, which impede the progress of human life.[33]

Jews, she insisted, are *bidden* to try to imitate God, not just through words but through social service. To be holy, she stated, is to work with and for God so as to ensure the triumph of His righteousness. Thus, she concluded, "I am called upon to labour . . . [for] the road to God's sanctuary is paved with deeds of loving kindness."[34]

FROM RELIGIOUS CALL TO THE FOUNDING OF THE J.R.U.

The establishment of the West Central Jewish Girls Club reflected this call to service. She felt compelled to share her education, faith and friendship with those who were less fortunate than she. "Our God," she maintained,

> . . . demands of us the giving of all we can spare
> of spirit and strength and time and material pos-
> sessions to the needs of the general community.[35]

"The more we have," she added, "the greater our self questioning--the more severe our responsibility."[36] Thus, despite her inexperience and lack of formal training, Lily Montagu formed a club which gave some working class Jewish girls an opportunity to develop themselves socially, intellectually and spiritually. Six years later, she worked to form an association aimed at revitalizing the religious life of the Anglo-Jewish community as a whole.

In "The Spiritual Possibilities of Judaism Today," Montagu asserted that the "call" to revivify Judaism by a "strongly organized religious movement" was unmistakeable and clear. This belief, she later wrote, "forced itself" upon her. She felt "driven" to write an essay through which these concerns might be expressed and eventually, with the support of those who similarly recognized the "working of the Spirit of Religion," sought to establish the Jewish Religious Union.[37]

Lily Montagu compared her own "call to service"[38] with those of the Hebrew prophets. She too felt called upon to combat "moral weakness and deceit," to warn against the miseries of sin and the "sadness of isolation" from God.[39] She, like them, cried out against the materialism of the age and the religious skepticism and indifference of those around her. Like the prophets, she felt compelled to spread God's moral teachings and to stress the importance of holiness, righteousness and truth. She too believed that God had called her to witness to His reality and to bring others closer to Him. Lily Montagu greatly admired the "unselfishness and uprightness" of the prophets and tried to emulate them both in thought and action. She also attempted to trust in God and to follow Him with courage and singleminded devotion. While she recognized that God demanded much self-sacrifice and effort, she insisted that "the pain of this sacrifice disappears" when one acknowledges "the privilege of service."[40] Thus, like the Hebrew prophets, she tried to face difficulties and disappointments with dignity and patience and, like them too, attempted to "act faithfully according to . . . [her] belief in God."[41]

She especially identified with Isaiah and his understanding of religion. She too felt that observances had no intrinsic value and therefore, like him, exhorted those around her to "do good, seek justice and correct oppression"

(Isaiah 1:17). Like Isaiah, Lily Montagu believed that she had an obligation to help others. "No man," she said, "can separate himself and stand detached, alone," for fulfillment can only be attained within a "social setting." Like Isaiah, Lily Montagu recognized her limitations and weaknesses. She too felt unworthy, yet eagerly and enthusiastically responded to God's call. We may not be "spiritual giants as was Isaiah," she asserted, but we can nevertheless "work for God in smaller ways."[42]

Lily Montagu frequently cited Isaiah 55 as her favorite chapter in the Bible. In 1941, in a letter to members of the West Central Club, she described the chapter in detail. It begins, she wrote, with the call of God, as issued through the prophet. Isaiah urges his people to approach God and hear Him and says that those who do so will become members of the everlasting covenant which God has promised to make. Isaiah, she continued, also establishes Israel's importance as witnesses to the reality of God. He tells his listeners that this revelation eventually will earn them the respect of other nations and will enable those who "live up to their faith" to attain righteousness and inner peace. Isaiah assures his people, she added, that God is merciful and ready to forgive those who repent of their wickedness. He is near us and therefore can hear our prayers. Yet finally, she stated, Isaiah maintains that God is ineffable. Though experience may convince us of His existence, neither His thoughts nor His actions can be comprehended.

While Lily Montagu's description closely followed the Biblical text, she clearly emphasized those elements which reflected her own religious thought. These included God's call to Israel, His nearness to humanity and the efficacy of prayer. Isaiah 55, she wrote, contains promise, bidding us to overcome doubt and fear. It reveals our "great purpose" as witnesses of God and calls us to a life of service.[43]

SENSE OF MISSION

Although Lily Montagu felt that she had received a personal call, she connected this revelation to her understanding of Jewish self-identity. God, she stated, had called her
to testify to His reality because it was her obligation, *as a
Jew*, to do so. She believed that the "definite calls to sacrifice"[44] which she had received were different from, though
not more important than, those received by non-Jewish men and
women. Each religion, she asserted, exists for a specific
purpose. Each has its own contribution to make to the spiritual treasury of the world.   Thus, in seeking to establish
the Jewish Religious Union, Lily Montagu attempted to act according to Judaism's "own method of service," its "own history," and its "own Divinely appointed purposes."[45] It is the
mission of all Jews, she wrote, to

> . . . stand as witnesses to the truth of the exist-
> ence of God, to the truth which we have inherited
> from our ancestors and which has been handed down
> from generation to generation.[46]

Much of this truth, she maintained, could be found within the Hebrew Bible. It affirms the reality of God as Creator
and Ruler of the universe and tells us to trust Him and acknowledge His saving power. It enjoins us to pursue righteousness and social justice and to dedicate ourselves to
God's service. Teaching us to enjoy life, it stresses the importance of work and the "Sabbath principle" of rest.[47] It
presents the concepts of atonement and sanctification and ex-
alts both love and beauty. These precepts, she stated, are
part of Judaism's spiritual contribution to the world. Yet,
to be understood fully, they must be supported by the testimony of a living faith.

In seeking God, Lily Montagu sought to apprehend for
herself that which He had revealed to her ancestors. While
"we do not claim," she insisted,

> . . . that our testimony alone is needed . . . we
> do claim that we have our own message to deliver in
> our own way, the Jewish way, and that this should
> be an essential contribution to the progress of
> humanity.[48]

She felt that once God's existence was universally recognized, it would neither be necessary nor desirable for Jews to exist as a separate religious group; but until then, she believed, Jews needed to remain apart, preserving the purity of their message of Divinely revealed truth.

Lily Montagu attributed her openness toward God to Judaism's own "religious inspiration."[49] Judaism, she wrote, "teaches that we can seek God at all times and call upon Him in prayer."[50] It encourages us to speak to God in confidence and faith and assures us of His loving kindness. Through Judaism, she maintained, she learned to rely upon God and to trust in His goodness and saving power. She learned to recognize Him as Father and King and to discover that which He commanded. It was through Judaism's teachings, she asserted, that her spiritual nature was awakened and that gradually she became aware of God's presence. She realized that her ancestors had been delivered from Egypt in order to serve God "for all time," a task which they could begin but which future generations had to continue. Therefore, she concluded, it was her obligation *as a Jew* to remain faithful to God and to serve Him "through truth, love and kindness."[51]

Lily Montagu's desire to form the Jewish Religious Union stemmed, at least in part, from this sense of mission. She hoped to convince other Jews that "our function, the purpose of our existence as a brotherhood," is to serve as messengers of God, bringing our live testimony before "the bar of humanity." Jews, she insisted, have a certain religious mission. Unless it is acknowledged and accepted, one cannot rightfully claim to be Jewish. In establishing the J.R.U., Lily Montagu

thus sought to make "the name Jew . . . synonymous with a
faith in the vitalising power of religion." Through her efforts, she attempted to strengthen the communal ideal of a
consecrated life, "inherited from the past," but "intended
for an infinite future."[52]

This sense of mission was intensified by Lily Montagu's
own understanding of what it meant to be a Jewish woman. Although she consistently maintained that men and women were
equal, she vigorously asserted that they were different. Men,
she said, were more analytical and methodical, making greater
use of logic and scientific reasoning, while women were more
imaginative and intuitive, more sensitive and creative.
Therefore, she concluded, because women's "contribution to
religion is distinctive,"[53] Jewish women had an obligation to
discover the nature of their own religious mission—a mission
which was similar to but somewhat different from that of Jewish men.

In numerous addresses specifically focusing on the spiritual contribution of Jewish women as women, Lily Montagu
described ways in which their religious mission was unique.
Like men, Jewish women had been called upon to witness the
reality of God, but the character of their testimony was to
reflect their own "special qualifications" rather than become
an "imitation" or "replica" of the testimony made by men.
Though later in her life Lily Montagu recognized that feminists might oppose her labelling certain qualities as inherently female, she continued to insist that humanity could
only be "enriched by the diversity between the sexes." She
assured her would-be opponents that she too believed in
women's complete social, political, economic and religious
equality and yet, she continued, it was essential that differences between men and women not be minimized or glossed
over, but instead made clear. In so doing, she felt, Jewish
women might understand their own place and responsibility

within the Jewish community more fully and might gain new awareness of the spiritual potential which they as women possessed.[54]

Lily Montagu believed that women were more intuitive. They were less likely, she wrote, to "sift and reason" and therefore tended to act on impulses which arose out of their own religious sensibilities. To illustrate this, she described the different ways in which a man and woman climb the mountain of God. A man, she said, "climbs step by step until he reaches the level within his reach." His spiritual path is thus "sure but rather slow." "Yet a woman," she maintained, "springs from ledge to ledge taking many risks." Her path is less sure perhaps, but it is more adventurous. Women, she continued, were more imaginative and consequently made better use of their creative power. A man, for example, might attempt to share his religious faith with his children by bringing them to the synagogue, discussing the worship service with them, and teaching them how to pray. A woman, however, might recall something that she and her children had admired on a walk together and thank God for having created something so beautiful or simply make a list of people whom they loved and ask God to bless them. Thus, the intention of the father would be to explain his faith; but the mother, intuitively realizing that faith must be experienced, would first seek to awaken within her children an awareness of God's presence.[55]

Lily Montagu maintained that women were more emotional than men. As a result, she felt, they were better able to emphasize Judaism's "emotional aspect," both within the synagogue and within the home. Though she failed to elaborate upon this aspect, she identified it as that which enriches Judaism and increases the "warmth of life."[56] Women too, she said, were more practical than men. While men might be interested in determining specific principles of Jewish law, women

primarily were concerned with satisfying the spiritual needs
of themselves and others, a concern stemming from women's
greater religious sensitivity. Consequently, she believed,
women were

> . . . expected by God Himself to act as guardians
> of the Divine gift of [moral] influence as express-
> ed in the power of the spirit.[57]

In a sermon entitled "Modern Woman's Greatest Duty," Lily
Montagu emphasized the significance of women's "spiritual
origin and direction." Spiritual power, she said, was one of
the "distinctive privileges" which women possessed. They were
to bring their husbands and children to a greater awareness
of God and to kindle the "sacred fires provided by institutional religion" by creating a religious atmosphere within
their homes.[58] Through an understanding of Jewish teachings,
Jewish women were to improve the religious training of their
sons and daughters and enthusiastically impress upon them the
vitality of Jewish faith.

Montagu believed that women could exert a further spiritual influence by harmonizing the world around them with
God's ways. Through social service and other "civic activities," women could combine physical with moral effort, bearing "witness to the reality of God's nearness" and power.[59]
Women, she maintained, were capable, in a way that men are
not, of taking *any* issue and lifting it into the sphere of
religion. Thus, for example, the existence of the atomic bomb
would not lead women, as it would men, to insist that their
country prepare for war. Rather, she said, it would lead them
to insist that their country turn away from war and work towards ensuring a lasting peace. Lily Montagu admitted that
men's concerns were more realistic. But optimistically, and
perhaps naively, she felt that women's spiritual concerns
could make a difference and ultimately, would lead to the

"triumph of righteousness" over evil and the recognition of
humanity's kinship as children of God.[60]

Lily Montagu's faith remained unshaken, even during the
Second World War. Though she was aware of German atrocities
and helped many Jews escape from Nazi Germany and the occu-
pied nations, she continued to insist that women exert their
moral influence so as to bring about peace. She didn't ignore
reality, but she viewed the world from a spiritual rather
than from a historical perspective. Her belief in God's goodness and love made it impossible for her to think or speak
badly of anyone, even the Germans. In May, 1941, after German
bombs had destroyed the West Central Club, Settlement House
and Synagogue, killing twenty-seven members and employees as
well, Lily Montagu wrote a letter to Club members expressing
her "sense of utter devastation." "These losses are shatter-
ing," she wrote, yet

> . . . there is obviously no use in calling our-
> selves Jews unless in this hour of disaster we feel
> that God, our Guardian, neither slumbers nor
> sleeps. His spirit fills the universe. Our tragedy
> does not affect our faith.[61]

Moreover, she maintained, we have been challenged "to turn
our hearts Godward, to listen to God, and to dedicate ourselves more earnestly than ever to the cause of peace and
freedom." We may represent only a "small group of ordinary
folk," but if all small groups share our sense of responsibility, "there is no doubt that a better life will be established." A man came over to her as she left the memorial service. Taking her hand, he sympathetically assured her that
they would have their revenge. But if he meant, she
continued,

> . . . that a Berlin woman who had given her life to
> some piece of work for nearly fifty years should

experience my kind of heartache . . . he offered me
a poor form of consolation.[62]
Thus, she concluded,

> . . . in memory of our dead I would urge you to
> cast hatred out of your hearts, as hatred is des-
> tructive, and through hatred we lose our standards
> and aspirations . . . . We are all mourning and our
> sense of loss is full of acute pain. But, for my-
> self, I feel more strongly than ever that God is
> allowing us the wonderful privilege of carrying
> on.[63]

Lily Montagu frequently acknowledged that it was emancipation which gave Jewish women the great opportunity for service which they now possessed. Her own work within the Club
and within the Liberal Jewish movement was made possible by
Judaism's entrance into modernity, the reevaluation of Jewish
identity and, subsequently, the increased participation of
women within public religious life. If, as a Jewish woman,
Lily Montagu felt a particularly strong call to service, it
was emancipation which enabled her to serve God so fully. "It
has taken countless generations," she said,

> . . . to prove that women are not unsexed by the
> possession of a liberty to follow any activity by
> which they can express their power of brain or
> heart or hand.[64]

Yet past conventions and repressions which grew out of ignorance and intolerance had now been overcome. Jewish women had
received new promise and hope, for with emancipation had come
greater possibilities for service.

In a Passover sermon delivered at the Liberal Jewish
Synagogue in 1929, Lily Montagu directly connected her establishing the Jewish Religious Union with this process of emancipation. Founding the J.R.U., she said, took courage, a
future vision, and a willingness to take risks. But, above

all, it took the "freedom for self development" which emancipation had provided. Thus, in founding the J.R.U., Lily Montagu sought not only to fulfill her spiritual mission but
also to achieve greater self-expression and growth.

"AMBITIOUS CALLING" AND THE CONCEPT OF VOCATION

Without denying the reality or authority of God, Lily
Montagu maintained that she had been called not just to better the world but to better herself as well. Alan Mintz, in
his study of George Eliot's *Middlemarch*, describes this late
nineteenth century merging of the "ideal of service" with the
"reality of ambition" as an ambitious calling.[65] Replacing
earlier notions of selfless dedication and self-denial, it
recognized the importance of self-realization, of discovering
one's own uniqueness and potential. The older ideal of calling viewed the individual as a "faithful steward," one who
had been called to work for God's greater glory. But the
ideal of ambitious calling perceived vocational aspiration as
a "vehicle of ennoblement . . . a course of action that
allows man to realize and objectify himself through his
labors."[66]

Lily Montagu's desire to create the Jewish Religious
Union clearly reflected this newer conception. Yet, unlike
George Eliot, Thomas Carlyle, John Stuart Mill and other late
Victorians, she refused to secularize what for her still remained a *religious* ideal. Rather than replacing the Divine
with either society or nature, she insisted that it was God
who had called her to a life of continuous labor. She acknowledged the importance of self-sacrifice and singleminded devotion. At the same time, however, she attempted to harmonize
her understanding of God's call with late nineteenth century
notions of selfhood. In so doing, Lily Montagu succeeded in

formulating a concept of calling which encompassed duty to
God and duty to one's self.

While for Lily Montagu, God remained, in Matthew Arnold's words, a "power not ourselves that makes for righteousness," she also believed that God influences and even
transforms those individuals who are open to Him. To experience the Divine, she said, is to feel a higher power within
us, to long for truth, revere wisdom and dedicate one's self
to justice.[67] Yet this experience does not obliterate the
uniqueness of the individual, but rather helps to develop it
more fully. God calls us, she insisted, to recognize our interests and capabilities, to know ourselves and strengthen
our personalities. Moreover, we are obligated to "stimulate
one another to find [this sense of] self and bring that self
consciously under the influence of God so that it may grow"
in usefulness and power.[68] Lily Montagu maintained that a
strong personality was to be prized above all else, for without it one could not begin to labor in God's service. Thus,
God's call, as she understood it, involved a coming *to* self,
rather than a surrender of self. It meant the discovery and
development of originality and potential and an awareness
that ultimately we are responsible to God, ourselves, and
each other.

Montagu believed that every individual who understood
and responded to his or her calling could be identified as a
hero. Like Thomas Carlyle, she viewed history as the biography of great men (sic), yet broadened the concept of greatness to include all those who through "force of character and
faith in something better than themselves . . . labour week
in and week out in the service of others."[69] Heroes, she
said, provide us with courage and inspiration. Without them,
we might well lose our power of reverence and worship.[70]
Using Carlyle's early depiction of the hero as a "wise,
gifted, noble-hearted man," she insisted that it is not

necessarily the "labelled people who are before the world"
who deserve to be worshipped as heroes. Equally, if not more,
deserving, she stated, are

> the working mother who establishes a real home, the
> school teacher who give[s] a character standard to
> his pupils, and the minister who give[s] himself to
> his congregation.[71]

What is essential, she said, is that we recognize our talents
and utilize them in a noble and responsible way. Ignoring
Carlyle's later writings on hero worship, Lily Montagu concluded that the hero does not need to possess physical or
political strength. Rather, she maintained, quoting Browning,
even the "low man [who] seeks a little thing to do, sees it
and does it" may well be worthy of reverence.[72]

Implicit within Lily Montagu's understanding of the hero
was the concept of vocation. For her, as for other men and
women of the Victorian era, it was not work in and of itself
that assumed major importance, but rather work as a way

> . . . in which the spirit becomes known to itself .
> . . in which the "inarticulate Self-consciousness"
> which dwells dimly within us can be rendered "ar-
> ticulate and decisively discernible."[73]

Work, she maintained, "justifies existence and develops character" as long as it is performed within the context of one's
true vocation.[74] Despite the leadership role which she assumed within the Anglo-Jewish community, Lily Montagu rarely
(and then only reluctantly) identified herself as a leader.
In part, this stemmed from her great sense of modesty, but it
also stemmed from the belief that she had been called to work
in smaller, less celebrated ways.

Her vocation, she believed, was to bring others to an
awareness of God's presence. In order to achieve this, she
immersed herself in social service, religious activities both
in England and abroad, and later in the work of the Juvenile

Courts in London. Yet Lily Montagu never aspired to become a
social worker, lay minister or justice of the peace. Unlike
many of her contemporaries, she refused to secularize that
which, to her, remained essentially religious. Without denying that one's profession could be one's vocation, Lily Montagu felt that *her* vocation simply was to demonstrate to
others the beauty of work "inspired by a living faith in
God."[75]

Through sermons, letters, books and most especially
through example, she attempted to reveal God's love and power. She had been called, she said, to be a witness, to testify
to the reality of the Divine. Her writings and spoken addresses were always personal in tone. In them, she shared her
thoughts, experiences and interests, encouraging her audience
to articulate their own. To do so, she believed, was to take
the first step towards self-knowledge, self-fulfillment and,
ultimately, towards God. Lily Montagu assumed that every individual possessed a spiritual nature. Moreover, she thought
it possible to awaken that nature through friendship, sympathy and understanding. Though often discouraged by the growth
of religious indifference, she refused to abandon that which
she considered to be her life's clear-cut purpose, namely,
"to seek from God guidance in the way of life and to introduce God's thoughts into the thoughts of men."[76] While recognizing that one couldn't force men and women to turn towards
religion, she optimistically, and naively, insisted that she
could "make" others want to do so, both by impressing upon
them the living influence of religion and by "expressing the
guiding principles of religious life in new forms suitable to
the [modern] age."[77]

In an address given in commemoration of her eightieth
birthday, Lily Montagu maintained that her life-long "work
for Judaism" had been made possible by her continual sense of
God's nearness and by the belief that He had a "special

purpose" for her to accomplish.[78] As her writings reveal, Lily Montagu identified this purpose as bringing the religiously indifferent back to God. Yet in what way did this purpose differ from that which she assigned to the Jews as a whole? All Jews, she maintained, were to be witnesses, bearing testimony to God's eternal presence. They had been chosen to spread God's teachings and were obligated, *as Jews*, to help awaken within others an awareness of the Divine. Indeed, on the surface, it seems impossible to distinguish Lily Montagu's sense of unique vocation from that of the "Jewish mission." It may well be that she herself never recognized the distinction. Moreover, even if she did, she would not necessarily have attempted to clarify it, for she showed little interest in systematizing her religious thought.

Given Lily Montagu's emphasis on originality and self-realization, however, it seems probable that, to her, at least, notions of Jewish missionhood and individual vocation were *not* identical to one another. Jewish missionhood was a general concept expressing the nature of Israel's relationship with God. Vocation, as she understood it, was far narrower, reflecting the aptitude and interests of a particular human being. Lily Montagu believed that her uniqueness was rooted in the *fulfillment* of her religious mission, rather than in the mission itself. God, she felt, had called her to bear witness in a specific, highly individualistic way. Thus, one could share a mission, but not a vocation. While her understanding of Jewish missionhood provided her with direction, it was only through her sense of vocation that this direction was given content and form. At times, Lily Montagu did not make this distinction clear. As I have already suggested, she herself may not have recognized this distinction. Yet she continually maintained that it was not by obliterating one's personality but by developing it that one succeeded in "touch[ing] God."[79] Accepting one's mission as a Jew, she wrote, is essential, but it is discovering one's *own* purpose in life "which will claim the best that is in you and which will challenge you to increase the powers and qualities of your personality."[80]

VIII. The Organization and Development of Liberal Judaism

By the end of the nineteenth century, encouraged by the success of her worship services at the West Central Club and the New West End Synagogue, Lily Montagu began to envision ways of broadening her religious endeavors. Believing that it was possible to awaken religious interest not only among children but also among adults, she convinced a number of men and women to help her form the Jewish Religious Union, an association which instituted Sabbath services of its own. Primarily intended for adults, these services (like those led by Lily Montagu at the West Central and the New West End), were conducted along Liberal lines. Though its stated intention simply was to revitalize Anglo-Jewry's religious life, the J.R.U. soon became identified as a specifically Liberal Jewish movement. It helped spread Liberal teachings throughout Great Britain with its founder, Lily Montagu, working to ensure its success.

While the J.R.U. was not established until February of 1902, Lily Montagu began to conceive of the idea for such an association several years before. In June of 1898, she attended a conference in London on Jewish Religious Education in which participants questioned whether traditional educational methods adequately met the spiritual needs of children. Some maintained that emphasis on class decorum, rote memorization of prayers and religion as history and geography did little to stimulate a sense of worship. Consequently, they argued, few young Jews felt close to God and eventually either identified Judaism with ceremonialism and viewed

ritual as an important end in itself, or held little if any
interest in religion.

According to Lily Montagu, this Conference was a "stirring accident," for its examination of Jewish education gave
her and others a broader understanding of Anglo-Jewry's current "spiritual state." It also gave those alarmed by the
growth of religious indifference an opportunity to meet and
voice their concerns. While the Conference confirmed Lily
Montagu's own experience that increasing numbers of Jews
lacked commitment to the Jewish community and its traditional
religious beliefs, it helped her to realize that there were
other men and women who, like herself, strongly opposed the
materialism and "self-aggrandisement" of the age.[1]

Several months later, she wrote an essay entitled "The
Spiritual Possibilities of Judaism Today." It appeared in the
January 1899 issue of the *Jewish Quarterly Review*. Pointing
to the religious indifference prevalent within the Jewish
community, she maintained that the reanimation of Judaism depended upon the reformulation of its religious ideals. Lily
Montagu insisted that her essay was nothing more than an "articulate expression" of "the rather vague thoughts and aspirations . . . seething in the minds and hearts" of many Jews,
including those whom she had met at the Conference.[2] Its intent, she wrote, was to describe the depth of Anglo-Jewry's
"spiritual degeneration," so that the previously apathetic or
unaware might support the kinds of aspirations revealed in
her essay.

Most English Jews, she began, belonged to one of two religious types. Some, best illustrated by the Jewish Eastern
European immigrants living in London's East End, attached
primary importance to external observance. They conscientiously followed traditional laws and customs, but made little if any effort to commune with the Divine. Others, she
continued, were exemplified by the wealthier, English-born

and "mostly indifferent" West End Jews. Though some belonged
to a synagogue and occasionally attended services, they were
"far more concerned in the length of the service than in its
adequacy to satisfy their spiritual needs," while those who
professed belief in some kind of "higher law" lacked faith in
a personal God.[3]

She argued that both types of Judaism weakened, and ultimately would destroy, the religious life of the community.
While many children of "East End Jews" followed the rigid observances of their parents, increasing numbers had begun to
doubt the moral and spiritual value of such "unquestioned
obedience." They might continue to uphold their parents' religion, but as observances became more inconvenient, and
their significance less clear, most would reject the East End
type of Judaism and subsequently lose all interest in religion. Children of West End Jews, she asserted, were equally
critical. They recognized that their parents, in making "no
demands on their Judaism" and denying it "real influence,"
had stripped Judaism of all meaning.[4] Thus, to young West End
Jews, religious indifference did not represent a rejection of
their spiritual inheritance, but rather an open acknowledgement that it had never been handed down to them.

In order to retain the loyalty of its young people, she
insisted, the Anglo-Jewish community needed to create a third
type of Judaism, comprised of "all that was valuable and
lovely in the ancient faith" in "forms acceptable to emancipated minds." Primary emphasis would be placed on the relationship between the individual and God and only those traditional observances which stirred the soul and led to a greater awareness of human and Divine kinship would be preserved.
To be a good Jew, it would maintain, necessitated good conduct, for while unquestioned obedience might help one "face
all earthly difficulties with courage and hope," it alone
could not make one righteous. Lily Montagu firmly believed

that through this type of Judaism, the religious life of the
Anglo-Jewish community would be revitalized and the growth of
secularism restrained. Once we have rediscovered our Judaism,
she wrote, "we shall be able to undertake with better heart
the instruction of our children" and "by the gladness and the
holiness of our lives," reveal the beauty and truth of its
teachings.[5]

This revitalization, she maintained, could best be effected through group effort. She thus proposed that religiously committed Jews form an association aimed at lifting
Judaism "from its desolate position by absorb[ing] it into
the lives" of the religiously skeptical and indifferent. Believing that the future of Judaism was at stake, she wrote:

> We English Jews can have no excuse for continued
> indifference and waiting. To us the call is clear
> and unmistakable. For our own sakes we must revive
> Judaism, and having reconciled its dogma with our
> highest conception of truth and beauty, allow it
> again to bind us to the God who cares for us.[6]

THE FOUNDING OF THE JEWISH RELIGIOUS UNION

Shortly after the publication of her essay, it was suggested to Lily Montagu by N. S. Joseph that she write to
leading members of the Anglo-Jewish community in order to ascertain how much support the proposal that she had outlined
might receive. Following this suggestion, she wrote a letter
dated March 24, 1899. Among the recipients were N. S. Joseph,
Claude Montefiore, Israel Abrahams and a number of her own
relatives. Stating the desire to formulate a program of those
Jewish elements which were consistent with truth and modern
moral standards, Lily Montagu asked four questions which she
hoped would help to develop her program further. Specifically, she asked:

1) What are the vital principles of the old Judaism
   that must be preserved in the new?

2) If those "vital principles" do not include belief in the miraculous Divine Revelation hereto-
   fore accepted, what is the authority on which we
   are to rely in judging right and wrong?

3) What forms and ceremonies should be retained on
   account of their historical or ethical or sani-
   tary value?

4) What is to be the special function of the Jew
   under the new Judaism?[7]

Though she failed to record either the names or number
of those who responded favorably (or the kinds of answers
that she received), the responses convinced her that there
was a significant group of Jews who shared her liberal religious views. A second letter, in which she asked those interested in helping "to strengthen the religious life in our
midst" to communicate with her was not sent out until November, 1901.[8] There are no clear reasons for the eighteen month
interval following the initial correspondence. The hostility
with which the community met Oswald Simon's attempts at reform may have temporarily discouraged her. Even more likely,
the disapproval of her father, and the realization that such
a movement needed the support of an individual with far
greater public stature than she, may have led Lily Montagu to
conclude that its formation would have to come about more
slowly.

Between 1899 and November 1901, Lily Montagu worked to
gain additional support. She urged Claude Montefiore to become leader of the group but, as she later wrote in her autobiography, because he viewed himself primarily as a scholar,
he "wasn't inclined to lead movements as a partisan, even in
the cause of religion."[9] He did, however, commit himself to
future participation.

On November 23, 1901, at a preliminary gathering of ten men and women, Lily Montagu asked those present to express their "willingness to associate together" and suggested that they: 1) establish special worship services for children; 2) organize special services for adults; 3) arrange lectures on religious subjects; and 4) issue publications that showed how their "ideas for a working religion" were "distinctly Jewish in . . . origin, methods and aspirations."[10] After some consideration, the group decided to focus their efforts on the creation of special worship services. They agreed, however, to support activities which similarly tried to strengthen the community's religious life. At Lily Montagu's instigation, this soon included public "propaganda" meetings as well as printed sermons and addresses.

Before the meeting's close, Lily Montagu's proposal that the group establish an organization which would work towards "adopt[ing] [sic] the ancient faith to the progressive needs of our contemporaries"[11] had gained formal approval. They also agreed to form an initial leadership committee on which all of them would serve. The members of that committee were: Lily Montagu; Claude Montefiore; Oswald Simon; Henrietta Franklin (Lily's eldest sister); Simeon Singer and A. A. Green (both Orthodox ministers); Morris Joseph; Albert Jessel (an Honorary Officer of the United Synagogue and cousin to Lily Montagu); N. S. Joseph; and Isidore Spielman (President of the Jewish Historical Society, an ex-warden of the New West End Synagogue and Lily Montagu's cousin).

At a second preliminary meeting two weeks later, formal elections were held. By then, encouraged by the support and enthusiasm of its founders (and pressured by Lily Montagu), Montefiore had agreed to serve as President of the association. Following Montefiore's election, Lily Montagu, Albert Jessel and Simeon Singer were elected as Vice-Presidents and Isidore Spielman, Honorary Secretary and Treasurer. The draft of a circular letter stating the objects of the group was approved and a third meeting scheduled. At the third meeting, it was agreed that the association be called the "Jewish Religious Union" in order to indicate its commitment to Judaism, religious faith and the unity of the Anglo-Jewish community. Shortly after, the circular letter was sent to over one hundred British Jews and several new individuals joined the leadership committee. Included were Israel Abrahams, A. Lindo Henry, Felix Davis (an honorary officer of the United Synagogue) and J. F. Stern (an Orthodox minister).

From December, 1901, until his death in 1938, Montefiore served as the J.R.U.'s official leader. Yet it was Lily Montagu who ensured its continued existence by assuming responsibility for its major activities and daily affairs. Had the organization's early goals been defined by Israel Abrahams, Oswald Simon, or even Montefiore himself, it is likely that they would have been more radical. Instead, they continued to reflect Montagu's vision of an inclusive religious organization of all British Jews. Reluctant to alienate herself from her family, Lily Montagu made it clear that she did not wish to form an independent Liberal Jewish movement. As we have seen, membership would not necessarily demonstrate one's allegiance to Liberal Judaism, but would merely reflect one's sympathetic understanding of the need to strengthen Anglo-Jewry's religious life by the most effective means possible.

The first official meeting of the Jewish Religious Union was held on February 16, 1902, at the home of Henrietta Franklin. It was attended by "upwards of 70 ladies and gentlemen." After an opening address by Montefiore, Lily Montagu's proposal "that this meeting sympathizes with the objects of the Jewish Religious Union and will endeavour to secure their fulfillment" was unanimously carried. The group agreed to institute special supplementary services to be held on Saturday afternoons, "conducted on lines specially adapted to

the requirements of those for whom the present synagogue services ordinarily fail to appeal." The initial members of the
leadership committee, reelected to their positions, were em-
powered to add new individuals to the committee and were to
decide, among themselves, how the objects of the Union could
best be fulfilled.[12]

In March, a services subcommittee was established. Its
members were Lily Montagu, Claude Montefiore, Simeon Singer,
A. A. Green, Oswald Simon, Israel Abrahams and H. R. Lewis
(who, along with F. H. Harvey-Samuel and H. S. Lewis, a social worker in the East End of London, had recently joined
the leadership committee). This committee decided that the
services would not exceed seventy-five minutes in length.
Services would include instrumental music; one Hebrew hymn
and a number of hymns sung in English; a selection of traditional Jewish prayers, most of which would be translated into
English and modified so as to appear more universalistic; a
brief Scriptural reading in English; a silent prayer; and a
sermon to be delivered by one of the various speakers chosen
by the leadership committee.[13] In addition, men and women
would sit together, prayer shawls and head coverings would be
optional (although the male members of the committee agreed
to wear hats), and a volunteer mixed choir was soon
established.

While the subcommittee hoped to hold the services at
a constituent congregation of the United Synagogue, the objections of the Chief Rabbi forced them to propose that the
services be held in a suitable hall. On October 18, 1902, the
Union's first service was held in the Wharncliffe Rooms of
the Hotel Grand Central, led by Simeon Singer with Montefiore
giving the address. Between 300 and 400 people attended, over
100 of whom had already become J.R.U. members. Although the
Jewish Chronicle described the service as "colourless" and
anemic,[14] subsequent services continued to attract large

numbers. By November, a provisional prayer book had been
written. The Chief Rabbi, while admitting that the motives of
the Jewish Religious Union were noble, criticized its services for not being sufficiently Jewish, warning that the existence of the J.R.U. would lead to a major schism within the
Anglo-Jewish community.[15] Within a year after its formation
the Chief Rabbi, Samuel Montagu and other Orthodox leaders
had pressured those members who were ministers of Orthodox
congregations into resigning.

By 1903, opposition to the Union had made it clear that
the kind of association envisioned by Lily Montagu would have
great difficulty in succeeding. However, the Union continued
to maintain that it was not a specifically Liberal Jewish
movement but simply an organization which held supplementary
Sabbath services as a means of revitalizing Jewish religious
life. In order to underscore this non-schismatic intent, the
proposal made by the West London congregation, in March of
1903, offering the Union use of its synagogue, was seriously
entertained. However, the Council of the West London Synagogue demanded that, during the services, men and women sit
separately, a portion of the Torah be read, and the form of
service be approved by them. Recognizing that such an agreement would substantially reduce the Union's independence and
would necessitate compromising on many essential points, the
overwhelming majority of J.R.U. members saw little choice but
to reject the West London Synagogue's offer.

While some feared that this rejection would be seen "as
a flag of defiance, and the act itself . . . as the starting
point of an entirely new division in their community,"[16] the
J.R.U. continued to include Orthodox, Reform and Liberal Jews
among its members. Between 1903 and 1909, it held Sabbath and
holy day services in the West End of London and, for several
years, successfully organized services in the East End as
well. Propaganda meetings were planned and led by Lily

Montagu in an attempt to increase Union membership, and pamphlets were issued explaining the Union's objects, methods
and aims. In addition, Lily Montagu began to conduct special
children's services, Henrietta Franklin instituted Bible
classes for children, and a number of essays were published,
most of which (like Lily Montagu's "The Relation of Faith to
Conduct") espoused Liberal Jewish ideas, although initially
these essays were to represent a variety of views.

As a woman and as a leader whose stature was overshadow-
ed by that of Montefiore, Lily Montagu was shielded from many
of the early accusations hurled against the Union. Yet it
was she who organized its meetings, handled its correspondence, and supervised its day-to-day activities and who, by
her own admission, "deserved to be the central target in the
attacks."[17] With characteristic energy and missionary zeal,
she sought to engender additional support for the Union and
urged others to give their all on its behalf. Montefiore jok-
ingly referred to her as his "gadfly" because she ceaselessly
pressed him into further involvement.

Lily Montagu remained naively hopeful that the Union
could promote liberal Jewish ideas without declaring itself
to be a Liberal Jewish movement. Were it to do so, she felt,
her father eventually would approve of the Union's existence.[18] Yet by 1908, though services were still fairly well
attended, interest in the J.R.U. had declined considerably
and the rate of new membership had become alarmingly low.
Communal pressure continued and the liberal bias of the Union's activities and publications led many to conclude that a
schismatic movement was, in fact, being created. Subsequently, many of the Orthodox and Reform Jews who were among the
J.R.U.'s original leaders resigned and, in November, the now
predominately Liberal leadership committee decided to consid-
er "the advisability and practicability of the establishment
of a Congregation on Liberal Jewish lines."[19]

THE CREATION OF THE LIBERAL JEWISH MOVEMENT

Although the formation of an independent, Liberal Jewish congregation violated the Union's original non-schismatic intent, the Jewish Religious Union had failed to become a strong and viable organization. Its goal of revitalizing Jewish religious life had barely been attained, opposition within the Anglo-Jewish community continued, interest steadily declined, and membership hardly exceeded two hundred. While the decision to reestablish the J.R.U. as an association specifically committed to the advancement of Liberal Judaism ultimately meant the resignation of all of its non-Liberal Jewish members, it was agreed that such a radical departure was the only means through which the Union could hope for substantial future success.

At a private members' meeting held on June 23, 1909, a resolution was passed stating that the time had come "for the establishment of the Jewish Religious Union into an independent, fully organized congregation."[20] By September, 110 members had expressed interest in joining the congregation and a letter, addressed to friends and members of the J.R.U., announced the suspension of the weekly West End services and presented the Union's new goals. Writing on behalf of the leadership committee, Claude Montefiore, President of the Union, Lily Montagu, its Vice-President, H. R. Lewis, its Treasurer, and A. Lindo Henry, its Honorary Secretary maintained that

> . . . the principles of Liberal Judaism, the organ-
> ization of a Jewish and sincere worship for those
> who cannot reconcile themselves to the old ortho-
> doxy, and fuller opportunity for cordial coopera-
> tion with other sections of the community in all
> the vital interests of our common Judaism . . . are
> objects worthy of a strenuous and sustained effort.[21]

Consequently, plans for establishing a Liberal Jewish synagogue were undertaken and a pamphlet by Montefiore outlining
the new principles of the Union was widely circulated and
labelled as the group's "manifesto."

In November, 1909, the title of the Union was formally
extended to become the "Jewish Religious Union for the Advancement of Liberal Judaism." Montefiore explained that the
association had made this change in order to

     . . . clearly indicate that its object was to con-
     solidate and promote Liberal Judaism in [Great
     Britain] . . . and thus bring the English movement
     into general line and sympathy with the correspond-
     ing movements in France, Germany and America.[22]

A small building on Hill Street, formerly a chapel, was acquired and Israel Mattuck, an American Reform rabbi, agreed
to serve as minister of the congregation. The J.R.U.'s leadership committee became the Liberal Jewish Synagogue Council
and by January 20, 1912, when Mattuck was formally inducted
as minister, synagogue membership had already exceeded three
hundred.[23]

THE GROWTH OF LIBERAL JUDAISM IN ENGLAND

In 1913, after the Liberal Jewish Synagogue had become a
constituent organization of the reestablished Jewish Religious Union, other sections of the Union were formed. The
first, the "West Central Section," developed out of the worship services organized by Lily Montagu at her West Central
Jewish Girls Club. Establishing Sabbath afternoon services on
a regular basis, Lily Montagu agreed to serve as the unoffi-
cial minister of the group and regularly preached sermons and
led the weekly prayers. She also helped conduct weddings and
funerals and prepared proselytes for conversion. In 1928,
the West Central Section became a fully established Liberal

Jewish Congregation. Sixteen years later, Lily Montagu's work
as a lay minister gained formal recognition at an induction
ceremony held at the Liberal Jewish Synagogue. At her instigation, additional constituent congregations of the J.R.U.
were formed and several elected her to serve as their President or Chairman.

Despite continued opposition from within the Jewish community, membership at the Liberal Jewish Synagogue steadily
increased and, in 1926, a larger synagogue was built in St.
John's Wood Road. Regular worship services were instituted
and weekly education classes for children and adults were
held. The congregation received permission to solemnize marriages, purchased a burial site in Willesden cemetery, and
began to publish a "Liberal Jewish Bulletin" (succeeded in
1929 by the *Liberal Jewish Monthly*). Eventually, a Liberal
Jewish prayer book was compiled and the J.R.U., reasserting
its separate identification, continued to search for new ways
in which the teachings of Liberal Judaism could best be
spread.

On October 1, 1925, it approved a proposal by Lily Montagu to form an international Union of Liberal Jewish organizations and supported her efforts to convene its first conference in July of the following year. Leaders from England,
France, Germany, India and the United States attended the
conference in London. The organization was named the "World
Union for Progressive Judaism." Montefiore was elected President, Mattuck, Chairman of its Executive Committee, and Lily
Montagu, Honorary Secretary, in charge of the organization's
daily affairs. One of her first duties was to organize an International World Union Conference to take place in Berlin in
1928. During the Conference a worship service was held in
Berlin's Reform Temple and Lily Montagu, as the first woman
to occupy a pulpit in Germany,[24] preached a sermon on "Personal Religion."

From 1926 until 1959, the offices of the World Union
(and the J.R.U. as well) were located in Lily Montagu's home.
Through her efforts, the number of World Union constituencies
steadily increased and, at her initiative, new Liberal Jewish
congregations in Europe, South America, Israel, South Africa
and Australia were created. In 1954, after the death of its
second President, Leo Baeck, Lily Montagu was elected President of the World Union. Despite her advanced age, she chair-
ed meetings, organized conferences, helped attract new members, and increased the Union's activities. Yet in 1958,
after unanimous agreement to transfer the World Union's head-
quarters to the United States, Montagu stated that she would
not seek reelection. At the recommendation of Solomon
Freehof, the Union's next President, she was made Honorary
Life President and was elected to chair the Union's newly-
established European Board.

In addition, from 1938 until 1961, Lily Montagu served
as President of the Jewish Religious Union. Elected to the
Presidency by acclamation following the death of Claude Montefiore, she also served, until December, 1945, as its Honorary Organizing Secretary. Under her leadership, a relationship of greater cooperation with the West London Synagogue
(begun by Montefiore) developed further and, by 1957, the Reform and Liberal movements agreed to train rabbis together.
Although the majority of British Jews continued to maintain
at least a formal attachment to Orthodox congregations, both
Reform and Liberal Judaism in England grew in numbers and in
vitality. Thus, by 1963, when Lily Montagu died, the Jewish
Religious Union--renamed the Union of Liberal and Progressive
Synagogues--successfully had established Liberal Judaism as
an important religious force within Anglo-Jewish life. At the
request of the U.L.P.S. and with the agreement of a Governing
Body of the World Union for Progressive Judaism, a Lily Montagu Center of Living Judaism, housing the West Central

Liberal Congregation, the European Board of the World Union and the offices of the U.L.P.S., subsequently was named in her honor.

IX. Lily Montagu as a Religious Thinker

Lily Montagu made little if any attempt to present her thoughts systematically. In most of her writings, she focused on specific topics (e.g., the relation of conduct to belief, the significance of ceremonialism, human and divine justice, the power of personality), while in others she randomly moved from one idea to the next. Her intent was not to offer clear-cut theological statements, but simply to share her faith with others. Yet there is a theme that runs throughout her works. Rooted in her profound sense of universalism, these works reveal the conviction that both Judaism in particular and religion in general need to be universal in order to be "true."

Universalism and "True Religion"

This emphasis on universalism stemmed from the conviction that "because God is one, humanity is one."[1] If God is our Father, Lily Montagu said, we all must be "brothers" and, as such, must "have in common a need for love, a thirst for righteousness, a knowledge of truth, a perception of beauty [and] a horror of sin."[2] True religion, she believed, helps us to satisfy those needs and realize those capabilities. Its veracity rests in its recognition of the Unity and holiness of all forms of life. Since this recognition may be expressed in different ways, there can be many true religions. Yet the goal of each must be the same. True religion, she concluded,

must aim at that which will benefit all of creation, for as
children of God we cannot shake ourselves free from one
another.

Lily Montagu thus viewed Judaism as a universalistic religion. To her, both its message and its mission transcended
the particular channels through which they gained expression.
Observances, she said, often served as aids to right living,
as "constant reminder[s] of God's teachings and of His presence,"[3] but they were not essential to Jewish life. Rather,
she insisted, the essentials of Judaism were its universal
teachings, i.e., the purity of its monotheism and its principle of "personal responsibility, social duty and communion
with God."[4]

She felt that Judaism, like Christianity, had certain
"good tidings" to bring to the world. She identified the good
tidings of Judaism with its universal teachings--its "message"--and maintained that the obligation to spread those
teachings was the universal mission of the Jews. To be a Jew,
she wrote, is to possess "faith in the vitalising power of
religion" and to increase the "spiritual life of humanity"
through personal conduct and love.[5]

This sense of universalism frequently led Lily Montagu
to address herself to Christians as well as Jews. One can see
this most clearly in her book, *Letters to Anne and Peter*,
published in 1944. Lily Montagu wrote *Letters to Anne and
Peter* as an introduction to the Hebrew Bible for "Christian
and Jewish boys and girls."[6] Focusing on specific characters
and stories, she discussed the contemporary significance of
the Bible, emphasizing critical issues which it raised and
moral lessons which could be discovered. She asked her readers, for example, to think about the dangers of war and materialism, the moral and social consequences of treating
others unfairly, and (describing Leah's marriage to Jacob)
the injustice of a society which only cared for the feelings

of men. She admonished them to be kind (as Abraham was to
Lot), hospitable (as Rebecca was to Eliezer, Abraham's ser-
vant), courageous (as Joseph was in Egypt), and loyal (as
David and Jonathan were to each other).

In her preface to parents, Lily Montagu stressed the
universal value of the Hebrew Bible. She expressed concern
that Christians not minimize its importance simply because it
was being introduced to their children by a Jew. Though the
Old Testament, she wrote,

> . . . gives the history of an ancient people and
> describes the development of the religion by which
> they have lived through all their generations even
> to this day . . . it may be well for Christian
> children, even while they are strengthening their
> own faith, to have some understanding of the faith
> of the Jewish children in their midst.[7]

Moreover, she continued, it is not merely a statement of Jewish faith, for while the Old Testament may emphasize God's
covenant with Israel, "Have we not all one father?" and "Hath
not one God created us all?"[8] In *Letters to Anne and Peter*,
Lily Montagu thus attempted to reveal the meaning of the
Hebrew Bible to both Christians and Jews. In so doing, she
hoped to demonstrate the universal nature of any religion
which maintained belief in a universal God.

Lily Montagu's universalistic vision found greatest expression in her short stories and novels. The heroines whom
she created, whether Christian or Jewish, possessed identical
notions of true religion. All acknowledged God's power and
beauty, the importance of social service and the significance
of love. Those who were Christian, like Joan Frankland in
Broken Stalks, never articulated specifically Christian beliefs. Nor did her Jewish heroines, like Naomi of *Naomi's
Exodus*, discover God through ritual observance. In order to
emphasize the universality of true religion, Lily Montagu

frequently left the particular religious identity of her
heroines undisclosed. At other times, she portrayed Jewish
and Christian characters as learning from one another. In
Naomi's Exodus, for example, it is Mrs. Finch, a Christian,
who helps Naomi understand the difference between outward
displays of faith and deep religious emotion. Similarly, it
is Sara Israelson, the Jewish heroine of the short story "A
Child Pays," who succeeds in awakening within her Christian
probation officer, Cicely Fane, a universal spirit of "love
and pity."[9]

In "A New Year Fantasy," privately published as a small
pamphlet, Lily Montagu dreamed of a time in which all men and
women would worship together. She began by envisioning a Jewish service, held in a large Temple one Saturday afternoon in
July. Present were "people of all races, colours and religions" with a rabbi, a priest, a bishop, Quakers, and Bud-
dhist seers all assuming an active role. Adorning the synagogue were symbols of the Old Testament, New Testament and
the Koran. Each religious group voiced its own prayers, yet
the result was harmonious.

In a second vision, she saw a group of Jews explaining
why they didn't worship on the Sabbath. Suddenly, a room was
filled with light and the group (whose location before this
had not been specified), began to enter from all sides, uniting together in worship as witnesses to God's reality and to
the truth of Judaism's religious teachings. Outside of the
building in which the room was contained, a number of "devout
looking Orthodox Jews" gathered together in prayer. Though
they remained separate, they were glad that those inside of
the building were helping to revitalize Jewish faith.

From a distance, the Orthodox worshippers heard men and
women of different "brotherhoods" praising their God and
again, they were gladdened. They realized that Judaism's
growing strength, made possible by those within the building,

had enabled Judaism's universal message to become more clear.
Eventually, they too would enter the building, just as the
worshippers of the first vision truly would pray "with one
accord." The first step, she concluded, was to establish
bonds of sympathy and understanding; the second to unite all
people together, "at one" with themselves, their neighbors,
and the Universal and Eternal God.[10]

Lily Montagu's fantasy revealed her confidence in the
J.R.U.'s future success. The description of a worship service
held in a room rather than in a sanctuary reflected the Union's activities, while its attracting religiously apathetic
Jews and gaining Orthodox approval reflected its goal. It was
not a question of whether this vision would become a reality,
she maintained, but simply when. Yet alongside of this vision
Lily Montagu added a dream of her own. Her fantasy of Jews
and non-Jews worshipping together exceeded the J.R.U's expectations, but brought to light her personal hope that one day
all would recognize God's unity and power. While in her fantasy religious distinctions remained, gradually, she added,
they too would disappear and the oneness of humanity would be
acknowledged.

This profound sense of universalism enabled Lily Montagu
to incorporate the ideas of non-Jews into her understanding
of both Judaism and true religion. She used their descriptions of God, faith, and human nature to underscore as well
as to articulate her experiences. Her justification for doing
so was the conviction that religious truths were universal
and as such were the possession of all human beings. At
times, Lily Montagu ascribed new meaning to that which she
quoted. Her intention, however, was not to misrepresent the
beliefs of others, but rather to express her own more
clearly.

Lily Montagu's belief in the universality of the Divine
Spirit convinced her that all human beings could testify to

the presence of God. Thus, in discussing the nature of revelation, she often referred not only to Biblical teachings and
to the thoughts of well-known individuals, but also to the
words of less prominent men and women. In 1953, she compiled
an anthology entitled *God Revealed*, a "book of devotion"
written by Jews "for themselves and their non-Jewish neighbors."[11] The book was divided into twelve sections, each
focusing upon a specific month of the year. Lily Montagu then
selected a number of themes relating to Divine revelation and
assigned one to each section. Among them were God revealed in
children, nature, human love, suffering, religious observance
and friendship.

    She began each section with appropriate Biblical verses,
followed by rabbinic dictates (which she presumably found in
Claude Montefiore's *A Rabbinic Anthology*) and quotations from
a variety of contemporary Jewish works, including those of
Montefiore and Mattuck. She then added the thoughts of various friends and family members, each of whom had been asked
to write a paragraph of their own. Included were numerous
rabbis (e.g., Leslie Edgar and John Rayner of the Liberal
Jewish Synagogue, Herbert Richter of the North London Synagogue, George Salzberger, founder of the Belsize Square
Synagogue in London, Julian Morgenstern, President Emeritus
of HUC-JIR, and David Wice, a leading member and later President of the World Union); her niece, Evelyn Peat, her nephew,
Eric Conrad, and her sister-in-law, Gladys Swaythling, as
well as Marjorie Moos, a teacher at the Liberal Jewish Synagogue; Peggy Lang, its Organizing Secretary; Sir Louis Gluckstein, its President; Rosina Drayton, a housewife and member
of the West Central Synagogue; Bruno Simon, an artist and
German refugee; Phyllis Jacobs, Lily Montagu's personal secretary; Bruno Woyda, Treasurer of the World Union, and Basil
Henriques, a social worker and major figure with the British

youth movement. Concluding each section was a prayer which
Lily Montagu had written relating to the month's particular
theme.

Most of the contributors to *God Revealed* remained un-
identified. Lily Montagu simply listed the name of each auth-
or, making no reference to either titles or achievements.[12]
In consciously failing to distinguish rabbis from lay people,
scholars from the uneducated and professionals from members
of the working class, Lily Montagu hoped to underscore the
universality of religious emotion. Moreover, in addressing
her book to Jews and Christians, Lily Montagu sought to emphasize the universality of Judaism's message. As she maintained, her intention was to create an anthology of "religious thoughts drawn from purely Jewish sources" which would
"enrich . . .[the] spiritual treasury" of the world.[13]

During her lifetime, Lily Montagu edited two other devotional works. One was *Thoughts About Home*, which she compiled
with her sister, Marian, and their friend, Constance Lewis;
the other, *Daily Readings from the Old Testament*, she edited
with her sister, Henrietta. Once again, her intention was to
awaken within others an awareness of God's presence and to
help them feel, as she did, the power of a living faith. A
similar intention lay behind the preparation of a series of
home worship services comprised of selections from the Liberal Jewish prayer book, suggestions for Bible readings, sermonettes on a wide range of topics and inspirational poems
and prayers that Lily Montagu had written. In addition, in an
effort to encourage Sabbath observance within the home, Montagu published a pamphlet entitled *Suggestions for Sabbath
Eve Celebrations.* Similar in content to the home worship services, it went through three editions, each of which stressed
the beauty of .the Sabbath and the seeds of "affection and
duty" which it planted, binding "families so closely together
that no subsequent separation" would be possible.[14]

Lily Montagu's identification of Judaism with universalism led her to oppose Zionism and the "chauvinistic, nationalistic attitude"[15] which she believed it represented. Since
to her Jews were a "spiritual brotherhood" rather than a political entity, she felt that regarding Palestine as the Jewish homeland was both unnecessary and unenlightened. It was
unnecessary, she stated, because emancipation had enabled
Jews to be at home in many countries and it was unenlightened
because it ignored the importance of giving testimony
throughout the world to the eternal presence of God.[16]

In 1917, in a sermon written in direct response to the
Balfour Declaration, Lily Montagu maintained that "the gift
of a POLITICAL home will not make JUDAISM live."[17] Recognizing that Political Zionism showed little interest in revitalizing Judaism as a "living [religious] faith," she urged her
listeners to direct their energies towards the creation and
growth of voluntary unions of "believers" (such as the
J.R.U.) rather than towards the creation of an independent
Jewish state. Thirty years later, reiterating these ideas,
she wrote:

> I hope and pray that political Zionists who are not
> religious will not have their way and induce Jews
> to create for themselves a political entity by sac-
> rificing the prophets' ideal of a spiritual fellow-
> ship of witnesses to the reality of a righteous God
> whom they must seek to imitate in the creation of
> justice and peace. That is, I think, what we stand
> for. That is our charge and our privilege.[18]

Lily Montagu's lifelong commitment to pacifism also developed out of her universalistic vision. In 1933, for example, she called for disarmament, maintaining that

> . . . surely, if the brotherhood of man is under-
> stood to depend on the Fatherhood of God, armaments
> seem altogether incongruous . . . . Since all men

have the same origin, since their mandate is the
same - their relations must be natural and friend-
ly. There can be no need to support them with
machine-guns, tanks and submarines.[19]

Eight years later, when the Germans destroyed her Club, Settlement and Synagogue, she urged the members of the West Central Congregation (as we noted in chapter eight) not to seek
retaliation but rather to see the war as a personal challenge
"to turn our hearts Godward, to listen to God, and to dedicate ourselves more earnestly than ever to the cause of peace
and freedom."[20] Though she admitted that England had had no
choice but to enter the war, she insisted that hating the
Nazis only lowered their *own* standards and aspirations. Thus,
she concluded, we must "purify our conduct and do loving,
merciful and good deeds," for, as children of God, it is our
obligation to uplift our feelings and actions.[21]

After the war, Lily Montagu encouraged the Governing
Body of the World Union to establish an annual Peace Festival
to be celebrated in progressive synagogues throughout the
world. She suggested that the celebration include a special
worship service centering around the "ideal of abiding
peace"[22] as well as a discussion of current political problems. Though the Governing Body, and later the World Union as
a whole, supported this suggestion, the Festival met with
only sporadic success. As late as 1958 (thirteen years after
her initial recommendation), Lily Montagu attempted to make
the Festival a more permanent institution. Apparently, however, her enthusiasm was not shared by many others and, gradually, the celebration of "Peace Day" disappeared.

AN ASSESSMENT OF HER THOUGHT

Much of Lily Montagu's religious thought can at best be
characterized as naive. Though she acknowledged the

significance of Palestine as a refuge for the "persecuted and
homeless," she continued to assert, even during the Second
World War, that Jews in "fully emancipated" countries were
already at home.[23] If there is evil in the world, she said,
it is because we have been Godless. Thus we frustrate this
"spirit of hatred" by renewing the faith of others and by infusing the world with love.

Remaining confident that ultimately God's righteousness
would triumph, Lily Montagu, as we have seen, frequently minimized the horrors of Nazi Germany. She spoke of evil as a
necessary consequence of human freedom and tried to convince
those around her that it was possible to work for a "future,
peaceful civilisation," even with the existence of a Hitler.
While she did not advocate passive acceptance of Nazi rule,
she constantly emphasized the humanity of each of Hitler's
"madmen." Quoting from Browning's The Ring and the Book, she
maintained that even if one could find no redeeming qualities, one could "be sure his mother loved him."[24]

The same sense of optimism which allowed her to ignore
the possibility of a German military victory led Lily Montagu
to proclaim that Liberal Judaism was the "Judaism of the future"[25] despite the movement's lack of great success. While
acknowledging that the vast majority of British Jews were
either Orthodox or religiously indifferent, she failed to
perceive that Liberal Judaism simply may have been incapable
of maintaining widespread appeal. Instead, Lily Montagu believed that the Liberal Jewish movement itself was at fault.
"We are not sufficiently positive. We are not pious and devoted enough," she insisted.[26] Crediting Liberal Judaism with
the ability to arrest the "present tendency to moral deteri-
oration," Lily Montagu concluded that "We cannot doubt . . .
[Liberal Judaism] will live." It is, she wrote,

. . . an integral part of human progress, widening
human vision and intensifying the sense of human
responsibility to God, the Father of all men.[27]

The most striking feature of Lily Montagu's religious
thought is that it never seemed to develop. Though she described Liberal Judaism as evolving from one age to the next,
her own ideas remained static. She vigorously denied that
"our present *form* of Liberal Judaism need necessarily be the
religion by which men and women will live" in the future, but
admitted that she herself could not conceive of a better
form.[28] In this sense, as Eric Conrad has observed, Lily Montagu was as "orthodox" as her father.[29] Once she formulated
her beliefs, they neither changed nor expanded. She continued
to see Judaism as a universal religion, constantly affirmed
the importance of her religious mission, and maintained that
"we can be Jews without paying heed to our observances, so
long as we are faithful to the teaching we have received."[30]
Lily Montagu refused to reconsider her position on Zionism,
even after the establishment of the State of Israel, and never wavered in her commitment to pacifism, acknowledging great
difficulty in admiring the Biblical Deborah.

Indicative of what best can be described as a lack of
intellectual growth was Lily Montagu's continual dependence
upon the Victorian writers who had influenced her. Though after 1930 she made fewer references to Carlyle, she never
tired of quoting either Browning, Eliot or Arnold. She continued to use Eliot's "Stradivarius," for example, to illustrate Divine and human kinship and consistently used Arnold's
"The power not ourselves that makes for righteousness" to express her belief in God.

Robert Browning remained as important to Lily Montagu in
1962 as he had been in 1900. Sermons written as late as the
1950s and early '60s centered around Browning's religious
ideas, with Lily Montagu citing, as she had forty years

earlier, poems such as "Abt Vogler," "Rabbi Ben Ezra" and
"Pippa Passes." Moreover, she continued to find new meaning
in Browning's poems. In June of 1962, only a few months before her retirement and seven months before her death, Lily
Montagu gave a sermon in which she reassessed the significance of "Self-Restraint and Self-Fulfillment." She discovered that Browning's "A Grammarian's Funeral," a poem to which
she had not referred before, reflected all that she had tried
to accomplish. Though scholars like the grammarian, the
"high" men of history, might pursue tasks of greatness, she,
like his disciples (the "low" men) had sought "little things
to do" and had done her best to achieve them.[31]

In quoting from Victorian essays, novels and poems, Lily
Montagu apparently made use of that with which she was most
familiar. Her taste in literature (as in clothing and art)
never underwent major change. There is little indication, in
fact, that Lily Montagu read many twentieth century works.
Short selections by Martin Buber and Hermann Cohen were included in *God Revealed*, but Lily Montagu failed to incorporate their ideas into her *own* religious vision.

Thus, while Lily Montagu lived for almost ninety years,
there seems to have been no real evolution in her conception
of either Liberal Judaism or that which she identified as
true religion. For this reason, one can view her writings as
a unified whole, attaching little if any significance to the
date of composition, the situation to which she was responding, or the audience being addressed. It is ironic that Lily
Montagu spent much of her life encouraging others to develop
their thought, yet was incapable of developing her own. She
admonished those around her to "harmonize the changes which
we sanction in daily life with the permanent values of Judaism,"[32] but she herself did not do so. In 1967, Eric Conrad
printed various extracts from Lily Montagu's letters and addresses. Though he arranged the material according to theme

(e.g., Jewish Worship, Liberal Judaism, Social Problems and Politics), he made no attempt to identify either when the selections were written or where they could be found. He did so not out of carelessness, but out of the conviction that such identifying information was unimportant.[33] While at times this omission is disconcerting, one can well understand the basis for Conrad's decision. A careful examination of Lily Montagu's thought leads one to conclude that the content of her religious vision was "progressive" only in comparison to British Orthodoxy and Reform. Its failure to respond either to historical circumstances or new ideas belied her own assertion that the task of Progressive Judaism was to develop and grow.

There are a number of possible explanations for the static nature of Lily Montagu's religious thought. The most obvious, i.e., that her intellectual capabilities were limited, cannot be dismissed lightly. One might argue that had Lily Montagu been more knowledgeable and had she possessed a keener, more inquisitive mind, her conception of Liberal Judaism *would* have evolved. She herself, in fact, minimized both her achievements and abilities, insisting that she was unimportant in the community and that there were others of far greater accomplishment and stature than she.[34]

While Lily Montagu recognized her success as a preacher, she felt that her success was due solely to the message which she conveyed rather than to any talent or ability of her own.[35] Compliments clearly embarrassed her. She tried, though unsuccessfully, to censor the manuscript of Eric Conrad's biographical study, asking that he delete all statements of praise.[36] Similarly, before her seventieth birthday, she wrote to Israel Mattuck, asking that he not plan anything special for the occasion. "*Please*," she added, "don't let people write nice things about me till they do my obituary notices."[37]

In part, Lily Montagu's modesty was due to her own intellectual insecurity. She realized that her knowledge of
Jewish sources and her understanding of Hebrew were limited.
While her parents had provided her with private tutors, her
brothers' more formal religious education had been more complete than her own. As we have seen, her studies consisted
almost entirely of Bible, focusing on the teachings of the
prophets. Later, she attempted to broaden her knowledge of
Jewish history and thought. Yet, by her own admission, she
never succeeded in becoming a scholar. In fact, she never
tried. Lily Montagu believed that she wasn't capable of becoming a scholar. She felt that she lacked the necessary intellectual rigor. While she may well have been correct, this
assessment served to weaken her sense of self-confidence and
discouraged her from exploring ways of promoting any further
intellectual growth.

As a result, Lily Montagu frequently relied upon the insights of others, rather than trusting insights of her own.
Though congregants and Club members frequently turned to her
for guidance, she relied almost completely upon Claude Montefiore and Israel Mattuck. During their lifetimes, she wrote
to both of them almost daily, looking up to them with what
was perhaps an exaggerated respect,[38] uncritical of everything they said and rarely critical of their actions.[39]

While Mattuck was much younger than she, she revered him
as her "leader." She continually turned to him for advice and
ceaselessly thanked him for having helped her. During the
1940s, when Mattuck seriously considered retiring from both
the Liberal Jewish Synagogue Council and the Chairmanship of
the World Union, Lily Montagu convinced him not to do so, for
the thought of working without him clearly terrified her.
While acknowledging his "longing to be free,"[40] she urged him
to reconsider. We cannot manage alone, she stated. We need

your wisdom, strength and guidance. When Mattuck persisted in
his decision to leave the World Union, she added:

> I hate putting forward the personal part but I do
> want to work for the Union for a little time more
> . . . [and] I simply cannot face the W.U. problems
> unless you promise [to continue].[41]

His decision, she told him, had made her "wretched." They
could not possibly find as brilliant a Chairman anywhere in
the world. I hope, she wrote, that you will come to my way of
thinking. "CGM," she concluded, in what must have been a
moment of desperation, "would want you to go on - I feel
sure."[42]

The development of Lily Montagu's religious thought was
further impeded by her great devotion to Claude Montefiore.
During his lifetime, he helped shape Lily Montagu's understanding of Judaism as a living faith. After his death, he
continued to live on "not only in her memory but in her actions."[43] As Eric Conrad has observed, "a spiritual union of
a unique and lasting nature was formed between them."[44]
Though Montefiore's death separated them physically, Lily
Montagu believed that, spiritually, they would be united
forever.

She continually referred to herself as Montefiore's disciple. As Chaim Bermant perceptively has noted, it was as
though he were St. Francis and she St. Clare.[45] She called
him (as she did Mattuck) her "leader," but more often, she
simply referred to him as her "teacher." Whenever she described her theological beliefs, she readily admitted his
great influence upon her. He was, she maintained, her chief
source of inspiration, for she had taken his vision of a living Judaism and made it the basis of her own. In awe of both
his scholarly achievements and his deep sense of humility,
she revered Montefiore as a prophet and a "priest of all
men."[46]

Had Montefiore lived longer, he might have encouraged
Lily Montagu to reevaluate her conception of Liberal Judaism.
Yet, with Montefiore's death in 1938, the possibility of Lily
Montagu's reformulating her faith disappeared completely. She
convinced herself that Montefiore's vision was timeless, that
it was eternally alive. In 1952, Lily Montagu wrote a second essay entitled "The Spiritual Possibilities of Judaism
Today." She described the efforts of Montefiore and his col-
leagues to help the Anglo-Jewish community "discover religious truth" and discussed at length the contemporary significance of Montefiore's religious ideas. Emphasizing Montefiore's sense of universalism, his belief in progressive revelation, and his exaltation of the prophetic over the "legal-
istic elements" of the Bible, she urged her readers to discover anew the spiritual legacy which Montefiore had left
them. It is our responsibility, she wrote, to make Liberal
Judaism an influence "in our own country and throughout the
world" by sharing this legacy with others. In it alone, she
concluded, rests our hope for the future.[47]

Lily Montagu's reliance upon Montefiore and Mattuck
clearly was as much emotional as it was intellectual. She
felt that she *needed* them, that she would be useless without their "full sympathy and faith."[48] Similarly, though she
might not have realized it, she remained intellectually and
emotionally attached to her father. While ostensibly rejecting his "rigid orthodoxy," Lily Montagu's own understanding
of Judaism was no less rigid. She was far more tolerant of
religious diversity than he, yet she too felt that certain
"presentments" of Judaism were inherently superior to others.

In her autobiography, Lily Montagu admitted that, as a
child, her religion was shaped by her father. The form of
this religion subsequently changed, yet the conviction that
faith demands intensity and self-sacrifice stayed with her.
Once she arrived at her own conception of a living Judaism,

she adhered to it as strictly as Samuel Montagu had to his own. Like him, she saw Judaism as all-embracing, absorbing her intellectual and spiritual natures, and, like him too, she recognized that true religion demands constant "commitment to service."[49]

Though well aware of her father's opposition to Liberal Judaism, Lily Montagu convinced herself that he simply had been born too soon to realize that it was the "logical outcome of principles as clear as his own."[50] As we have seen, she insisted that there was an "essential sympathy" between them and that he knew (if only in death) that she "was carrying on *his* work in preserving the inheritance he had given" her.[51]

Lily Montagu's great love for her father led her to view traditional observances in a surprisingly positive light. While neither identifying such observances as essential nor in any other way compromising her beliefs, she tried to discover new meaning in rituals which seemed hopelessly outdated. Claude Montefiore asserted that, to the Liberal Jew, traditional observance was simply a matter of "individual sentimentalities and idiosyncrasies."[52] He recommended the optional retention of Biblical but not rabbinic law, maintaining that the latter encouraged anti-social behavior. Lily Montagu, however, insisted that

> . . . ritual observances help us to be at peace in
> the midst of the anxiety of everyday life. We clear
> a space in our hearts for the love of God to rest
> there, and in trying to cherish this love, we are
> able to resist the temptation to greed and self-
> indulgence, which may assail us.[53]

Though, like Montefiore, she attached greater significance to Biblical law, she felt that both Biblical and rabbinic precepts served as aids towards holiness, helped stimulate the power of prayer, were important educational instruments,

strengthened the bonds of Jews throughout the world, and suggested "possibilities of self-development and service."[54]

Out of loyalty and respect for her father, Lily Montagu
retained observances which she otherwise might have abandoned. She and Marian, for example, refrained from riding on the
Sabbath, walking a distance of several miles from their home
in Bayswater to the services at the West Central Club. Eventually, however, advanced age made it impossible for them to
continue their walks and their sister, Henrietta, arranged
for her chauffeur to drive them. Lily gratefully accepted
such rides, but steadfastly refused to travel on the Sabbath
"for any lesser occasion."[55]

Lily and Marian Montagu similarly adhered to the Jewish
dietary laws. Recalling the great trouble which their father
had taken "even on his travels to deny himself any forbidden
food," they too refrained from eating food which was not
kosher.[56] Significantly, they later gave up eating meat altogether. According to Phyllis Jacobs, Lily Montagu's personal
secretary for many years, Lily Montagu refused to eat non-
kosher meat in deference to the beliefs of her father, yet
refused to eat kosher meat "on principle," maintaining that
she failed to see the value of such observance.[57]

Each year, on the anniversaries of their parents'
deaths, Lily and Marian Montagu walked to the New West End
Synagogue to say *kaddish* (though silently) for them. Lily did
not enjoy the services. They were in Hebrew and thus she
could barely understand them. Moreover, since she was relegated to the women's gallery, she could barely hear and see.
Yet she went "as a sign of reverence to her parents and the
Orthodox faith by which they lived."[58] She believed that her
father would have wanted her to do so.

Lily Montagu's intolerance towards intermarriage further
reveals her great emotional attachment to her father. Samuel
Montagu had vehemently opposed such marriages and had

stipulated in his will that if any of his children married a
non-Jew, he or she would receive no future financial support.
Lily Montagu shared her father's sentiments, using the idea
of the Jewish mission to justify that which seemed to contra-
dict her own universalistic vision. She insisted that intermarriage endangered the purity of Judaism's message. "The
[Jewish] man or woman who marries someone of a different
faith," she wrote,

> . . . denies the importance of his mission and by
> breaking the chain of witnesses does as much harm
> as is in the power of an individual human being to
> weaken the value of his ancestral faith.[59]

She argued that intermarriage among Jews and Christians would
not lead to a blending of the religions, but rather to the
disappearance of both. Moreover, she doubted whether such
marriages would be successful, for she believed that homes
could only be founded on the unity of faith. As she wrote to
the members of the West Central Club:

> A home, if worthy of its name must be founded on
> complete spiritual unity; man and wife can differ
> intellectually and be very happy, but real marriage
> is a spiritual at-onement and no complete merging
> is possible between a Christian and a Jew.[60]

Claude Montefiore and Israel Mattuck also opposed intermarriage, yet their objections were neither as vocal nor as
sustained. To Lily Montagu, however, intermarriage was "hardly less than an act of betrayal."[61] It revealed, she said, a
desire to extinguish the life of Judaism and thus threatened
the Jewish community as a whole. As stubborn as her father,
Lily Montagu refused to compromise her position. Insisting
that Jews and non-Jews could "like one another and respect
one another and work side by side," she nevertheless maintained that God had called her to be separate. "It is hard to
understand," she confessed, "why God made Jews and like this,

but I believe it's because he loves us all." There are two "separate truths" which we've been given and to preserve them, we must remain apart.[62]

Rejecting the notions of Jewish peoplehood and national- ity, Lily Montagu thought it possible for a non-Jew to enter Judaism's "community of witnesses." She enthusiastically ac- cepted converts whose motivations were religious and main- tained that they were more Jewish than men and women who sim- ply were Jewish by birth. Moreover, she felt that marriage between "one who is devoted to Judaism" and a Jewish "materi- alist who has led a secular life" was in itself a form of in- termarriage "nearly as dangerous as any other." It too, she believed, endangered the "stability of the Judaism of the fu- ture" and therefore was to be condemned.[63] In thus broadening her definition of intermarriage, Lily Montagu succeeded in placing her objections solely upon religious grounds. In so doing, she remained faithful both to her father and to the teachings of Liberal Judaism. Though, like her father, she strongly opposed such marriages, her concern was not to pre- serve the Jewish "race" but rather the Jewish "message."

Lily Montagu's experience of God served to reinforce her attachment to Montefiore, Mattuck and her father. It con- vinced her that her conception of Judaism was as "true" as her father's and, as we have seen, led her to believe that if he'd been born later, *his* experience of God (and therefore his understanding of Judaism) might have been closer to her own. Moreover, it transformed Montefiore's liberal present- ment of Judaism into a personal, living faith. She and Monte- fiore became more than disciple and teacher. They (and Mat- tuck) became kindred spirits, united in their visions of God.

In attempting to understand the nature of Lily Montagu's religious thought, one should not ignore Lily Montagu's own conception of religion. She shared Friedrich Schleiermacher's conviction that religion was "not knowledge and science,

either of the world or of God," but rather "immediate consciousness of the Deity as He is found in ourselves and in
the world."[64] Thus, for her (as for Schleiermacher), rational
principles and systems of belief remained outside the sphere
of true religion. If Lily Montagu seemed unconcerned with (or
unaware of) the static nature of her thought, it was perhaps
because her sole interest lay in *feeling* the Divine presence.
Her conception of Liberal Judaism may have failed to develop,
then, not because she was rigid in her thinking, but because
her experience of God (and His message to her) simply--and
necessarily--remained the same.

CONCLUSION

In evaluating the historical significance of Lily Montagu, one needs to turn to both her life and thought. As a
leader, she possessed a forceful, perhaps charismatic personality. Drawing others to her, she exerted a strong influence
over many, giving direction to their lives and helping to
shape their ideas. As an organizer, she succeeded in establishing and maintaining not only the Jewish Religious Union
and the World Union for Progressive Judaism but also a handful of Liberal Jewish synagogues throughout Great Britain,
including the West Central Liberal Jewish Congregation, which
she served as lay minister for well over thirty years. Finally, as a religious thinker, she took the ideas of others
and sought to imbue them with her personal experiences and
concerns. Her intent was to emphasize the ways in which Liberalism was emotionally as well as intellectually satisfying,
a form of Judaism capable of promoting spiritual awakening
and growth.

LIBERAL JUDAISM, SPIRITUALITY AND MODERNITY

Those who knew Lily Montagu felt that she lived in two
worlds. Although she possessed outstanding organizational
abilities and ceaselessly worked for practical change, she
seemed surrounded by a "spiritual aura" from which radiated a
serene and quiet glow.[1] Consequently, many claimed that she
was a prophet. Her spiritual power, they said, filled them
with both reverence and awe. When she spoke, she seemed to

tower over them physically, her chin expressing her determination, her "gift for endurance and leadership and . . . in-
domitable will power."[2] Through her personality, she influenced their beliefs and conduct, exerting a mysterious hold
upon them.

In his biography (which, significantly, he chose to sub-
title *Prophet of a Living Judaism*), Eric Conrad maintained
that listening to his aunt preach was a unique and memorable
experience. Her rich, deep voice "with its fine modulation"
carried "a message of peace and love to every heart, and a
call to service to every conscience." And yet, he continued,
the "deep impression and emotion" which Lily Montagu's sermons created rested neither on oratory nor on structure. "By
means impossible to analyze," he wrote, she roused the indifferent and made "her congregation take part in her own exalt-
ed spiritual life."[3]

At the same time, however, the kindness and warmth which
Lily Montagu displayed enabled others to feel close to her.
Her dark, deep set eyes glowed with goodness and loving sympathy while her "firm mouth, set in a serious and meditative
face" often gave way to a smile that lit up "her whole coun-
tenance and . . . [lent] to her features a wonderful soft-
ness."[4] Lily Montagu took a great interest in everyone she
knew and sympathetically and eagerly offered her assistance.
Under her leadership, the West Central Congregation became a
"recognisable whole" rather than an "amorphous mass, dissolv-
ed as soon as a service . . . [was] over."[5] Following her example, members learned to care for one another, and those ab-
sent from services wrote letters of apology for, justifiably,
they felt that "Miss Lily" would miss them. Her enthusiasm
and sense of dedication made her a hero to the girls of the
West Central Club and several members consciously modelled
their lives after her own. Even her critics acknowledged the
strength and sincerity of her convictions and they, like her

followers, recognized Lily Montagu's magnetism and personal appeal.[6] Thus, paradoxically perhaps, Lily Montagu was held in both awe and affection. She was admired not only for her love of God and Judaism but also for her love of humanity. Subsequently, she succeeded in exerting influence and power through what Max Weber, in his study of religious leadership and charisma, identifies as the "personal gifts" of revelation and friendship.[7]

These "gifts" help to explain why Lily Montagu, despite her own intellectual and emotional dependence on others, was able to make a contribution not just to the organizational growth of Liberal Judaism but to its intellectual growth as well. First, using the "realities of modernity," both as a starting point for spiritual discovery and as a means of illuminating the universal nature of true religion, she sought to reveal Judaism, and in particular Liberal Judaism, as a living faith. Second, viewing spirituality as central to existence, she continually emphasized not only the importance of living each day in constant awareness of God's presence, but also the spiritual basis upon which the Liberal Jewish movement was founded and upon which a Liberal Jewish identity needed to be maintained.

It is tempting, perhaps, to criticize Lily Montagu for what seems to be a lack of original thought. Often, she incorporated the ideas of others into her understanding of religion, placing as much emphasis upon their visions (and particularly that of Claude Montefiore) as she did on her own. Yet I would argue that her books and sermons were not simply popularized versions of Claude Montefiore's religious works. While Montefiore focused upon abstract concepts like beauty, truth and justice, Lily Montagu focused upon poems, movies, books, works of art, nature, even people, as that through which these concepts could best be revealed. In part, perhaps, she did so because she lacked the scholarly expertise

of Montefiore and even Mattuck. She wrote about what she knew
best, e.g., secular literature, contemporary plays, friends,
and family members. To conclude, however, that Lily Montagu
would have deleted such references had she possessed a greater knowledge of Jewish sources is to miss what she believed
to be the significance of Liberal Jewish teachings.

To her, Liberal Judaism was a living faith precisely because its teachings could be found within the ordinary, the
everyday. Montefiore's chief concern was to articulate the
principles of Liberal Judaism; hers was to show the ways in
which those principles could be discovered. Though other conceptions of Judaism might be equally valid, none, she believed, had greater relevance to the modern age. Seeking to share
this insight with others, she focused upon the "realities" of
modernity, presenting the principles of Liberal Judaism as
theological reflections of them. These "realities" included
Jewish political emancipation, social interaction between
Jews and non-Jews, the participation of Jews within European
and American cultural life, and economic, educational and political opportunities available to women within the secular
world. Reflecting these realities were Liberal Judaism's rejection of Jewish nationality, replaced by the concept of
Jews as members of a religious brotherhood, the rejection of
traditional ceremonies and observances which made social interaction difficult if not impossible, the universalistic belief that beauty and truth could be found in all types of
literature and art and could be articulated by non-Jewish as
well as Jewish authors, and Liberal Judaism's commitment to
the religious equality of women. In making the connection between Liberal Judaism and modernity clear, Lily Montagu hoped
to persuade others to open themselves (as she had) to the
teachings of Montefiore and those articulating similar religious views.

This appropriation of the realities of modernity reveals Lily Montagu's own particularly modern sensibility. Were she to have lived several hundred years earlier, she would have been either unable or unwilling to incorporate non-Jewish literature, music and art into her spiritual vision. Those "realities" would have appeared--to her and others--not merely as "un-Jewish," but as part of an explicitly Christian culture from which Jews, by definition, were excluded.

By the nineteenth century, however, most Jews (and Christians) had come to see culture as neutral. This understanding of culture reflects both a new perspective and a new form of civilization itself. While one might argue that not all of modern civilization is secular, the growing separation of religion from culture made it possible for Jews and Christians to develop a number of common "realities" from which both could gain insight and inspiration. To Lily Montagu, then, drawing upon the works of Eliot, Browning, Carlyle and Arnold simply meant drawing upon literature which she, as an Englishwoman, could claim as her own. Similarly, the paintings to which she referred (almost all of which were either at the Tate Gallery or in her father's private collection and almost all of which were modern and British) were "her" works of art. Moreover, her beliefs that women were equal and that she and her co-religionists were English by nationality and Jews only by religious conviction were not drawn from traditional Jewish understandings of self-identity, but from enlightened notions of individual equality and the "brotherhood of man." Lily Montagu felt that the modern Jew could freely appropriate these beliefs because they reflected (even more than those of rabbinic Judaism) the values of the civilization to which she (and her non-Jewish neighbors) belonged.

To Lily Montagu, however, it was not enough for Jews to appropriate the realities of modernity and claim them as

their own. Instead, she insisted that one see those realities
as means of discovering and giving expression to the eternal
presence of God. As leader of the West Central Club, the West
Central Liberal Congregation and the Jewish Religious Union,
Lily Montagu tried and to a great extent succeeded in convey-
ing this belief to others. Consequently, while the Liberal
Jewish movement in England is indistinguishable in many respects from American Reform, in practice if not also in theory, the Liberal Jewish movement places greater emphasis upon
personal religion, expecting each of its members to formulate
his or her *own* vision of what Liberal Judaism is and should
be.

In America, identifying oneself as Reform most often de-
signates the type of synagogue to which one belongs. In England, this may also be true, but there seems to be a greater
awareness of and commitment to the ideology of Liberal Judaism. As Eric Conrad has maintained, Lily Montagu's "lasting
achievement" was that she gave the Anglo-Jewish community a

> . . . living Judaism; a Judaism which is not only
> kept alive by the few, but which must be kept alive
> in every individual Jew as a compelling all-
> powerful force.[8]

It was her belief that one's Jewish life was worthless unless
it revealed the "search after truth, the practice of righteousness and justice, the giving of love, [and] the reverence of beauty."[9] By infusing the Liberal Jewish movement
with this conviction, Lily Montagu helped make it unique.

LILY MONTAGU'S ROLE IN THE GROWTH OF LIBERAL JUDAISM

Lily Montagu used her organizational talent to transform
Liberal Judaism from a way of thinking to a way of life. In
founding the Jewish Religious Union, she gave the religious

ideas of Claude Montefiore greater public expression and support. Subsequently, she worked to disseminate these ideas further, devoting most of her time and energy to that which she identified as the Liberal Jewish "cause."

She thus deserves recognition as both the founder and driving force of the Liberal Jewish movement in England. Though the movement might have developed without her, its date of origin and the character which it assumed would have been different. As we have seen, earlier attempts to stem the tide of religious indifference within the Anglo-Jewish community had been unsuccessful. Even the most popular, namely the Sabbath afternoon services initiated by the Hampstead group, had failed to sustain interest and, after a period of three years, the group was forced to disband. The J.R.U., however, continues to exist today. Renamed the Union of Liberal and Progressive Synagogues in 1944, it remains a small but vital organization, boasting twenty-four member synagogues.[10] Since 1909, it has been representative of a specific religious movement, committed to the advancement of Liberal Judaism through the creation of institutions and the propagation of Liberal Jewish ideas.

One might argue, with some justification, that the relatively small size of the Liberal Jewish movement (representing less than ten percent of British Jewry) indicates that Lily Montagu achieved only moderate success. Yet Lily Montagu never sought to establish a movement that would rival Orthodoxy either in numbers or in claims of authenticity. Her efforts were aimed exclusively at those Jews for whom Orthodoxy had no appeal. Liberal Judaism, for her, represented an alternative to, rather than a supplanting of, Orthodoxy. While she herself identified Liberalism with real or true religion, she made it clear that Orthodoxy could be (and was) equally true for others. Her concern was simply that Jews recognize the "spiritual possibilities" of Judaism. Thus, in forming

the J.R.U. (and, later, Liberal Jewish synagogues throughout
Great Britain), she sought to give those who (like herself)
were unable to find Judaism's spiritual possibilities within
Orthodoxy another equally valid path through which these
might be discovered.

THE PLIGHT OF THE MODERN JEWISH WOMAN

Lily Montagu's appreciation of Orthodoxy undoubtedly
stemmed from her relationship with her father. While her involvement within the Liberal Jewish movement served to alienate her from him, she herself retained an emotional attachment to Samuel Montagu that lasted throughout her life. Her
walking to synagogue on the Sabbath and refraining from eating non-kosher meat (neither of which held any religious significance for her) are only two small indications of her emotional dependence upon him. To have envisioned a Liberal Jewish movement that would render Orthodoxy obsolete would have
meant calling into question the legitimacy of her father's
faith. It would also have brought about his disapproval.
Though Samuel Montagu died in 1911, Lily Montagu continued to
seek both his approval and his respect. As we have seen, she
wanted, indeed *needed* to believe that he understood that she
was carrying out his work. By identifying this "work" with
the revitalization of Anglo-Jewry's religious life, she
glossed over or ignored her father's own insistence that a
Jewish religious life could *only* be attained through adherence to Jewish law.

In many respects, Lily Montagu's relationship with her
father can be seen as paradigmatic of the relationship of
many modern Jewish women towards Judaism itself. As early as
the eighteenth century, many discovered (as did Lily Montagu
two hundred years later) that they could not "worship with
their father's heart." Some (like Lily Montagu) tried to

discover a spiritual path that would be both personally meaningful *and* acceptable to their fathers, while others, recognizing the futility of such an attempt, abandoned Judaism
completely.

Yet most, if not all, of these women struggled against
leaving their fathers' world. Thus, it may well have been a
desire for familial (and communal) acceptance that first led
Dorothea Mendelssohn, in the late eighteenth century, to marry her father's disciple, Simon Veit, and that led the salon
Jewess, Henriette Herz, to remain a Jew for much of her lifetime. Indeed it was only after her father's death that Dorothea left her husband for Friedrich Schlegel and Christianity; similarly, Henriette deliberately refrained from converting to Christianity until after her mother had died. Both
Dorothea and Henriette struggled, it seems, against literal
and symbolic "fathers" who represented a religious tradition
in which they could find no personal meaning. Yet both, like
Lily Montagu, were reluctant to leave their "fathers" behind.

The growth of religious liberalism in the late nineteenth and early twentieth centuries afforded Jewish women a
new means of resolving this dilemma. Many, like Lily Montagu,
found it possible to establish a personally meaningful bond
with the world of their fathers either by accepting or formulating a new definition of Judaism itself. I would suggest,
for example, that the religious liberalism of Rebecca Kohut,
a communal worker and early leader of the American National
Council of Jewish Women; the late nineteenth century journalist and preacher, Ray Frank; and Tehilla Lichtenstein, a
founder and leader of the twentieth century movement, Jewish
Science, need to be seen in light of the kind of father-
daughter paradigm which Lily Montagu's life represents. Each
of these women rebelled against the religious traditionalism
--the "Judaism"--of their fathers. Yet each, like Lily Montagu, sought to redefine their understanding of Jewish

self-identity in a way that would be acceptable both to their families and to themselves.

For many Jewish women, the dilemma of creating a modern Jewish identity took on greater proportions than it did for Jewish men. There were numbers of men who also struggled against leaving the world of their fathers. Like their female counterparts, many of them attempted to harmonize the Jewish and modern worlds, in both of which they wanted to play a part. Yet Jewish women, unlike Jewish men, found themselves confronted with a *double* identity crisis. As they began to reevaluate the roles which traditional Judaism had assigned them, many began to question not only whether they could be fully modern and fully Jewish but also whether, as women, they had *ever* been fully Jewish. The conversions of Dorothea Mendelssohn, Henriette Herz, and other wealthy Jewish women stemmed, it seems, from a negative resolution to both queries. Believing that it was *not* possible to be fully modern and fully Jewish and, at the same time, recognizing that they had relatively little at stake in remaining Jewish, these women decided to convert to a Christianity which seemed to offer both acceptance within the modern world and an opportunity to develop their own spiritual potential (an opportunity which traditional Judaism seemed to deny them).

By the nineteenth century, as we have seen, religious liberalism appeared to offer many Jewish women a mediating resolution. Were such a resolution available one hundred years earlier, perhaps Dorothea Mendelssohn and Henriette Herz would not have found it necessary to convert to Christianity. Yet while religious liberalism provided Lily Montagu and others with a means of resolving their religious dilemma, the dilemma itself remains paradigmatic of the plight of many Jewish women, even today.

Twentieth century Jewish women, no less (and perhaps more) than eighteenth and nineteenth century Jewish women, have felt the pull of two seemingly irreconcilable sets of expectations: those created by modernity and those rooted in the Jewish tradition itself. If traditional Jewish society promised Jewish women personal and spiritual growth, it did so only within the confines of a specifically defined sex-differentiated role. Modernity, on the other hand, held out (and continues to hold out) the promise of seemingly unlimited intellectual and spiritual freedom, emphasizing individualism over community and autonomy over externally imposed obligations. Before the era of emancipation, Jewish women were excluded from much of Judaism's public religious life, playing out their own religious roles primarily within the home as wives and mothers. The education of these women was limited. Few knew Hebrew and only the rarest of Jewish women became a scholar. Yet Jewish women *did not expect* to learn Hebrew. Neither did they expect to study the intricacies of Jewish law.

Emancipation, however, offered Jewish women new educational and social opportunities. As they began to learn foreign languages and the languages of their neighbors-- French, German, English, Latin, Greek, and for Henriette Herz even Sanskrit--it is not surprising that many also demanded to learn Hebrew. Similarly, as they began to take part in the non-Jewish intellectual circles of their day, many began to demand participation in Jewish intellectual circles as well. Lily Montagu certainly was not one of the best educated Jewish women of the nineteenth century. Yet her knowledge of literature (especially English literature), philosophy, politics and religion in general remains impressive. Clearly, she felt part of the modern world and the knowledge contained within it. In contrast, her early relationship to the Jewish world seems to have been characterized neither by personal commitment nor conviction but merely by a sense of family loyalty. The modern world promised Lily Montagu freedom (in

particular, intellectual freedom), while the Jewish world
seemed to be asking her to curtail her self-development for
the sake of a tradition that appeared to have been created by
and primarily for Jewish men.

This estimate of traditional Judaism as created by and
for men is echoed by Elisabeth Stern in her autobiography, *I
am a Woman - and a Jew*, published (under the pseudonym of
Leah Morton) in 1926. The daughter of a cantor and rabbinical
assistant, Stern received a religious education that seemed
to have been limited to Hebrew lessons given by her father.
One of her earliest memories was of her father rising at dawn
to "read the Torah." "All through my girlhood," she wrote, "I
lived with the sound of his chanting voice, at night the last
sound, in the morning, the first as background."[11] Her father's world was one of religious study and prayer. Elisabeth
longed to be part of that world. Yet like Lily Montagu her
lack of religious education (in contrast to the secular educational opportunities available to her) led her to find her
heroes "in Tennyson's poems, in the novels of Thackeray and
George Eliot and Zangwill"[12] rather than in the writings of
the rabbis.

Through her early teens, Elisabeth conscientiously followed the dictates of her father. She prayed three times a
day, and observed the dietary laws and the Sabbath regulations. Yet while she faithfully observed "all the rules of
religious life," she began to realize, again like Lily Montagu, that "they no longer meant anything" to her.[13] She soon
concluded that despite the beauty of her father's faith, she
no longer believed in it and, by nineteen, was convinced that
she had no religion at all.

At the age of twenty-one, wanting to enter into a world
in which her "mind counted" and in which she could use the
intelligence that she knew she possessed, Stern left home to
continue her education. Marrying a non-Jew (who, like

herself, was a social worker), she became estranged from her
family and apparently never saw her father again. Once, however, her mother came to visit. At the time, Elisabeth was
expecting her second child but she refrained from telling her
mother that she was pregnant. Her mother, she felt, could accept her first child--a girl--even though she was a "Gentile
baby." But suppose, she thought,

> . . . I were to be the mother of a son, now? A
> girl, after all, was to her just a female. But a
> boy, a man - he ought to be a Jew, taught Hebrew
> from babyhood, confirmed in the covenant at thir-
> teen - he ought to be made a Jew at his birth![14]

Unlike Lily Montagu, Elisabeth Stern never found personal meaning in Judaism. After her father's death, as a means
of feeling closer to him, she tried to return to the "old Judaism" with no success. Although for a while she succeeded in
finding meaning within the "newer Judaism"--Reform--she discovered that its Temple held "no religious faith warm enough,
beautiful enough, to take the place of the old orthodox Judaism" that she had lost in her girlhood. Thus, Stern said
"good-bye to the Temple," reciting the prayers for her father
(the Kaddish) by herself, at home. Though she continued to
identify herself as a Jew, she admitted that she could not
believe its teachings. Unable to overcome her early sense of
alienation from a religion that seemed to exclude her, she
concluded that, for her, being a Jew was simply "part of the
life which poured through . . . [her] veins," having come to
her in her "mother's womb," before she had either thought or
being.[15]

One finds similar strains of alienation and exclusion
running through the novels of Anzia Yezierska, written during
the early decades of the twentieth century. They reflect
Yezierska's own sense of alienation from traditional Judaism,
which she, like Montagu and Stern, saw as holding out few if

any spiritual possibilities for women. Again, like Montagu
and Stern, Yezierska's struggle against the "old Judaism" coalesced in her struggle with her father, a struggle which for
her--as for Montagu and Stern--ended in their estrangement.
Yet in her novel *Bread Givers*, published in 1925, Yezierska
envisioned the reconciliation that might have been. Like Lily
Montagu, it seems, she too wanted and perhaps *needed* her
father's approval.

Sara Smolinsky, the heroine of *Bread Givers*, struggles
to free herself from the tyranny of her father and the religion that is the source of her oppression. Judaism, as she
perceives it, is a religion by and for men. Her father had
taught her that "women had no brains for the study of God's
Torah" and yet, she notes with bitterness and anger,

> . . . they could be the servants of men who studied
> the Torah. Only if they cooked for the men, and
> washed for the men and didn't nag or curse the men
> out of their homes; only if they let the men study
> Torah in peace then, maybe, they could push them-
> selves into Heaven with the men, to wait on them
> there.[16]

Seeking freedom and the chance to develop her own potential,
Sara leaves home. Recognizing that "dreams of any understanding from [her] Father" are futile,[17] she sets out on her own,
eventually graduating from college and receiving certifica-
tion as a teacher. Six years after her departure, Sara re-
turns only to find that her mother is about to die and that
her father is already looking for another woman who will cook
his meals, wash his clothes and light "his" Sabbath candles.

The reconciliation that takes place between father and
daughter at the end of the novel is brought about by Sara's
coming to understand her father. She begins to realize that
he is as much a product of his world and its expectations as
she is of her own. His view of women as inferior is not, she

sees, his own view but that of "generations who made [him] .
. . whose weight was still upon" her and other Jewish
women.[18] Though she cannot accept her father's faith, she begins to see that it is from him that she inherited the
strength, the "iron," to undergo her own personal struggle.
Having come to this realization, Sara, for the first time,
begins to love him. She introduces him to her fiance, Hugo,
who asks Mr. Smolinsky if he might study Torah with him. For
Sara (as for Yezierska), Judaism remains tied to the old
world--a religion by and for men. Yet in reaching out to her
father and his world, albeit through Hugo, Sara hopes that,
finally, she will gain her father's approval.

Within the last fifty years, especially in the United
States, change has made it possible for increasing numbers of
Jewish women to feel that there *is* an equal place for them
within Jewish religious life, that it is possible, in other
words, for women to be "fully Jewish." Orthodoxy's upgrading
and encouraging of women's religious education, the building
of new synagogues where women, though still seated separately
from men, are no longer relegated either to a second floor
gallery or to the back of the synagogue, the gradual acceptance of the Bat Mitzvah ceremony, and the institution of separate women's prayer groups, have led a number of American
Orthodox women, like Blu Greenberg, to conclude that it is
possible for women not only to be fully Jewish but also to be
both a feminist *and* an Orthodox Jew.[19]

Similarly, within the Conservative movement, the decision of its Committee on Jewish Law and Standards to grant
women *aliyot* (being called to the Torah) and to count them in
the *minyan* (the quorum necessary for communal prayer), the
equalization of the Bar and Bat Mitzvah ceremonies within
many Conservative synagogues (also in Reform but not Orthodox
congregations), and the careful consideration of women's
ordination as rabbis have given many women hope that

Conservatism is well on its way towards recognizing them as
"fully Jewish."[20] While at present, the ordination issue has
been "tabled indefinitely," even its detractors admit that
the issue will continue to be raised. In fact, many if not
most further admit that the question is no longer *whether*
women will be ordained as Conservative rabbis, but rather
when.

The Reform movement's Central Conference of American
Rabbis approved a resolution calling for the ordination of
women as rabbis as early as 1922. Nevertheless, it has only
been within the last eleven years that the movement has begun
to ordain women. Since then, the number of women seeking ordination has grown. Other women, again in increasing numbers,
have begun seeking investiture as cantors. The Reform movement, like Orthodoxy and Conservatism, has yet to grant women
equal access to leadership roles within all of its organizations. At present, however, Reform women do have the opportunity to function within a wide variety of religious and
communal roles.

Yet despite these advances, many women still feel that
they, as women, are little more than religiously "peripheral
Jews."[21] This perception is rooted not only in women's exclusion from what Paula Hyman has called the "heart and soul" of
traditional Judaism, namely study and communal prayer,[22] but
also in the kind of language that we use in worship. As Jews
address "Our God and God of our Fathers, God of Abraham,
Isaac and Jacob," it is difficult if not impossible for women
to remind themselves that this God is also the God of our
mothers. Similarly, as Jews imagine this God as Father, Lord
and King (and not as Mother, Queen or Mistress of Heaven), it
becomes tempting to conclude that perhaps only men have been
created in *His* image. The liturgy thus excludes women both as
members of the congregation of Israel and as human beings
created in the image of God. Any sense of alienation and

exclusion is heightened by Judaism's traditional lack of life cycle ceremonies celebrating either the birth of a girl or her formal entrance into the covenant and is further exacerbated by the traditional lack of ceremonies celebrating specifically female life cycle events (including menarche and menopause). While women have begun to create new ceremonies, including those surrounding the celebration of the New Moon, and while women and men have begun to create formal ceremonies for the naming of a daughter, the plight of the modern Jewish woman has not ended. Like Lily Montagu, many Jewish women feel the pull of both modernity and tradition and are trying, with varying degrees of success, to arrive at a mediating resolution. They too have had to ask: "To what extent must I sacrifice individualism for the sake of a community that often seems to exclude me?" Yet many, perhaps most, again like Lily Montagu, are neither ready nor willing to leave the world of their fathers completely.

Lily Montagu's religious dilemma clearly does not provide us with a paradigm through which we can view *all* modern Jewish women. Some have based their sense of Jewish self-identity solely on secular grounds without ever recognizing what Lily Montagu would have maintained was their own spiritual potential. Golda Meir, for example, claimed that, even as a child, she could not remember "ever having thought very much about God or praying to a personal deity."[23] Her Zionist activities were rooted in her concern for (and love of) the Jewish people and their political, economic and social need to establish Palestine as a Jewish state. Similarly, Hannah Senesh, who left Budapest for Palestine in 1939, later forfeiting her life in an attempt to rescue Hungarian Jews from Nazi persecution, saw Zionism as a secular solution to a social, political and economic problem, namely the growth of anti-Semitism and the Nazi rise to power. Unlike Meir, Senesh was not a secularist. Yet unlike Lily Montagu she remained

untroubled, apparently, by her own lack of clarity as to
where she stood regarding "synagogue, religion and the question of God."[24]

One obviously needs additional paradigms through which
to examine the lives of Meir, Senesh and others like them.
Though Meir and Senesh, like Lily Montagu, felt more at home
in the modern world than in the traditional "world of their
fathers," neither seem to have undergone any real spiritual
dilemma. Yet for modern Jewish women who *have* thought about
God and who *have* experienced a religious dilemma, the paradigm which Lily Montagu's life suggests may help them--and
others--in understanding their struggle better.

SUMMARY

As we have seen, Lily Montagu resolved her dilemma
through religious liberalism and that which she identified as
"personal religion." Her plight, as she understood it, was
twofold. First, she needed to discover a means of remaining
fully modern while becoming fully Jewish. Second, she needed
to redefine what it meant to *be* fully Jewish so as to identify Judaism with what she viewed as "real religion." It is my
contention that this plight was not Lily Montagu's alone, for
it arose out of particular historical circumstances that
transcend Montagu's biography. Indeed, Lily Montagu's plight,
as I have described it, arose out of the confrontation between tradition and modernity, a confrontation which affected
women in a particular way.

For many eighteenth and nineteenth century Jewish women,
the struggle to establish a modern Jewish identity took on
greater proportions than it did for men. First, the reevaluation of their traditional religious role led many to conclude
that Judaism saw women as subordinate if not inferior; second, in weighing opportunities available to them in the

non-Jewish world against those available even in modern Jewish communities, many recognized (albeit for some with reluc-
tance) that the former seemed to offer women far greater opportunities for self-expression and growth than did the latter; and third, a limited knowledge of Jewish texts (compared
with a far greater knowledge of non-Jewish literary works)
led many to consciously or unconsciously assimilate Protestantized notions of religion, placing greatest stress on inner piety and communion with God. For many of these women,
unable to follow the Hebrew liturgy and excluded from much of
public religious life, the idea of redefining Judaism so as
to include both these Protestantized notions of religion and
themselves--as women--as full participants in the worship
service seemed problematic at best. In short, while eighteenth and nineteenth century Jewish men, struggling to discover a balance between modernity and Judaism, may have seen
participating in the modern and Jewish worlds as positive, in
reevaluating the roles to which Judaism continued to assign
them, many women felt a greater sense of ambivalence towards
Judaism than they did towards modernity. Seeking to resolve
this ambivalence, wanting to feel more positive towards Judaism and their role within it, wanting, in other words, to
truly feel at home in the "world of their fathers," yet unsure as to how this could be done, many women found themselves confronted with a real and, for some, insoluble
dilemma.

Many twentieth century Jewish women, including the Orthodox women to whom I previously have referred, may not
share Lily Montagu's Protestantized notions of religion.
However, their exclusion from much of Judaism's public religious life remains. What's more, their reexamination of Judaism not only through the eyes of modernity but also through
the critical eye of feminism has created, for many, an even

greater ambivalence towards Judaism, serving to exacerbate
their plight as Jewish women.

For Lily Montagu, Liberal Judaism became a way out of
this dilemma. It enabled her to develop her spiritual potential within a specifically Jewish context, to express her *own*
understanding of the religious, and to draw upon religious
texts in which she found the greatest meaning. The discovery
of this solution was shared by Rebecca Kohut, Ray Frank and
other nineteenth and twentieth century Reform Jewish women.
While they may not have identified Jewish liberalism with
personal religion, both Kohut and Frank felt that Reform enabled them, in a way that Orthodoxy did not, to become fully
Jewish, by providing them with new opportunities to discover
and develop their own spiritual natures.

Yet for other Jewish women, Reform remained an inadequate or unthinkable solution. For some, Reform seemed too
universalistic, too "un-Jewish," while others found that the
spiritual opportunities promised by Reform were more theoret-
ical than real. Indeed, while nineteenth century German Reformers maintained that the role of women within Judaism
should be equal to that of men, this role, as Riv-Ellen Prell
recently has observed,

> . . . was not actively addressed [by the Reform
> movement] until the last decade of feminist activ-
> ism in America, despite its prominence in Reform's
> initial program. [This] is as much because social
> reality lags behind ideology as it is because the
> women's issue for Reformers was a logical conse-
> quence of their [enlightenment] ideology, not a
> central cause. [25]

The Reformers offered women a new legal status, i.e.,
they declared that legally women were "men." Yet by simply
dismissing the issue of gender, they failed to examine how
this new legal status could be put into practice, how women's

traditional role, in other words, could be transformed in
light of both Reform ideology *and* existing social conditions.
Consequently, they left it to the host culture to determine
what women's religious role should be. It is not surprising,
then, that in 1922, when the Central Conference of American
Rabbis concluded that there was no reason why women should be
denied ordination, Hebrew Union College's Board of Governors
voted against the CCAR resolution. They did so solely on the
grounds that "social conditions" did not yet permit such a
step to be taken.

Jewish women who rejected religious liberalism began to
search for other solutions. Some, like Elisabeth Stern, resigned themselves to exploring their spirituality alone, some
attained an uneasy truce with traditionalism, while others,
like Anzia Yezierska, abandoned spirituality altogether.
Consequently, although many women simply denied or dismissed
their Jewish self-identity, others began to seek secular def-
initions of Jewishness through such activities as Zionism,
communal service and participation in Jewish (and/or Yiddish)
culture. To explore these options in depth--and to determine
whether women have been (and continue to be) less excluded in
Zionist, communal and cultural circles than in traditional
Jewish religious life requires further study. Perhaps in the
future this study will be undertaken.

Yet even if, as I suspect, women engaged in secular Jewish pursuits still feel a sense of alienation, rooted in
their continued exclusion either from full participation in
these activities or from equal access to leadership positions, all of these options do remain viable for Jewish
women, even today. Perhaps what unites these women with those
still seeking a spiritual resolution is the discovery that it
is easier to articulate a religious dilemma than it is to
find a solution. Undoubtedly, one reason why Liberal Judaism
became such a satisfying solution for Lily Montagu was that

she herself helped define and shape what Liberal Judaism in
England came to be. Thus, unlike most Jewish women, she was
able to resolve her spiritual dilemma through the creation of
a movement that she formed and helped lead for over fifty
years.

To Lily Montagu, Liberal Judaism held out for women a
new sense of equality and access to all spheres of religious
life. Like other nineteenth and early twentieth century Reformers, however, she rarely suggested specific ways in which
new roles for women could be created. Indeed, she herself believed that her role of religious leadership was second best
to women's more "natural" roles of wife and mother. Yet while
Lily Montagu (unlike, for example, Bertha Pappenheim, founder
of the Jewish Feminist Movement in early twentieth century
Germany) can hardly be labelled a feminist theorist, she became what Joan Kelly has identified as a "feminist in action." Like the Christian sectarians to whom Kelly refers,
Lily Montagu's feminist ideas primarily remained "in the context and in the service of religious dissent."[26] In founding
the Jewish Religious Union, leading its early propaganda
meetings and later becoming its President; in creating the
World Union for Progressive Judaism and preaching from the
pulpit at the Reform Temple in 1928; and in assuming the religious and organizational leadership of the West Central
Liberal Jewish Congregation, Lily Montagu transformed into
reality that which, for other Jewish women, could only be a
hope for the future.

ABBREVIATIONS

CL   Club Letter (sermonettes in the form of open letters from Lily Montagu to members of the West Central Club).

JAAR   *Journal of the American Academy of Religion.*

JJS   *Jewish Journal of Sociology.*

JQR   *Jewish Quarterly Review.*

JRU   Jewish Religious Union, London, England.

LJM   *Liberal Jewish Monthly.*

LJS   Liberal Jewish Synagogue, London, England.

PJP   *Papers for Jewish People.*

WCC   West Central Congregation.

NOTES

INTRODUCTION

1. References to Reform unless otherwise noted (or directly implied) refer to those individuals affiliated with the West London Synagogue of British Jews founded in 1840. See p. 47ff.

2. Albert M. Hyamson, *A History of the Jews in England* (London: Methuen & Co., Ltd., 1928), 2nd ed., p. vii.

3. Todd M. Endelman, *The Jews of Georgian England 1714-1830: Tradition and Change in a Liberal Society* (Philadelphia: The Jewish Publication Society of America, 1979), pp. ix-x.

4. Ibid., p. ix.

5. Chaim Bermant, *The Cousinhood: The Anglo-Jewish Gentry* (New York: Macmillan Co., 1971), p. 1.

6. While in theory the nineteenth century Reform movement in Germany also expressed a willingness to expand women's religious role, in reality little change occurred. In America, Reform women did begin to assume new communal and religious roles but, by the 1870s, the establishment of Hebrew Union College as the movement's ordaining institution made it difficult for women to become religious leaders. To do so, in effect, they had to become Reform rabbis. Yet it wasn't until 1972 that the movement began to ordain women.

7. Jacob Katz, *Out of the Ghetto: The Social Background of Emancipation, 1770-1870* (New York: Schocken Books, 1978), p. 111.

8. Gentz, quoted in Hannah Arendt, *Rahel Varnhagen: The Life of a Jewess* (London: The East & West Library, 1957), p. 25.

9. Michael A. Meyer, *The Origins of the Modern Jew: Jewish Identity and European Culture in Germany, 1749-1824* (Detroit: Wayne State University Press, 1967), p. 92.

10. Ibid., p. 92.

11. Henriette Herz, quoted in Meyer, p. 105.

12. Katz, p. 120.

13. Meyer, p. 107.

14. See David Rudavsky, *Modern Jewish Religious Movements: A History of Emancipation and Adjustment*, rev. 3rd ed. (New York: Behrman House, Inc., 1979), footnote 29 in NOTES TO CHAPTER THREE, p. 408. According to Rudavsky, the daughters of Moses Isaacs were to be cut off from their inheritance if they married non-Jews. When they did so they contested their father's will, maintaining that in converting to Christianity "they did not repudiate God or religion . . . and that their father the testator could, therefore, not have intended to exclude them from their inheritance for joining the church."

CHAPTER I

1. Lily H. Montagu, "Spiritual Possibilities of Judaism Today," *JQR* 11 (January 1899):222.

2. Stephen S. Sharot, "Native Jewry and the Religious Anglicization of Immigrants in London, 1870-1905," *JJS* 16, no. 1 (June 1974):41.

3. General references in this chapter to "Jews" and "native born Jews" (unless otherwise noted) refer to members of the upper classes, that segment of society to which Lily Montagu belonged and from which the leadership of the Anglo-Jewish community was drawn.

4. Jacob Katz, "Religion as a Uniting and Dividing Force in Modern Jewish History," in *The Role of Religion in Modern Jewish History*, ed. J. Katz (Cambridge, MA: Association for Jewish Studies, 1975), p. 15.

5. Kenneth Scott Latourette, *A History of Christianity* (New York: Harper & Row, 1953), 2:1065.

6. H. S. Q. Henriques, *The Jews and English Law* (London: The Bibliophile Press, 1908?), p. 199.

7. Isaiah Friedman, "Dissentions Over Jewish Identity in West European Jewry," in Katz, *Role of Religion*, p. 128.

8. Ibid. pp. 128-29.

9. Monk Gibbon, *Netta* (London: Routledge & Kegan Paul, 1960), p. 63.

10. Bermant, p. 13.

11. Stephen S. Sharot, "Religious Change in Native Orthodoxy in London 1870-1914: The Synagogue Service," *JJS* 15, no. 1 (June 1973):72.

12. Stephen S. Sharot, "Religious Change in Native Orthodoxy in London, 1870-1914: Rabbinate and Clergy," *JJS* 15, no. 2 (December 1973):171.

13. Edward Jamilly, "Synagogue Art and Architecture," in *A Century of Anglo-Jewish Life, 1870-1970*, ed. Salmond S. Levin, (London: United Synagogue, 1973?), p. 1.

14. Sharot, "Rabbinate and Clergy," p. 180.

15. Lord Rothschild, quoted in Sharot, "Rabbinate and Clergy," p. 178.

16. Ibid., p. 182.

17. Sharot, "Synagogue Service," p. 67.

18. Ibid., p. 72.

19. Jamilly, p. 83.

20. Ibid.

21. Sharot, "Native Jewry," p. 39.

22. Henriques, p. 211.

23. Ibid., p. 213.

24. Sharot, on page 74 of his article, "Synagogue Service," notes that "it was considered remarkable and a little odd for someone who had been born into a rich family and had gone to Oxford to remain orthodox."

25. Beatrice Webb, *My Apprenticeship* (New York: Longmans, Green & Co., 1926), p. 214.

26. The Rt. Hon. Viscount Samuel, *Memoirs* (London: The Cresset Press, 1945), p. 4.

27. Ibid., pp. 18, 19.

28. Owen Chadwick, *The Secularization of the European Mind in the Nineteenth Century* (Cambridge: Cambridge University Press, 1975), pp. 27-29.

29. Sharot, "Synagogue Service," p. 65.

30. Quoted in Sharot, "Synagogue Service," p. 65.

31. Bermant, p. 370.

32. Aubrey Newman, "Setting the Scene: Anglo-Jewry in 1870," in Levin, p. 1.

33. Katz, *Out of the Ghetto*, p. 84.

34. Meyer, p. 94.

35. Martha Vicinus, "Introduction: New Trends in the Study of Victorian Women," in *A Widening Sphere: Changing Roles of Victorian Women*, ed. Martha Vicinus (Bloomington: Indiana University Press, 1977), p. lx.

36. Janet Murray, *Strong Minded Women and Other Lost Voices from Nineteenth Century England* (New York: Pantheon Books, 1982), p. 259.

37. Ibid., p. 283.

38. Richard D. Altick, *Victorian People and Ideas* (New York: W. W. Norton & Co., 1973), p. 51

39. Martha Vicinus, "Introduction: The Perfect Victorian Lady," in *Suffer and Be Still: Women in the Victorian Age*, ed. Martha Vicinus (Bloomington: Indiana University Press, 1972), p. ix.

40. Murray, p. 425.

41. Geoffrey Best, *Mid-Victorian Britain, 1851-1875* (New York: Shocken Books, 1972), p. 134.

42. Ibid.

43. Lily H. Montagu, *My Club and I: The Story of the West Central Jewish Club* (London: Neville Spearman, Ltd., 1954), p.30.

44. Michael Hill, *The Religious Order: A Study of Virtuoso Religion and its Legitimation in the Nineteenth Century Church of England* (London: Heinemann Educational Books, 1973), p. 300.

45. Lily H. Montagu, *The Faith of a Jewish Woman* (Keighley, Yorkshire: Wadsworth & Co., 1943), p. 13.

46. Jessie Boucherett, "How to Provide for Superfluous Women" (1869), quoted in Murray, p. 56.

47. Carol Dyhouse, *Girls Growing Up in Late Victorian and Edwardian England* (London: Routledge & Kegan Paul, 1981), p. 162.

48. Montagu, *Faith*, p. 13.

49. Dyhouse, pp. 120, 140.

50. Ibid., p. 175.

51. *Report of the Conference of Jewish Women, London, May 13 and 14, 1902* (n.p.: n.d.), p. iv, New York Public Library, Judaica Collection.

52. Ibid., p. 74.

53. Hill, p. 254.

54. Ibid., p. 280.

55. Ibid., p. 199.

56. Cecilia Robinson (1914), quoted in Hill, p. 150.

57. Olive Anderson, "Women Preachers in Mid-Victorian Britain," *Historical Journal* 12, no. 3 (1969):468.

58. Owen Chadwick, *The Victorian Church, 1860-1901* (London: Adam & Charles Black, 1970), p. 289.

CHAPTER II

1. Gunther Plaut, *The Rise of Reform Judaism: A Source-book of its European Origins* (New York: World Union for Progressive Judaism, 1963), p. 138.

2. Abraham Geiger, "Die Stellung des weiblichen Geschlechtes in dem Judenthume unseren Zeit," *Wissenschaft Zeitschrift fur judische Theologie* 3 (Stuttgart, 1837):13-14.

3. Plaut, p. 254.

4. Ray Frank, "Women in the Synagogue," *Papers of the Jewish Women's Congress, 1893* (Philadelphia: Jewish Publication Society of America, 1894), p. 63.

5. Montagu, *Faith,* p. 23.

6. David Philipson, "The Progress of the Jewish Reform Movement in the United States," *JQR* 10 (October 1897):99.

7. Montagu, *Faith,* p. 28.

8. Eric Conrad, *Lily H. Montagu: Prophet of a Living Judaism* (New York: National Federation of Temple Sisterhoods, 1953), p. 43.

9. Lily H. Montagu, *The Jewish Religious Union and Its Beginnings. Papers for Jewish People No. 27.* (London: Jewish Religious Union, 1927), p. 2.

10. Cecil Roth, *The Great Synagogue, London, 1690-1940* (London: Edward Goldston & Sons, 1950), p. 255.

11. Quoted in Albert Hyamson, *The Sephardim of England* (London: Methuen & Co., 1951), p. 280.

12. Bermant, p. 76.

13. Robert Liberles, "The Origins of the Jewish Reform Movement in England," *AJS Review* 1 (1976):125.

14. Ibid., p. 127.

15. Ibid., p. 135.

16. Michael Leigh, "Reform Judaism in Britain," in *Reform Judaism: Essays on Reform Judaism in Britain*, ed. Dow Marmur (Oxford: Reform Synagogues of Great Britain, 1973), p. 40, and David Philipson, *The Reform Movement in Judaism*, rev. ed. (New York: Ktav Publishing House, 1967), p. 402.

17. From the preface by Morris Joseph in the Hampstead Sabbath Afternoon Service's Order of Prayer, quoted in Philipson, *Reform Movement*, p. 403.

18. Oswald J. Simon, "Reformed Judaism," *JQR* 6 (January 1884):276.

19. Israel Abrahams, "Appendix," in Oswald Simon "The Mission of Israel," *JQR* 10 (January 1897):196.

20. Claude G. Montefiore, *Lectures on the Origin and Growth of Religion as Illustrated by the Religion of the Ancient Hebrews. The Hibbert Lectures, 1892*, 3rd ed. (London: Williams & Norgate, 1897), p. 552.

21. Claude G. Montefiore, "Mr. Smith: A Possibility," *JQR* 6 (October 1893):105.

22. Claude G. Montefiore, "Liberal Judaism in England: Its Difficulties and Duties," *JQR* 12 (July 1900):649.

CHAPTER III

1. John Ruskin, *Sesame and Lilies* (New York: Charles E. Merrill & Co., 1891), pp. 13, 15, 104.

2. Montagu, *My Club and I*, p. 13.

3. Montagu, *Faith*, p. 11.

4. Ibid., p. 12.

5. Mrs. Humphrey Ward, *Robert Elsmere* (1888; rpt. London: Smith, Elder & Co., 1906), pp. 318, 365, 530.

6. Montagu, *Faith*, p. 12.

7. Patricia Otto Klaus, "Women in the Mirror: Using Novels to Study Victorian Women," in *The Women of England: From Anglo-Saxon Times to the Present*, ed. Barbara Kanner (Hamden, CT: Archon Books, 1979), p. 301.

8. Linda Gertner Zatlin, *The Nineteenth Century Anglo-Jewish Novel* (Boston: Twayne Publishing, 1981), p. 105.

9. [Lily H. Montagu], CL 60 (June 1944), private collection, Hannah Feldman, London.

10. Miss Lily H. Montagu, "The Girl in the Background," in *Studies of Boy Life in Our Cities*, ed. E. J. Urwick (London: J. M. Dent & Co., 1904), p. 233.

11. Montagu, *Faith*, p. 2.

12. Matthew Arnold, *Literature and Dogma* (1873; rpt. London: Smith, Elder & Co., 1909), p. 42.

13. [Lily H. Montagu], CL 140 (January 1952), Feldman Collection. The phrase "germ of religious consciousness" was Arnold's, found in *Literature and Dogma*.

14. [Lily H. Montagu], "Immortality in Literature," sermon, 16 February 1924, LJS Archives.

15. Ibid.

16. Thomas Carlyle, *Sartor Resartus* (London: J. M. Dent & Sons, Ltd., 1908), pp. 148-49.

17. Ibid., pp. 50, 142.

18. Thomas Carlyle, *On Heroes, Hero-Worship and the Heroic in History* (1840; rpt. London: J. M. Dent & Sons, Ltd., 1908), p. 358.

19. George Eliot, letter to J. W. Cross, 11 November 1874, in *George Eliot's Life as Related in her Letters and Journals*, ed. J. M. Cross (New York: Harper & Bros., 1885) 3:179-180.

20. [Lily H. Montagu], "The Power of Personality in a Democratic Age," sermon, 31 October 1925 (draft), LJS Archives.

21. Lily H. Montagu, "How Much Do I Count," sermon, November 1943 (London: West Central Liberal Jewish Congregation, n.d.), LJS Archives.

22. George Eliot, letter to Charles Bray, 15 November 1857, in Cross, 1:339-340.

23. George Eliot, letter to Harriet Beecher Stowe, 8 May 1869, in Cross, 3:67.

24. George Eliot, *Scenes of Clerical Life* (1858; rpt. Harmondsworth, Middlesex: Penguin Books, 1973), pp. 43, 85, 113, 374.

25. Zatlin, p. 71.

26. George Eliot, letter to Harriet Beecher Stowe, 29 October 1876, in Cross, 3:241.

27. [Lily H. Montagu], "Honest Doubt," sermon, March 1934, LJS Archives.

28. [Lily H. Montagu], "Immortality in Literature."

29. Amy Cruse, *The Victorians and Their Reading* (Boston: Houghton Mifflin Co., 1935), p. 219.

30. [Lily H. Montagu], CL 24, March 1941, Feldman Collection.

CHAPTER IV

1. Joseph Mazzini, "The Duties of Man" (1860), in *The Duties of Man and Other Essays by Joseph Mazzini*, ed. Ernest Rhys (London: J. M. Dent & Sons, 1910), p. 25.

2. Claude G. Montefiore, *Liberal Judaism: An Essay* (London: Macmillan & Co., Ltd., 1903), pp. 11, 89.

3. Claude G. Montefiore, *A Justification of Judaism* (n.p., 1885), p. 26.

4. Claude G. Montefiore, "Mystic Passages in the Psalms," *JQR* 1 (January 1889):146.

5. Montefiore, *Hibbert Lectures*, pp. 64, 122-156, 343ff.

6. Though Montefiore may have been the first British Jew to articulate these views publicly, these ideas were already common within American and German Reform circles.

7. Montefiore, *Hibbert Lectures*, pp. 551-552.

8. Claude G. Montefiore, *The Bible for Home Reading* (London: Macmillan & Co., 1925), 2:781.

9. Claude G. Montefiore, "Liberal Judaism and Jewish Nationalism," *Papers for Jewish People No. 16* (London: JRU, 1917), pp. 23-24.

10. Claude G. Montefiore, "The Religious Teaching of Jowett," *JQR* 12 (January 1900): 301, 310.

11. Israel Abrahams, "The Open Door," sermon, April 1890, in *Aspects of Judaism: Being Sixteen Sermons* (London: Macmillan & Co., 1895), p. 39.

12. Montagu, *Faith*, p. 42.

13. Cruse, p. 108.

14. [Lily H. Montagu], letter to Israel Mattuck, 13 May 1918, LJS Archives.

15. Mazzini, p. 43.

16. Ibid., pp. 19, 57ff.

17. Joseph Mazzini, "From the Pope to the Council" (1850), in *Mazzini's Essays*, ed. Ernest Rhys (London: Walter Scott, 1887), p. 248.

18. Lily H. Montagu, "Mazzini: The Man and the Teacher," *Present Day Papers* 4 (June 1901):188.

CHAPTER V

1. Conrad, p. 17.

2. Nellie G. Levy, *The West Central Story and Its Founders* (London: Leeway Business Services, Ltd., 1968?), p. 19.

3. Leslie I. Edgar, "Memorial Tribute" (from an address at LJS, 10 February 1963) in "Lily H. Montagu, 1873-1963," *LJM Memorial Tribute*, p. 3, LJS Archives.

4. Samuel, p. 2.

5. Lily H. Montagu, *Samuel Montagu, First Baron Swaythling: A Character Sketch* (London: Truslove & Hanson, n.d.), p. 59. As an illustration of Samuel Montagu's ethical principles, Lily Montagu notes (p. 60) that he never "held South African shares because he thought them 'unclean.'"

6. Ibid., p. 72.

7. See V. D. Lipman, "Synagogal Organization in Anglo-Jewry," *JJS* 1 (April 1959):91 and Bernard Homa, *Orthodoxy in Anglo-Jewry: 1880-1940* (London: The Jewish Historical Society of England, 1969), p. 43.

8. Montagu, *Samuel Montagu*, p. 41.

9. *The Complete Diaries of Theodor Herzl*, ed. Raphael Patai, trans. Harry Zohn (London: Thomas Yoseloff; New York: Herzl Press, 1960), 1:411ff.

10. Amos Elon, *Herzl* (New York: Holt, Rinehart & Winston, 1975), p. 206.

11. Bermant, p. 1.

12. Paul H. Emden, *Jews of Britain: A Series of Biographies* (London: Sampson Low, Marston & Co., 1944), p. 176.

13. V. D. Lipman, *Three Centuries of Anglo-Jewish History* (London: The Jewish Historical Society of England, 1961), p. 91.

14. Montagu, *Faith*, p. 17.

15. Ibid.

16. Ibid.

17. Montagu, *My Club and I*, p. 30.

18. Ibid., p. 15.

19. Ibid., p. 30.

20. Ibid., p. 29.

21. Ibid., p. 10.

22. Ibid., p. 154.

23. Levy, p. 7.

24. Lily H. Montagu, *Broken Stalks* (London: R. Brimley Johnson, 1902), p. 137.

25. [Lily H. Montagu], CL 16 (June 1940), Feldman Collection.

26. Montagu, *Broken Stalks*, p. 240. The semi-autobiographical references in her novels as well as references in other published works and letters indicate that Lily Montagu at one time may have been in love with Claude Montefiore. When she first met him, he was a widower. However, he married soon after, ending the possibility of a romance developing between them. There is no evidence to suggest that Lily Montagu ever was engaged. Though she admired and respected men, she showed no interest in becoming involved romantically. As her secretary Jessie Levy confided, once the man that she loved (presumably Montefiore) married, she directed her love towards God and humanity in general   (interview with Jessie Levy, 21 July 1977, West Central Liberal Congregation, London).

27. [Lily H. Montagu], letter addressed to "Mr. Hartog" (typed carbon), 24 March 1899, private collection, Eric Conrad, London.

28. Magnus was married to Isidore Spielman's daughter, Dora, and Hartog was related through marriage to Kate Schlesinger, one of Ellen Montaqu's sisters.

29. [Lily H. Montagu], draft of questionnaire (n.d.) and carbon copies (dated 24 March 1899), Conrad Collection.

30. Lily Montagu in fact maintained, although historical evidence suggests otherwise, that Samuel Montagu was "quite sympathetic" to the J.R.U.'s early activities and did not object to the supplementary Sabbath services which they held (Montaqu, *Faith*, p. 35).

31. Montagu, *Samuel Montagu*, p. 16.

32. Montagu, *Faith*, p. 36.

33. Ibid., pp. 37-38.

34. Lily Montagu, letter to Louis Montagu, 8 March 1911 (typed carbon), Conrad Collection.

35. Lily H. Montagu, letter dated 2 September 1919, Conrad Collection.

36. Lily H. Montagu, letter, 1 September 1939 ("Short Paper with Outline of what I want done with regard to my work if I pass away"), Conrad Collection.

CHAPTER VI

1. Conrad, p. 18.

2. Montagu, *My Club and I*, pp. 21, 24.

3. Montagu, *Faith*, p. 19.

4. The fact remains, however, that one of Lily Montagu's major goals was to bring upper middle class culture to Jewish girls of the working classes. Thus, opportunities for self-expression were channeled in a number of specific, appropriate directions, including those which would help "her" girls become more "refined."

5. Montagu, *My Club and I*, p. 34.

6. Ibid., p. 38.

7. Ibid., p. 111.

8. Levy, p. 7; and Lily H. Montagu, Letter to Girls of Girls' Club, October 1913, Conrad Collection.

9. Montagu, *My Club and I*, p. 53.

10. Levy, p. 6.

11. Montagu, *My Club and I*, p. 44.

12. Ibid., p. 46.

13. Ibid. (In her writings, the only prayer to which she explicitly referred was the *Shema*. A note included in *The Faith of a Jewish Woman*, justifying its retention, described the prayer as "taken from Dt. vi., et seq." and embodying "the commandments of the complete surrender of the human soul in love to the Creator" [p. 21]).

14. Ibid., p. 48.

15. Ibid., pp. 41-42.

16. Lily H. Montagu, *Prayers for Jewish Working Girls* (London: Wertheimer, Lea & Co., 1895), pp. 6-7.

17. See Montagu, *My Club and I*, p. 49; and Levy, p. 7.

18. While this account of Lily Montagu as a Club leader
is based primarily upon Lily Montagu's own recollections, her
account is corroborated by statements made by Eric Conrad in
his biography and by Nellie Levy in her brief history of the
West Central Club. They have been corroborated further
through my own conversations with former members of the Club
(now among the members of the Liberal Jewish Synagogue and
the West London Liberal Congregation).

19. Lily H. Montagu, "The Condition of the Individual in
a Socialist State," *Westminster Review* 146 (October 1896):
339-40.

20. Ibid., pp. 442, 444. It is interesting to note that
Lily Montagu made no further reference to socialism in any of
her addresses or later writings.

21. Montagu, "Spiritual Possibilities," p. 217.

22. Lily H. Montagu, "The Relation of Faith to Conduct
in Jewish Life," *Papers for Jewish People No. 2.* (London:
Jewish Religious Union, 1907), pp. 5, 10.

23. See *Prayers, Psalms, and Hymns for Jewish Children*,
ed. Lily H. Montagu and Theodora Davis (London: Eyre & Spot-
tiswoode, 1901).

24. Lily H. Montagu, "Kinship With God," printed sermon,
15 June 1918, LJS Archives.

25. Lily H. Montagu, *Thoughts on Judaism* (London: R.
Brimley Johnson, 1904), p. 60.

26. Montefiore, *Liberal Judaism*, p. 129.

27. Montagu, *Thoughts*, p. 60.

28. Ibid., pp. 1, 6.

29. Lily H. Montagu, *Naomi's Exodus* (London: T. Fisher
Unwin, 1901), p. 194. In the book's epilogue, the reader
learns that after Mrs. Saul's death, Naomi became a nurse in
a hospital. One day, she met Clement Marks there. He had become a County Councillor and a candidate for Parliament, but
was an unhappily married man. He begged Naomi to see him
again but she refused. Although she still loved him, her life
was now dedicated to service.

30. Ann Douglas, *The Feminization of American Culture* (New York: Alfred A. Knopf, Inc., Avon Books, 1977), p. 137, quoting a reviewer for the *Christian Examiner* in 1839 who was castigating women novelists in general.

31. Ibid., p. 4.

32. Ibid., p. 8.

33. Cover of *Present Day Papers* 4 (June 1901).

34. A "Scrap book of Press Notices of her Books" assembled by Marian Montagu, Conrad Collection.

CHAPTER VII

1. Chadwick, *Secularization*, pp. 46-47.

2. Lily H. Montagu, "Draft of Letter Which Started J.R.U.," November 1901, Conrad Collection.

3. William James, *The Varieties of Religious Experience* (New York: New American Library, Mentor Books, 1958), p. 58.

4. Montagu, *Faith*, pp. 7-8.

5. Ibid., p. 7.

6. Montagu, *Thoughts*, pp. 6, 50, 60, 79.

7. Montagu, *Faith*, p. 8.

8. Ibid., p. 12.

9. Conrad, p. 14.

10. Montagu, *Faith*, p. 13.

11. Conrad, p. 8.

12. Montagu, *Thoughts*, p. 143.

13. Ibid.

14. Lily Montagu never mentioned the exact duration of her illness. It may have lasted only a few months or perhaps as long as two years (when she began to involve herself in social service and, by her own admission, was by this time fully recovered).

15. James, p. 83ff.

16. Ibid., p. 162.

17. Lily H. Montagu, "The Peace of God," sermon, n.d., LJS Archives.

18. Carol P. Christ, *Diving Deep and Surfacing: Women Writers on Spiritual Quest* (Boston: Beacon Press, 1979), pp. 14-17.

19. Ibid., p. 15.

20. Ibid., p. 16.

21. [Lily H. Montagu], Address on Club Holiday, Little-hampton, 12 August 1916, LJS Archives.

22. Montagu, *Faith*, p. 6.

23. Montagu, Address on Club Holiday.

24. Ibid.

25. Ibid.

26. Montagu, *Faith*, p. 9.

27. Ibid., p. 10.

28. Montagu, Address on Club Holiday.

29. Montagu, *Exodus*, p. 41.

30. According to Carol Christ, women's spiritual awaken-ings are often followed by such insights.

31. Montagu, *Thoughts*, p. 33.

32. Montagu, "Kinship With God."

33. Lily H. Montagu, "The Social Teachings of Judaism," paper read to the Society of Jews and Christians, 23 October 1928, LJS Archives.

34. Ibid.

35. Lily H. Montagu, "Religion and Private Possession," sermon, 10 January 1925, LJS Archives.

36. Ibid.

37. See Montagu, "Spiritual Possibilities," p. 229; "Draft of Letter Which Started J.R.U."; and *J.R.U. and Its Beginnings*.

38. Lily H. Montagu, "The Typical Jew," sermon, n.d., LJS Archives.

39. Montagu, *Thoughts*, p. 58.

40. Ibid., p. 28.

41. Lily H. Montagu, *Letters to Anne and Peter* (London: Mamelok Press, 1944), p. 133.

42. Lily H. Montagu, "Here Am I: Send Me," sermon, Brighton, 17 June 1944, LJS Archives.

43. [Lily H. Montagu], CL 25 (April 1941), Feldman Collection.

44. Lily H. Montagu, "If Winter Comes," sermon, 10 March 1923, LJS Archives.

45. [Lily H. Montagu], CL 35, "What is Judaism? (3) Belief in Spiritual Progress" (March 1942), Feldman Collection.

46. Montagu, "Here Am I."

47. [Lily H. Montagu], CL 45 (February 1943), Feldman Collection.

48. Ibid.

49. Lily H. Montagu, "Who are the Hypocrites?" sermon, North London Synagogue, 11 December 1926, LJS Archives.

50. [Lily H. Montagu], CL 36, "What is Judaism? (4) Man's Relation to God" (April 1942), Feldman Collection.

51. Montagu, *Letters*, pp. 41-42.

52. See CL 45 and Montagu, *Faith*, pp. 69-70.

53. Lily H. Montagu, "Jewish Women's Contribution to the Spiritual Life of Humanity," n.d., LJS Archives.

54. Lily H. Montagu, "The Spiritual Contribution of Women as Women," address given at Jewish Education Building, Chicago, 26 November 1948, LJS Archives.

55. Ibid.

56. Montagu, "Jewish Women's Contribution."

57. Lily H. Montagu, "Modern Woman's Greatest Duty," sermon, 4 April 1938 at LJS and 7 May 1938 at West Central Congregation, LJS Archives.

58. Ibid.

59. Lily H. Montagu, address to National Federation of Temple Sisterhoods, Temple Emanu-el, New York City, 7 November 1948, LJS Archives.

60. Montagu, "Spiritual Contribution of Women."

61. [Lily H. Montagu], CL 26 (May 1941) in Conrad, p. 81.

62. Ibid.

63. Ibid.

64. Lily H. Montagu, "Divinity in Freedom," sermon, 4 May 1929, LJS Archives.

65. Alan Mintz, *George Eliot and the Novel of Vocation* (Cambridge: Harvard University Press, 1978), pp. 30, 37.

66. Ibid., p. 150.

67. [Lily H. Montagu], "Paper to be Read on October 13, 1918," LJS Archives.

68. [Lily H. Montagu], "Acting and Real Life," sermon, 16 May 1925, LJS Archives.

69. [Lily H. Montagu], "Who is Self-Made," sermon, 2 February 1924, LJS Archives.

70. [Lily H. Montagu], "Hero Worship and Modernity," sermon, 30 March 1928 (draft), West Central Congregation, LJS Archives.

71. Montagu, "Who is Self-Made."

72. Lily H. Montagu, "Self-Restraint and Self Fulfillment," sermon, West Central Congregation, 16 June 1962, LJS
Archives.

73. Mintz, p. 27 (discussing and quoting Carlyle).

74. [Lily H. Montagu], "Immortality in Literature."

75. Lily H. Montagu, "Address" (At the New Theatre, on
the Occasion of the Annual Display of Work, West Central
Girls' Club, April 9, 1911), LJS Archives.

76. [Lily H. Montagu], CL 171 (February 1955), Feldman
Collection.

77. Lily H. Montagu, "I Will Not Let Thee Go Except Thou
Bless Me," (address delivered at last afternoon service held
at Old Club, 8 Dean Street, 21 June 1913), LJS Archives; and
Montagu, "Strengthen the Things That Remain," (address at
LJS, 2 January 1954), Conrad Collection.

78. Montagu, "Strengthen the Things That Remain."

79. Montagu, "The Power of Personality in a Democratic
Age."

80. [Lily H. Montagu], CL 171.

CHAPTER VIII

1. Montagu, "Spiritual Possibilities," pp. 216, 233; and
Lily H. Montagu, "Paper Read At First Meeting of J.R.U. Con-
ference Invited to Start Movement," 23 November 1901, Conrad
Collection.

2. Montagu, *J.R.U. and Its Beginnings*, p. 3.

3. Montagu, "Spiritual Possibilities," p. 219.

4. Ibid., pp. 218-219.

5. Ibid.

6. Ibid., p. 229.

7. [Lily H. Montagu], letter to "Mr. Hartog."

8. A draft of a second letter was written as early as 1900 but apparently never sent. The letter that was sent in November 1901 is not identical to (though does not differ significantly from) the earlier draft ([Lily H. Montagu], handwritten drafts of letter dated 1900 and "Letter Which Started the J.R.U.").

9. Montagu, *Faith*, p. 28.

10. Montagu, "Paper Read at First Meeting of J.R.U."

11. Ibid.

12. *Minute Book of J.R.U. Committee 1902-1909*, minutes of J.R.U. meeting, 16 February 1902, LJS Archives.

13. Ibid., minutes of Committee meeting, 17 March 1902.

14. *J.R.U. and the Press, 1902-1914* (scrapbook of press clippings relating to the establishment and growth of the J.R.U.). See clipping from *Jewish Chronicle*, 24 October 1902, WCC.

15. Ibid., clipping from *Jewish Chronicle*, 12 December 1902.

16. *Minute Book*, minutes of members' meeting, 5 April 1903.

17. Montagu, *Faith*, p. 37.

18. While Lily Montagu agreed to serve as Vice-President of the Union, it is unlikely that she would have done so had not Simeon Singer and Albert Jessel, both well-respected Orthodox leaders, agreed to serve with her. Similarly, after the Union had announced its reestablishment as a specifically Liberal Jewish organization, she resigned from the position, so as not to further alienate her father.

19. *Minute Book*, minutes of special members' meeting, 8 April 1908.

20. Ibid., minutes of Committee meeting, 28 June 1909.

21. Ibid., minutes of Committee meeting, 23 September 1909.

22. Ibid., minutes of Committee meeting, 13 November 1909.

23. *Minute Book J.R.U.-L.J.S. 1909-1912*, Liberal Jewish Synagogue First Annual Report, 1912, LJS Archives.

24. Conrad, p. 58.

CHAPTER IX

1. Lily H. Montagu, "Justice, Human and Divine," sermon, n.d., LJS Archives.

2. [Lily H. Montagu], "Contribution of the Jews to the Spiritual Life of the World," Quaker Conference, 30 June 1928, LJS Archives.

3. [Lily H. Montagu], CL 180 (January 1956), Feldman Collection.

4. Lily H. Montagu, *Home Worship and Its Influence on So-cial Work*, paper read at Conference of Jewish Women, May 1902 (Southamptom: Cot & Sharland, n.d.), p. 14.

5. Montagu, *Faith*, p. 69.

6. A. A. Cock, "Introduction," in Montagu, *Letters*, p. iii.

7. Montagu, *Letters*, p. v.

8. Ibid., p. 133.

9. Lily H. Montagu, *What Can A Mother Do? And Other Stories* (London: George Routledge & Sons, 1926), p. 209.

10. Lily H. Montagu, *A New Year Fantasy*, n.p.: n.d., LJS Archives.

11. Lily H. Montagu, "Foreword," in Lily H. Montagu, ed., *God Revealed* (Keighley, Yorkshire: John Wadsworth, 1953).

12. I am therefore indebted to Jessie Levy, Lily Montagu's personal secretary for over twenty years, for identifying many of the contributors (interview with Jessie Levy, 21 July 1977).

13. Montagu, "Foreword," in Montagu, ed., *God Revealed*.

14. Lily H. Montagu, *Suggestions for Sabbath Eve Celebrations*, 3rd. ed. (n.p.: 1958), Klau Library, Hebrew Union College-Jewish Institute of Religion, Cincinnati, Ohio.

15. [Lily H. Montagu], CL 91 (April 1947), Feldman Collection.

16. In this regard, Lily Montagu was unusual if not unique. Though British Jewry in general (especially prior to World War II) adopted an anti-Zionist stance, most Jews did so for political reasons. Lily Montagu's anti-Zionism, however, was primarily theological, rooted in the conviction that Jews, no longer a nation, were a "spiritual brotherhood," with a specific *religious mission* to carry out, one that required their living in all parts of the world.

17. Lily H. Montagu, "Out of Zion Shall the Law Go Forth and the Word of the Lord from Jerusalem," sermon, West Central Club, 17 November 1917, LJS Archives.

18. [Lily H. Montagu], CL 91, n.d.

19. Lily H. Montagu, "Let the Hebrew Prophets Tell," *The Inquirer* (and *Christian Life*) 4742 (20 May 1933):241.

20. [Lily H. Montagu], CL 26, n.d.

21. Ibid.

22. Lily H. Montagu, minutes, Executive Committee and Governing Body, World Union for Progressive Judaism, 16 December 1945, American Jewish Archives, Cincinnati, Ohio.

23. Montagu, *Faith*, p. 56.

24. CL 86 (November 1946), LJS Archives.

25. Lily H. Montagu, "Presidential Address," Annual General Meeting, Union of Liberal and Progressive Synagogues, 11 May 1958, LJS Archives.

26. [Lily H. Montagu], "The Position of Liberal Judaism in Anglo-Jewry," Annual General Meeting, Union of Liberal and Progressive Synagogues, 29 April 1956, LJS Archives.

27. [Lily H. Montagu], "Will Liberal Judaism Live as a Religion," n.d., LJS Archives.

28. Montagu, "Presidential Address."

29. Interview with Eric Conrad, 20 July 1977.

30. CL 62 (September 1944), Feldman Collection.

31. From Robert Browning, "A Grammarian's Funeral," quoted in Lily Montagu, "Self-Restraint and Self Fulfill-ment."

32. Lily H. Montagu, "The Task of Progressive Judaism," undated paper given in U.S. at a conference [CCAR? 1931?], LJS Archives.

33. Interview with Eric Conrad, 20 July 1977.

34. At times, she even insisted that it was Claude Mon-tefiore and not she who had founded the Jewish Religious Union.

35. Lily Montagu, letter to Israel Mattuck, 16 December 1922, LJS Archives.

36. Interview with Eric Conrad, 20 July 1977.

37. Lily Montagu, letter to Israel Mattuck, 18 July 1943, LJS Archives.

38. Interview with John Rayner, Senior Minister of the Liberal Jewish Synagogue, 13 July 1977, at LJS.

39. When she *did* criticize them, she did so privately. In a letter to Claude Montefiore dated 13 November 1913, for example, she criticized him for planning to resolve at the next LJS Council meeting that application forms for member-ship should indicate that those without money *could* become members of the synagogue but would be "tolerated as paupers." It is sufficient, she wrote, to explain this to prospective members without putting it on the membership form. Moreover, those unable to pay dues should not simply be "tolerated" since they can contribute to the synagogue in other ways (Conrad Collection).

40. Lily Montagu, letter to Israel Mattuck, 23 January 1943, LJS Archives.

41. Lily Montagu, letter to Israel Mattuck, 19-20 May 1949, LJS Archives.

42. Ibid.

43. Conrad, p. 47.

44. Ibid., p. 46.

45. Bermant, p. 210.

46. Lily Montagu, letter to Marian Montagu, 20 July 1931, Conrad Collection.

47. Lily H. Montagu, "The Spiritual Possibilities of Judaism Today 1952," *LJM* 23, no. 7 (July 1952): 85-89.

48. Lily Montagu, letter to Israel Mattuck, 21 April 1920, referring to her dependence upon both Mattuck and Montefiore, LJS Archives.

49. Montagu, *Samuel Montagu*, p. 24.

50. Ibid., p. 22.

51. Montagu, *Faith*, p. 36.

52. Montefiore, *Liberal Judaism*, p. 129.

53. Montagu, *Thoughts*, p. 65.

54. Ibid., p. 67.

55. Bermant, p. 214.

56. Montagu, *Faith*, p. 4.

57. Interview with Phyllis Jacobs, 27 August 1977, London.

58. Conrad, p. 66.

59. [Lily H. Montagu], CL 139 (December 1951), Feldman Collection.

60. Ibid.

61. Ibid.

62. Montagu, *What Can A Mother Do?*, p. 132.

63. [Lily H. Montagu], CL 185 (June 1956), Feldman Collection.

64. Friedrich Schleiermacher, *On Religion: Speeches to its Cultured Despisers* (New York: Harper & Row, 1958), pp. 36, 101.

CONCLUSION

1. Interview with Hannah Feldman, 25 July 1977, West Central Club, London.

2. Conrad, p. 5.

3. Ibid., pp. 4, 64.

4. Ibid., p. 65.

5. Ibid., p. 63.

6. Interview with Eric Conrad, 22 July 1977 (and reiterated during subsequent conversations).

7. See Max Weber's discussion of religious leadership and charisma in *The Sociology of Religion*, introd. Talcott Parsons, trans. Ephraim Fischoff (Boston: Beacon Press, 1963), p. 47.

8. Conrad, p. 44.

9. [Lily H. Montagu], CL 28 (July 1941), Feldman Collection.

10. Figures supplied by John D. Rayner, Senior Minister, Liberal Jewish Synagogue, London (November 1982).

11. Elisabeth Stern [Leah Morton, pseud.], *I am a Woman - and a Jew* (1926; rpt. New York: Arno Press & The New York Times, 1969), p. 9.

12. Ibid., p. 20.

13. Ibid., p. 11,

14. Ibid., p. 102.

15. Ibid., p. 360.

16. Anzia Yezierska, *Bread Givers* (1925; rpt. New York: Persea Books, 1975), pp. 9-10.

17. Ibid., p. 208.

18. Ibid., p. 297.

19. See Blu Greenberg, *On Women and Judaism: A View From Tradition* (Philadelphia: Jewish Publication Society of America, 1982).

20. The fact, however, that some Conservative synagogues still do not count women in the *minyan*, but when a quorum is needed and no men available, will count each women present as "one half," indicates that the struggle of Conservative women to be recognized as fully Jewish is hardly over!

21. Rachel Adler, "The Jew Who Wasn't There: Halacha and the Jewish Woman," *Response. The Jewish Woman: An Anthology* 18 (Summer 1973):77ff.

22. Paula Hyman, "The Other Half: Women in the Jewish Tradition," in *The Jewish Woman: New Perspectives*, ed. Elizabeth Koltun (New York: Schocken Books, 1976), p. 107.

23. *My Life by Golda Meir* (Jerusalem: Steimatzky's Agency, Ltd., 1975), p. 3.

24. *Hannah Senesh: Her Life and Diary*, introd. Abba Eban, trans. Marta Cohn (New York: Shocken Books, 1973), p. 26.

25. Riv-Ellen Prell, "The Vision of Women in Classical Reform Judaism," *JAAR* 50, no. 4 (December 1982):576.

26. Joan Kelly, "Early Feminist Theory and the *Querelle des Femmes*, 1400-1789," *Signs: Journal of Women in Culture and Society* 8, no. 1 (Autumn, 1982):6 (see footnote 4).

BIBLIOGRAPHY

WORKS BY LILY H. MONTAGU

I. Published Works

Broken Stalks. London: R. Brimley Johnson, 1902.

"The Conception of Prayer." *Aspects of Progressive Jewish Thought*. Introd. Israel Mattuck. London: Victor Gollancz, 1954, pp. 94-98.

"The Condition of the Individual in a Socialist State." *Westminster Review* 146 (October 1896):439-445.

The Faith of a Jewish Woman. Keighley, Yorkshire: Wadsworth & Co., 1943.

"The Girl in the Background." *Studies of Boy Life in Our Cities*. Ed. E. J. Urwick. London: J. M. Dent & Co., 1904, pp. 233-254.

"The History of Liberal Judaism in England." *The Judaeans* 4 (1933):152-162.

Home Worship and Its Influence on Social Work. Paper read at Conference of Jewish Women, May 1902. Southampton: Cox & Sharland, n.d.

In Memory of Lily H. Montagu: Some Extracts from her Letters and Addresses. Ed. Eric Conrad. Amsterdam: Polak & Van Gennep, 1967.

"In The Beginning." *The First Fifty Years: A Record of Liberal Judaism in England, 1900-1950*. Keighley, Yorkshire: John Wadsworth, 1950, pp. 3-6.

The Jewish Religious Union and Its Beginnings. PJP 27. London: JRU, 1927.

"The Jewish Religious Union in War Time." *LJM* 10, no. 6 (November 1939): 55-56.

"The Just Shall Live by His Faith." *LJM* 17, no. 4 (April 1946): 29-30.

"The Letter Which Started the Jewish Religious Union." *LJM* 27, no. 1 (January 1956):4.

Letters to Anne and Peter. Introd. Rev. A. A. Cock. London: Mamelok Press, 1944.

Introduction to *Max Dienemann: Ein Gedenkbuch, 1875-1939,* by Mally Dienemann. Plymouth: Latimer, Trend & Co., 1946.

"Mazzini: The Man and the Teacher." *Present Day Papers* 4 (June 1901):188-209.

My Club and I: The Story of the West Central Girls Club. 2nd ed. London: Neville Spearman & Herbert Joseph, 1954.

Naomi's Exodus. London: T. Fisher Unwin, 1901.

A New Year Fantasy. N.p.: n.d.

Notes on the Life and Work of Claude G. Montefiore. N.p., 1938.

"Pioneer Personalities of the J.R.U." *LJM* 10, no. 7 (December 1939):64-67.

"The Place of Judaism in the Club Movement." *LJM* 1, no. 3 (June 1929):27-29.

"The Power of Quiet." *LJM* 5, no. 4 (July 1934):28-30.

Prayers for Jewish Working Girls. London: Wertheimer, Lea & Co., 1895.

The Relation of Faith to Conduct in Jewish Life. PJP 2. London: JRU, 1907.

Religious and Social Service. PJP 18. London: JRU, 1918.

Religious Education in the Home. PJP 26. London: JRU, 1925.

"The Russian Jew: A Character Study." *Living Age* 301 (1919): 141-149.

Samuel Montagu, First Baron Swaythling: A Character Sketch. London: Truslove and Hanson, n.d.

"Social Teaching of Judaism for To-Day." *In Spirit and In Truth: Aspects of Judaism and Christianity*. Ed. George A. Yates. London: Hodder & Stoughton, 1934, pp. 105-119.

"Some Thoughts on Home Worship." *LJM* 8, no. 4 (June 1937): 22-23.

"Spiritual Possibilities of Judaism Today." *JQR* 11 (January 1899):216-231.

"The Spiritual Possibilities of Judaism Today." *Lily H. Montagu: Prophet of a Living Judaism*, by Eric Conrad. New York: National Federation of Temple Sisterhoods, 1953, pp. 90-101.

A Story of the "Black Fast." N.p.: n.d.

Suggestions for Sabbath Eve Celebrations. 2nd ed. London: Wightman & Co., 1944.

Thoughts on Judaism. London: R. Brimley Johnson, 1904.

What Can A Mother Do? And Other Stories. London: George Routledge & Sons, 1926.

"Why Pray? An Answer." *LJM* 3, no. 1 (April 1931):4-5.

Ed.   *God Revealed: An Anthology of Jewish Thought*. Keighley, Yorkshire: John Wadsworth & Co., 1953.

Ed. with Netta Franklin. *Daily Readings from the Old Testament*. London: Williams & Norgate, 1922.

Ed. with Theodora Davis. *Prayers, Psalms and Hymns for Jewish Children*. London: Eyre & Spottiswode, 1901.

With Claude G. Montefiore. *Judaism and Authority*. *PJP* 10. London: JRU, 1927.

With R. Brasch. *A Little Book of Comfort for Jewish People In Times of Sorrow*. London: Wightman & Co., 1946?

II. Unpublished Works

      A. American Jewish Archives, Cincinnati, Ohio

LETTERS

To Sheldon H. Blank (re: the establishment of a Liberal Jew-
    ish seminary in Paris), 20 April 1955, 10 May 1955, 13
    May 1955.

To Nelson Glueck, 6 June 1977 (Box 2382).

To Julian Morgenstern, letters dating between 1929 and 1959
    (Box 3207).

      B. Private Collection of Eric Conrad, London, England

DIARY, 22 December 1886 to December 1890.

LETTERS

To the Editor of *The Nation*, 16 December 1917.

To Girls of Girls Club, October 1913.

To Mr. Goldstein, 21 July 1903.

To Louis Montagu, 8 March 1911.

To Marian Montagu, 20 July 1931.

To Claude Montefiore, 13 November 1913,

To be opened upon her death, 2 September 1919.

To be opened upon her death, December 1939.

In case of her death, 15-17 June 1940 (handwritten and typed
    copies).

To Whom It May Concern, 20 April 1954.

Letter entitled "Short Paper With Outline of What I Want Done
    with Regard to My Work If I Pass Away," 1 September
    1939.

MANUSCRIPTS

Draft of *Faith of a Jewish Woman*, handwritten, n.d.

"Draft of Letter Which Started J.R.U.," November 1901.

Draft of questionnaire, n.d., handwritten ("Questionnaire"
    sent to Mr. Hartog, 24 March 1899, carbon copy).

SERMONS AND ADDRESSES

"Faith in God," n.d.

"C. G. Montefiore--As Man and Prophet," sermon, LJS, 5 July
    1941.

"A New Year's Talk to Girls," January 1912.

"Paper Read At First Meeting of J.R.U. Conference Invited to
    Start Movement," 1902.

    C. Private Collection of Hannah Feldman, London, England

Club Letters, No. 3-236 (March 1939 to October 1961).

             D. LJS Archives, London, England

Instructions for Religious Services, titled "Home Worship
    Services," 1935-1938.

LETTERS

To Israel Mattuck, letters dating 13 May 1918 to 24 December
    1953.

To Club Leaders on Religion, 1 April 1943.

To Julian Morgenstern, 19 March 1929, 23 May 1929, 5
    September 1929, and 20 March 1930.

SERMONS AND ADDRESSES

"Acting and Real Life," 16 May 1925.

"Address," at the New Theatre, on the occasion of the Annual
    Display of work, West Central Girls Club, 9 April 1911.

"Address," Germany, January 1930.

"Address," Service of Induction for Lay Ministers of J.R.U.,
    19 November, 1944.

"Address," National Federation of Temple Sisterhoods, Temple
    Emanu-el, New York City, 7 November 1948.

"Address," at service of National Federation of Temple Youth,
    Sinai Temple, Boston, MA, 13 November 1948.

"Address," Induction of Rev. Vivian Simmons, Wembley
    Synagogue, 5 October 1956.

"Address," South London Women's Service, 26 October 1958.

"Address on Club Holiday," Littlehampton, 12 August 1916.

"Address at L.J.S. Exhibition, 1911-1951," 5 November 1951.

"Address to New Liberal Jewish Congregation," 12 May 1961.

"Address to Federation of Liberal and Progressive Jewish
    Youth Groups," 29 October 1961.

"Address Given at the West Central Jewish Working Girls
    Club," 28 February 1914.

"After Ten Years," anniversary sermon, 27 October 1935.

"All Before Us Lies the Way," Day of Atonement, 1929.

"Am I My Brother's Keeper?" sermon, LJS, 21 August 1943.

"Are You Ready," Day of Atonement, 24 September 1958.

"Arise! Shine!", WCC, 11 October 1959.

"Backwards and Forwards," 29 March 1924.

"Before the New Year Begins," WCC, 8 September 1934.

"The Best Is Yet To Be," Day of Atonement, 1927.

"Bow Down Thine Ear, O Lord," Eve of the Day of Atonement,
    1934.

"Can We Possibly Be Mistaken?" 1939.

"Capital Punishment and the Old Testament," n.d.

"The Contribution of the Jews to the Spiritual Life of the
      World," July 1941?

"Courage, Gaiety and A Quiet Mind," January 1935.

"Day of Atonement," 1925.

Draft of sermon for Day of Atonement, 1961.

"Divinity in Freedom," LJS, 4 May 1929.

"Effort in Religion," n.d.

"Environment and Personality," WCC, 7 February 1948.

"The Eve of Pentecost," WCC, 6 April 1938.

"Evidences of God in Everyday Life," 14 November 1925.

"Faith in God in the Face of Evil," Rodeph Sholom, New York
      City, 5 December 1948.

"Faith in this World and the Next," 12 December 1925.

"The Festival of Dedication," WCC, 1 December 1945.

"The Festival of Happiness," South London Synagogue, 11
      October, no year.

"The First Service of the Jewish Religious Union," Fiftieth
      Anniversary, 1952.

"The Future of Judaism," Pavilion Theatre, Brighton, 20 June
      1943.

"Give Unto the Lord," LJS, n.d.

"The Greatest Thing Ever Known," n.d.

"Here Am I: Send Me," Brighton, 17 June 1944.

"Hero Worship and Modernity," WCC, 30 March 1928.

"Honest Doubt," WCC, March 1934.

"How Can the Synagogue Exercise Its Influence in the Modern
      World?" Presidential Address, U.L.P.S., n.d.

"How Much Do I Count," November, 1943.

"How To Combat Indifference," n.d.

"I Am the Lord Thy God," LJS and WCC, May 1947.

"I Will Not Let Thee Go Except Thou Bless Me," West Central
    Girls Club, 21 June 1913.

"If I Had Only One Sermon To Preach," WCC, 26 February 1944.

"If I Had Time," 27 May 1961.

"If Winter Comes," 10 March 1923.

"Immortality in Literature," 16 February 1924.

"Influence and Self Realisation," January 1926.

"Influence of Great Lives," n.d.

"Inter-Marriage," 18 April 1925.

"Introductory Address at the Central Jubilee Service," Octo-
    ber 1952.

"Jewish Thoughts Found in Wordsworth's 'Ode to Duty,'" July
    1956.

"Jewish Women in the Rabbinate," July 1956.

"Jewish Women's Contribution to the Spiritual Life of Human-
    ity," n.d.

"Joy and Suffering," 3 October 1925.

"Judaism and Social Service," 15 May 1921.

"The Just Shall Live By His Faith," n.d.

"Justice, Human and Divine," n.d.

"Justice, Mercy and Humility," WCC, 2 June 1962.

"Kinship With God," LJS, 15 June 1918.

"Know Before Whom Thou Standest," 27 December 1930.

"The Liberal Outlook," 16 February 1936.

"Loneliness," West Central Jewish Girls Club, 2 December 1916.

"Lot's Wife," n.d.

"Man's Ambition and God's Law," LJS, 18 January 1919.

"The Meaning of Pentecost in Modern Life," WCC, 15 May 1937.

"Memories and Hopes (2)," WCC, 3 January 1959.

"Modern Woman's Greatest Duty," LJS, 30 April 1938 and WCC, 7 May 1938.

"Mother's Talk, Number 2," August 1933.

"My Religious Beliefs," North London Synagogue, 28 November 1945.

"New Liberal Jewish Congregation Dedication," 12 May 1961.

"Out of Zion Shall the Law Go Forth and the Word of the Lord from Jerusalem," West Central Club, 17 November 1917.

"Pacifism--From a Jewish Woman's Point of View," n.d.

"Paper to be Read on October 13, 1918."

"Parents: Characters Ancient and Modern," WCC, 27 November 1943.

"The Peace of God," LJS, n.d.

"Peace, Peace Where There Is No Peace," LJS, April 1947.

"Personal Religion," 4 March 1928.

"The Place and Responsibility of the Jewish Woman in her Community," Breslau, Germany, n.d.

"The Position of Liberal Judaism in Anglo-Jewry," LJS, 29 April 1956.

"The Possible You," WCC, 19 May 1962.

"The Power of Personality in a Democratic Age," 31 October 1925.

"Power of Religion," North London Synagogue, 2 June 1928 and
    WCC, 9 June 1928.

"Prayer for the Day of Atonement," 1 October 1941.

"Presidential Address," Annual General Meeting of U.L.P.S.,
    1 November 1953.

"Presidential Address," Annual General Meeting of U.L.P.S.,
    11 May 1958.

"Presidential Address," Annual General Meeting of U.L.P.S.,
    8 April 1962.

"Problems of Family and Home," 28 October 1945.

"Psalms as Poems of Today," WCC, 21 January 1928.

"Public Worship--Can It Be Made More Acceptable To Our Young
    People?" address to Federation of Women's Societies,
    LJS, 16 February 1956.

"The Question of Punishment," LJS, 8 February 1947.

"Reconsecration Service," West Central Club, 23 September
    1925.

"Religion and Private Possessions," 10 January 1925.

"Religious Experience," Women's Federation Meeting, 13 Decem-
    ber 1956.

"Religious Faith and the Children's Courts," LJS, n.d.

"Religious Perplexities," 3 February 1923.

"Religious Responsibility in Public Life," 28 June 1950.

"The Responsibility of Leisure," paper read at Conference of
    the National Union of Women Workers, Oxford, England,
    October 1912.

"Right or Wrong?" WCC, 27 June 1953.

"The Right to Doubt," WCC, 7 January 1928.

"The Sabbath," n.d.

"Seek Ye The Lord," August 1936.

"Seen At The Tate Gallery," West Central Hall, 7 February 1925.

"Self-Restraint and Self-Fulfillment," WCC, 16 June 1962.

"Sensational Journalism and Judaism," November 1928.

"Original English Draft of Sermon at Berlin Reform Synagogue," August 1928.

"Service of National Prayer," Brighton and WCC, 26 May 1940.

"Should We Enjoy Life," LJS, n.d.

"Social Service Yesterday and Today," Rockdale Avenue Temple, Cincinnati, Ohio, 19 November 1948.

"The Social Teachings of Judaism," read to Society of Jews and Christians, 23 October 1928.

"Some Of Our Puzzles," WCC, 21 December 1961.

"Strengthen the Things That Remain," LJS, 2 January 1954.

"The Sun as Preacher," 23 May 1925.

"Taking Risks," 28 April 1928.

"The Spiritual Contribution of Women as Women," Jewish Education Building, Chicago, Illinois, 26 November 1948.

"Talk to Mothers, Number 1," Summer 1933.

"The Task of Progressive Judaism," Central Conference of American Rabbis?, 1931?

"Thoughts Left By Shevuoth," WCC, 27 May 1939.

"The Typical Jew," LJS, n.d.

"The Ultimate Decencies of Life," 17 October 1925.

"Unfinished Man," 13 June 1925.

"What I Owe to the Synagogue," LJS, 18 October 1950.

"What Some of Our Critics Are Saying," 13 December 1924.

"What Would You Miss Most?" WCC, 3 June 1961.

"Who Are The Hypocrites?" North London Synagogue, 11 December 1926.

"Who Is Self Made," 2 February 1924.

"Why Do We Bother?" 21 February 1925.

"Will Liberal Judaism Live As A Religion?" n.d.

E. Private Collection of Hans Woyda, London, England

Letters from Lily Montagu to Bruno Woyda (Treasurer of the World Union for Progressive Judaism), 26 October 1950 to 16 December 1960.

WORKS ABOUT LILY MONTAGU

I. Published Works

Conrad, Eric. *Lily H. Montagu: Prophet of a Living Judaism.* New York: National Federation of Temple Sisterhoods, 1953.

Lelyveld, Arthur. "Lily Montagu--The Lady Rabbi: Progressive Judaism's Dynamo," *The Jewish Record*? (1938?). Conrad Collection.

Levy, Nellie G. *The West Central Story and Its Founders.* London: Leeway Business Services, n.d.

"Lily H. Montagu, 1873-1963," *LJM Memorial Supplement*, n.d.

Sayle, Anne. "The Service of the Institution of Lay Ministers," *The World Union for Progressive Judaism Bulletin*, no. 16 (March 1945).

II. Unpublished Works

Jacobs, Bertram. "Personal Memories of the Hon. Lily Montagu." Private collection of Ellen Umansky, New York.

Rayner, John D. "The Next Chapter," sermon, LJS, 2 February 1963. LJS Archives.

_____. "Remembering Lily Montagu," sermon, LJS, 1969. Private collection of John D. Rayner, London, England.

III. Interviews

Personal interviews were conducted with the following people in London, England, during the summer of 1977:

Eric Conrad (nephew and biographer of Lily Montagu)

Rabbi Leslie Edgar (former Minister of the Liberal Jewish Synagogue)

Hannah Feldman (former member of West Central Club, organizer of Montagu Circle)

Dr. Israel Feldman (former Joint Chairman of Children and Youth Aliyah Committee for Great Britain, involved in West Central Club)

Rabbi Albert Friedlander (Minister of Westminster Synagogue)

Sir Louis Gluckstein (President of Liberal Jewish Synagogue)

Rabbi Hugo Gryn (Minister of West London Synagogue)

Rabbi Bernard Hooker (Minister of North London Progressive Synagogue)

Rabbi Harry Jacobi (former youth leader within World Union for Progressive Judaism)

Bertram Jacobs (Chairman of European Board, World Union for Progressive Judaism)

Phyllis Jacobs (former personal secretary of Lily Montagu)

Jessie Levy (former personal secretary of Lily Montagu, now deceased)

Dr. Charles Lewsen (former Treasurer of World Union for Progressive Judaism and physician to Lily and Marian Montagu)

Jeremy Montagu (nephew of Lily Montagu)

Marjorie Moos (former teacher at Liberal Jewish Synagogue and West Central Club)

Rabbi John D. Rayner (Senior Minister of Liberal Jewish
    Synagogue)

Rabbi Herbert Richter (former Minister of North London Pro-
    gressive Synagogue)

Lawrence Rigal (Minister of West Central Liberal Congrega-
    tion)

Hans Woyda (son of Bruno Woyda, former Treasurer of the World
    Union for Progressive Judaism)

WORKS RELATING TO THE DEVELOPMENT OF
LIBERAL JUDAISM IN ENGLAND

I. Published Works

Abrahams, Israel. *The Union and The Festivals.*   *PJP* **11.**
    London: JRU, 1909.

_____ and Claude Montefiore. *Aspects of Judaism: Being
    Sixteen Sermons.* London: Macmillan & Co., 1895.

Cohen, Lucy. *Some Recollections of Claude Goldsmid Montefi-
    ore, 1858-1938.* London: Faber & Faber, 1940.

*Directory of Progressive Jewish Congregations in Europe and
    Israel, 1976.* London: The Montagu Centre, n.d.

Joseph, N. S. *Essentials of Judaism.* *PJP* **1.** London: JRU,
    1906.

_____. *Immortality.* *PJP* **5.** London: JRU, 1909.

_____. *Why I Am Not a Christian: A Reply to the Conver-
    sionists.* *PJP* **3.** London: JRU, 1908.

Lazarus, Olga. *Liberal Judaism and Its Standpoint.*   London:
    Macmillan & Co., 1937.

Mattuck, Israel. *The Essentials of Liberal Judaism.*   London:
    Routledge & Kegan Paul, 1947.

_____. *Religion and Society.* *PJP* **14.**   London: JRU,
    1917.

_____ and Claude G. Montefiore. *Jewish Views on Jewish Missions*. PJP 31. London: JRU, 1933.

Montefiore, Claude G. *Assimilation: Good and Bad*. PJP 9. London: JRU, 1914.

_____. *The Bible for Home Reading*. 2 vols. London: Macmillan & Co., vol. 1, 1896, vol. 2, 1899.

_____. *The Dangers of Zionism*. PJP 20. London: JRU, 1918.

_____. "The Desire for Immortality." *JQR* 14 (October 1901):96-110.

_____. "The Expression of Faith Drawn Up By Claude Montefiore for the Jewish Religious Union, 1902." *LJM* 27, no.1 (January 1956):5-6.

_____. "Dr. Friedlander on the Jewish Religion." *JQR* 4 (January 1892):204-244.

_____. "Dr. Wiener on the Dietary Laws." *JQR* 8 (April 1896):392-413.

_____. *Great Is Truth and Strong Above All Things*. Address delivered at the service of the JRU, 4 March 1905. Edinburgh: Ballantyne, Hanson & Co., n.d.

_____. *Is There a Middle Way?* PJP 23. London: JRU, 1920.

_____. *Jewish Conceptions of Immortality*. PJP 30. London: JRU, 1932.

_____. *The Jewish Religious Union: Its Principles and Its Future*. PJP 19. London: JRU, 1918.

_____. *Judaism and Democracy*. PJP 13. London: JRU, 1917.

_____. "Mr. Smith: A Possibility." *JQR* 6 (October 1893):100-110.

_____. *A Justification of Judaism*. N.p., n.d.

_____. *The Justification of Liberal Judaism*. PJP 21. London: JRU, 1919.

_____. *Lectures on the Origin and Growth of Religion As Illustrated by the Religion of the Ancient Hebrews. The Hibbert Lectures, 1892.* 3rd ed. London: Williams & Norgate, 1897.

_____. *Liberal Judaism: An Essay.* London: Macmillan & Co., 1903.

_____. "Liberal Judaism." *JQR* 20 (April 1908):363–390.

_____. *Liberal Judaism and Authority.* PJP 22. London: JRU, 1919.

_____. *Liberal Judaism and Convenience.* PJP 25. London: JRU, 1924, pp. 1–9.

_____. *Liberal Judaism and Hellenism and Other Essays.* London: Macmillan & Co., 1918.

_____. *Liberal Judaism and Jewish Nationalism.* PJP 16. London: JRU, 1917,

_____. "Liberal Judaism in England: Its Difficulties and Duties." *JQR* 12 (July 1900):618–650.

_____. *The Meaning of Progressive Revelation.* PJP 8. London: JRU, 1914.

_____. "Nation or Religious Community?" *JQR* 12 (January 1900):177–194.

_____. *The Old Testament and After.* London: Macmillan & Co., 1923.

_____. *The Old Testament and Its Ethical Teachings.* PJP 15. London: JRU, 1917.

_____. *Outlines of Liberal Judaism.* London: Macmillan & Co., 1912.

_____. *The Place of Judaism in the Religions of the World.* PJP 12. London: JRU, 1916.

_____. *The Question of Authority in Liberal Judaism.* PJP 33. London: JRU, 1936.

_____. *Some Rough Notes About Liberal Judaism.* PJP 28. London: JRU, 1928.

_____. *Truth in Religion and Other Sermons*. London: Macmillan & Co., 1906.

Rayner, John D. *The Practices of Liberal Judaism*. Keighley, Yorkshire: John Wadsworth, 1958.

Simmons, Vivian. *The Path of Life: A Study of the Background, Faith, and Practice of Liberal Judaism*. London: Vallentine-Mitchell, 1961.

Simon, Oswald J. "Jews and Modern Thought." *JQR* 9 (April 1899):387-399.

_____. "The Mission of Judaism." *JQR* 9 (January 1897): 177-223.

_____. "Reformed Judaism." *JQR* 6 (January 1894):262-277.

II. Unpublished Works

Letters from male members of LJS Council, re: women on the pulpit. 1918. LJS Archives.

Minute Book, Jewish Religious Union, 1902-1909. LJS Archives.

Minute Book, Liberal Jewish Synagogue Council, 1910-1919. LJS Archives.

Minute Book, Liberal Jewish Synagogue Council, 1920-1937. LJS Archives.

J.R.U. Council Current Minutes, 1937-1948. LJS Archives.

Rigal, Lawrence. *History of Liberal Judaism*. Private collection, Lawrence Rigal.

ANGLO-JEWISH HISTORY

I. Published Works

Abrahams, Israel, ed. *The Literary Remains of the Rev. Simeon Singer*. 2 vols. London: George Routledge & Sons, 1908.

Bermant, Chaim. *The Cousinhood: The Anglo-Jewish Gentry.*
New York: Macmillan Co., 1971.

Emden, Paul H. *Jews of Britain: A Series of Biographies.*
London: Sampson Low, Marston & Co., 1971.

Endelman, Todd M. *The Jews of Georgian England 1714-1830:
Tradition and Change in a Liberal Society.* Philadelphia: The Jewish Publication Society of America, 1979.

Gibbon, Monk. *Netta.* London: Routledge & Kegan Paul, 1960.

Henriques, H. S. Q. *The Jews and the English Law.* London:
The Bibliophile Press, 1908?

Homa, Bernard. *Orthodoxy in Anglo-Jewry, 1880-1940.* London:
The Jewish Historical Society of England, 1969.

Hyamson, Albert M. *A History of the Jews in England.* 2nd
ed. London: Methuen & Co., 1928.

_____. *The Sephardim of England.* London: Methuen &
Co., 1951.

Levin, Salmond S., ed. *A Century of Anglo-Jewish Life, 1870-
1970.* London: United Synagogue, 1973?

Liberles, Robert. "The Origins of the Jewish Reform Movement
in England." *Association for Jewish Studies Review* 1
(1976):121-150.

Lipman, V[ivian] D[avid]. *Social History of the Jews in England 1850-1910.* London: Watts, 1954.

_____. "Synagogal Organization in Anglo-Jewry." *JJS* 1
(April 1959):80-93.

_____, ed. *Three Centuries of Anglo-Jewish History: A
Volume of Essays.* London: The Jewish Historical Society
of England, 1961.

Loewe, L. L. *Basil Henriques: A Portrait.* London: Routledge
& Kegan Paul, 1976.

Marmur, Dow, ed. *Reform Judaism: Essays on Reform Judaism in
England.* London: Reform Synagogues of Great Britain,
1973.

Newman, Aubrey. *The United Synagogue, 1870-1970*. London: Routledge & Kegan Paul, 1976.

Roth, Cecil. *The Great Synagogue, London, 1690-1940*. London: Edward Goldston & Son, 1950.

_____. *A History of the Jews in England*. London: Oxford University Press, 1941.

Samuel, Rt. Hon. Viscount. *Memoirs*. London: The Cresset Press, 1945.

Sharot, Stephen. "Native Jewry and the Religious Anglicization of Immigrants in London, 1870-1905." *JJS* 16 (June 1974):39-56.

_____. "Religious Change in Native Orthodoxy in London, 1870-1914: The Synagogue Service." *JJS* 15 (June 1973): 57-78.

_____. "Religious Change in Native Orthodoxy in London, 1870-1914: Rabbinate and Clergy." *JJS* 15 (December 1973):167-187.

Zatlin, Linda Gertner. *The Nineteenth Century Anglo-Jewish Novel*. Boston: Twayne Publishing, 1981.

II. Unpublished Works

Montagu, Ellen. Letter, "For My Children to be Opened after My Death." 6 April 1911. Conrad Collection.

Montagu, Samuel. Letter to Ellen Montagu, "To Be Opened Only After My Death." 27 February 1875. Conrad Collection.

ENGLISH LITERATURE AND HISTORY

I. Primary Sources

Arnold, Matthew. *Literature and Dogma*. 1873; rpt. London: Smith, Elder & Co., 1909.

Browning, Robert. *The Complete Poetic and Dramatic Works of Robert Browning*. Ed. Horace E. Scudder. Boston: Houghton, Mifflin & Co., 1895.

Carlyle, Thomas. *On Heroes, Hero Worship and the Heroic in History*. 1840; rpt. London: J. M. Dent & Sons, 1908.

_____. *Sartor Resartus*. 1831; rpt. London: J. M. Dent & Sons, 1908.

Cross, J. M., ed. *George Eliot's Life as Related in Her Letters and Journals*. 3 vols. New York: Harper & Brothers, 1885.

Eliot, George. *Daniel Deronda*. Ed. Barbara Hardy. 1876; rpt. Baltimore: Penguin Books, 1967.

_____. *Middlemarch*. 1872; rpt. New York: New American Library, Signet Classics, 1964.

_____. *Scenes of Clerical Life*. 1858; rpt. Harmondsworth, Middlesex: Penguin Books, 1973.

Jowett, Benjamin. "On the Interpretation of Scripture." *Essays and Reviews*. 7th ed. London: Longman, Green, Longman & Roberts, 1861.

Ruskin, John. *Sesame and Lilies*. 1865; rpt. New York: Charles E. Merrill & Co., 1891.

Ward, Mrs. Humphrey. *Robert Elsmere*. 1888; rpt. London: Smith, Elder & Co., 1906.

Webb, Beatrice. *My Apprenticeship*. New York: Longman, Green & Co., 1926.

II. Secondary Sources

Altick, Richard D. *Victorian People and Ideas*. New York: W. W. Norton & Co., 1973.

Anderson, Olive. "Women Preachers in Mid-Victorian Britain." *Historical Journal* 12, no. 3 (1969):467-484.

Banks, J. A. and Olive Banks. *Feminism and Family Planning in Victorian England*. New York: Schocken Books, 1964.

Basch, Francoise. *Relative Creatures*. New York: Schocken Books, 1974.

Bentley, Eric. *A Century of Hero-Worship*. 2nd ed. Boston: Beacon Press, 1957.

Best, Geoffrey. *Mid-Victorian Britain, 1851-1875.* New York: Schocken Books, 1972.

Bott, Alan and Irene Clephane. *Our Mothers: A Cavalcade in Pictures, Quotations and Descriptions of Late Victorian Women, 1870-1900.* New York: Benjamin Blom, 1932.

Brown, E. K., ed. *Victorian Poetry.* New York: The Ronald Press, 1942.

Chadwick, Owen. *The Secularization of the European Mind in the Nineteenth Century.* Cambridge: Cambridge University Press, 1975.

_____. *The Victorian Church, Part II, 1860-1901.* London: Adam & Charles Black, 1970.

Cruse, Amy. *The Victorians and Their Reading.* Boston: Houghton Mifflin Co., 1935.

Dyhouse, Carol. *Girls Growing Up in Late Victorian and Edwardian England.* London: Routledge & Kegan Paul, 1981.

Elliot-Binns, L. E. *Religion in the Victorian Era.* London: The Lutterworth Press, 1936.

Evans, R. J. *The Victorian Age, 1815-1914.* 2nd ed. London: Edward Arnold, 1968.

Hill, Michael. *The Religious Order: A Study of Virtuoso Religion and its Legitimation in the Nineteenth Century Church of England.* London: Heinemann Educational Books, 1973.

Houghton, Walter E. *The Victorian Frame of Mind, 1830-1870.* New Haven: Yale University Press, 1957.

Hynes, Samuel. *The Edwardian Turn of Mind.* Princeton: Princeton University Press, 1968.

Kanner, Barbara, ed. *The Women of England: From Anglo-Saxon Times to the Present.* Hamden, CT: Archon Books, 1979.

Kasuya, Yoshi. *A Comparative Study of the Secondary Education of Girls in England, Germany and the United States.*

Kitson-Clark, G. *The Making of Victorian England.* New York: Atheneum Press, 1976.

Mintz, Alan. *George Eliot and the Novel of Vocation*. Cambridge: Harvard University Press, 1978.

Murray, Janet, ed. *Strong Minded Women and Other Lost Voices from Nineteenth Century England*. New York: Pantheon Books, 1982.

Strachey, Ray. *"The Cause": A Short History of the Women's Movement in Great Britain*. London: G. Bell & Sons, 1928.

Vicinus, Martha, ed. *A Widening Sphere: Changing Roles of Victorian Women*. Bloomington: Indiana University Press, 1977.

_____. *Suffer and Be Still: Women in the Victorian Age*. Bloomington: Indiana University Press, 1972.

WOMEN IN JEWISH LIFE

Arendt, Hannah. *Rahel Varnhagen: The Life of a Jewess*. London: The East and West Library, 1957.

Baum, Charlotte, Paula Hyman and Sonya Michel. *The Jewish Woman in America*. New York: The New American Library, 1975.

Frank, Ray. "Women in the Synagogue." *Papers of the Jewish Women's Congress, 1893*. Philadelphia: Jewish Publication Society of America, 1894.

Greenberg, Blu. *On Women and Judaism: A View from Tradition*. Philadelphia: Jewish Publication Society of America, 1982.

"The Jewish Woman: An Anthology." *Response: A Contemporary Jewish Review* 7, no. 2 (Summer 1973).

Kaplan, Marion A. *The Jewish Feminist Movement in Germany: The Campaigns of the Judischer Frauenbund, 1904-1938*. Westport, CT: The Greenwood Press, 1979.

Kohut, Rebecca. *My Portion*. 1925; rpt. New York: Arno Press, 1975.

Koltun, Elizabeth, ed. *The Jewish Woman: New Perspectives*. New York: Schocken Books, 1976.

Litman, Simon. *Ray Frank Litman: A Memoir*. New York: American Jewish Historical Society, 1957.

Meir, Golda. *My Life by Golda Meir*. Jerusalem: Steimatzky's Agency, 1975.

Prell, Riv-Ellen. "The Vision of Woman in Classical Reform Judaism." *JAAR* 50, no. 4 (December 1982):575-589.

Senesh, Hannah. *Hannah Senesh: Her Life and Diary*. Trans. Marta Cohn. Introd. Abba Eban. New York: Schocken Books, 1973.

Shulman, Gail B. "View from the Back of the Synagogue: Women in Judaism." *Sexist Religion and Women in the Church*. Ed. Alice L. Hageman. New York: Association Press, 1974, pp. 143-166.

Stern, Elisabeth [Leah Morton, pseud.]. *I Am A Woman - And a Jew*. 1926; rpt. New York: Arno Press and the New York Times, 1969.

Yezierska, Anzia. *Bread Givers*. 1925; rpt. New York: Persea Books, 1975.

GENERAL JEWISH HISTORY

Elon, Amos. *Herzl*. New York: Holt, Rinehart & Winston, 1975.

Geiger, Abraham. "Die Stellung des Weiblichen Geschlechtes in dem Judenthume Unseren Zeit." *Wissenschaft Zeitschrift fur Judische Theologie* 3 (1837):1-14.

Herzl, Theodor. *The Complete Diaries of Theodor Herzl*. 4 vols. Ed. Raphael Patai. Trans. Harry Zohn. London: Thomas Yoseloff; New York: Herzl Press, 1960.

Katz, Jacob. *Out of the Ghetto*. Cambridge: Harvard University Press, 1973.

_____, ed. *The Role of Religion in Modern Jewish History.* Cambridge, MA: Association for Jewish Studies, 1975.

Meyer, Michael. *The Origins of the Modern Jew.* Detroit: Wayne State University Press, 1967.

Philipson, David. "The Beginnings of the Reform Movement in Judaism." *JQR* 15 (April 1903):475-521.

_____. "The Progress of the Jewish Reform Movement in the United States." *JQR* 10 (October 1897):52-99.

_____. *The Reform Movement in Judaism.* Rev. ed. New York: Ktav Publishing House, 1967.

Plaut, Gunther. *The Rise of Reform Judaism: A Sourcebook of its European Origins.* New York: World Union for Progressive Judaism, 1963.

Rudavsky, David. *Modern Jewish Religious Movements: A History of Emancipation and Adjustment.* Rev. 3rd ed. New York: Behrman House, 1979.

Weiner, Max. *Abraham Geiger and Liberal Judaism: The Challenge of the Nineteenth Century.* Philadelphia: Jewish Publication Society of America, 1962.

SELECTED BIBLIOGRAPHY OF OTHER CONSULTED WORKS

I. Published Works

Christ, Carol P. *Diving Deep and Surfacing: Women Writers on Spiritual Quest.* Boston: Beacon Press, 1979.

Douglas, Ann. *The Feminization of American Culture.* New York: Alfred A. Knopf, Avon Books, 1977.

James, William. *The Varieties of Religious Experience.* New York: New American Library, Mentor Books, 1958.

Kelly, Joan. "Early Feminist Theology and the *Querelle des Femmes* 1400-1789." *Signs: Journal of Women in Culture and Society* 8, no.1 (December 1982):4-28.

Latourette, Kenneth Scott. *A History of Christianity*. 2 vols. New York: Harper & Row, 1953.

Mazzini, Joseph. *The Duties of Man and Other Essays By Joseph Mazzini*. Ed. Ernest Rhys. London: J. M. Dent & Sons, 1920.

_____. *Mazzini's Essays*. Ed. Ernest Rhys. London: Walter Scott, 1887.

Schleiermacher, Friedrich. *On Religion: Speeches to its Cultured Despisers*. Trans. John Oman. 1893; rpt. New York: Harper & Row, 1958.

Tulloch, John. *Movements of Religious Thought During the Nineteenth Century*. New York: Charles Scribners Sons, 1893.

Weber, Max. *On Charisma and Institution Building*. Ed. and introd. S. N. Eisenstadt. Chicago: University of Chicago Press, 1968.

_____. *The Sociology of Religion*. Introd. Talcott Parsons. Trans. Ephraim Fischoff. Boston: Beacon Press, 1963.

Willey, Basil. *Nineteenth Century Studies*. London: Chatto & Windus, 1949.

II. Unpublished Works

World Union for Progressive Judaism Minutes: Executive Committee and Governing Body, 1930-1965. American Jewish Archives, Cincinnati, Ohio. World Union for Progressive Judaism Boxes.

Index

STUDIES IN WOMEN AND RELIGION

12-12-07

BM
755
M57
U46
1983